D0478853

DETECTIVE MARIE CIRILE
Memoirs of a Police Officer

DETECTIVE MARIE CIRILE

Memoirs of a Police Officer

Doubleday & Company, Inc., Garden City, New York
1975

Library of Congress Cataloging in Publication Data

Cirile, Marie.
    Detective Marie Cirile.

    1. Cirile, Marie. 2. Policewomen—New York (City)—Correspondence,
reminiscences, etc. 3. Detectives—New York (City)—Correspondence, rem-
iniscences, etc. I. Title.
HV7911.C57A34   363.2'0924 [B]
ISBN 0-385-07621-5
Library of Congress Catalog Card Number: 74-18787

Portions of news stories reprinted on pages 57–59 are used
by permission of the New York *Daily News.*

For every cop, out There, doing the job.

In memory of, "Used to be"
and "Should have been";
so often heard,
but no longer seen.

"You should've been in this office when it used to be. . . ."

And to:
Cindy and Jim, my favorite twigs
Patrick Spagnuolo, my friend, husband, and blue-eyed slave driver.

DETECTIVE MARIE CIRILE

Memoirs of a Police Officer

Some hotshot cop!

Dejectedly I slumped into the unyielding couch in the police surgeon's waiting room, my neck encased in a three-inch brace as a result of an auto accident. I looked like a patch on a blown-out tire that wasn't sticking right, and nobody could figure out why. The impatience with the pain and enforced inactivity was starting to wear thin and a listless despondency was beginning to take hold. I barely noticed the weak spurt of April sun that was to be the spring of 1973.

The Police Department has a medical bureau to supervise all members who are on sick report, and going sick can only be compared with going sick in the Army with its attendant red tape. A grand pain in the ass!

If you go sick from your residence, you have to notify your command and then the sick desk in the medical office. You report sick as of 1034 hours. You are suffering from, say, diarrhea, which you must plainly state, have been treated by Dr. Kumquat of 444 Pleasant Avenue, have no outstanding complaints pending or court appearances, and will report to your police surgeon within twelve hours.

So you call your assigned surgeon and he queries your complaint and asks how it is being treated. He'll ask how many times you've trotted to the john, and you'll be greeted with something like, "You call that diarrhea? When you go ten or twelve times in a couple of hours, you've got something to worry about. Report to my office tomorrow."

1

While on sick report, regardless of whether you have a cast on your leg, or have just been discharged from the hospital after a heart attack, you have to report to your assigned surgeon at least once a week. He is now the master of your future. He doesn't actually examine or treat you; his main function seems to be finding out what kind of treatment you've been getting on your own, and keeping records to this effect. He has the power to keep you out sick, return you to duty, or further still to report that you might be malingering.

In addition to this the real beauty is that while on sick report you are confined to your home and not allowed to leave.

The medical office has a special investigative unit of sergeants whose sole function is to run around and do house checks. If you're not in to sign their little logbooks, you've had it. They can issue an official complaint which can result in an appearance before the trial board with a resultant five to ten days' loss of pay and the complaint is entered and becomes part of your official file. Any time you're transferred, or up for a promotion or grade money, one of the first questions you are asked is, "Do you have any complaints?"

They also double back on you by having checkup phone calls, both from the medical bureau and from your command office.

We call it house arrest. Suppose you break your arm . . . you can't work, right? But what's to prevent your going to a movie with your family or out to dinner? The rules will prevent you, that's what. If you've got to wear that cast or brace for an extended period of time, you've had it. You start to feel like a substandard member of the human race. I've taken baths with the bathroom door open, when alone in the house, because of the fear of not hearing the doorbell or the phone and missing a house check. You go stir crazy and paranoid.

I've had my doctor tell me, "You've got to get out and get some air, go for slow walks, your muscle tone is deteriorating." I repeat this to the surgeon and he says, "Yes, that's a good idea."

"Can I have a permission slip to leave the residence?"

"Well, no. As long as you're wearing that neck brace, I don't feel free to issue permission. Why don't you just walk in front of your house, so you can see if anyone comes to check on you."

"That's fine, except that my house is on top of a big hill. You

2

have to climb down over thirty steps to get to street level, which I'm not up to doing yet. I'd like to do my walking on the back street, which is level, but I can't see if any cars come from there."

"Well, if you take off your brace I can give you a slip."

"But, Doctor, my doctor says it must remain on."

"Then you'd better stay in, I can't take a chance in your condition."

So there I sat on my weekly visit. I looked around at my fellow officers; one was a pretty gal. That was a switch. Usually I'm the only female around.

When she was leaving she went to sign out in the attendance book and read my sign-in entry. She whirled, bright-eyed, and said, "Marie Cirile . . . you're Marie Cirile . . . I never thought I'd ever get to meet you. I've heard so much about you! . . . All the guys talk about you . . . they call you the lady tiger . . . you're a legend . . . really a legend."

"I don't know if I like that. It makes me sound like I'm a hundred and eighty years old!"

"Oh, I don't mean it that way. It's just that when the guys get talking on the subject of working with women, your name usually pops up and you'll hear, 'Well, if I have to be assigned with a woman, the only one I'd want to work with would have to be Marie Cirile.'"

Dr. Grossnon's curt "Next" interrupted and I was in his office giving him the latest neurological findings, but my mind kept going back to the word *legend, legend,* and I started to smile.

You should be dead about fifty years before someone calls you that. But I was flattered and feeling expansive. A legend in my own time! Ha! That's a good one!

Take a skinny little Italian girl, first-generation Italian-American. This automatically means she was brought up to believe that any man knows better than any woman.

Her entire upbringing prepares her to serve this God creature she will marry: to obey, to cook, to clean, to bear children (boys, preferably), and to keep her mouth shut, because after all everyone knows women were put on earth to suffer.

Can a "lady cop," or better yet a "police tigress," as quoted from newspaper headlines, evolve from this background?

I was a quiet little mouse. Even Mrs. Waller, my eighth-grade teacher in P.S. 77, wrote in my autograph book, "Too shy and re-tiring for a good pupil." I was one of the four girls born to Michele and Rosa Panzarino, formerly of Bari, Italy.

Mom miscarried her first child, a boy. This was followed by a procession of females—Antonietta Benedetta, Maria Teresa, Paolina Lina, and Elvira Concetta. Pop never did forgive her for this rotten trick and at eighty-three when he's been at the wine a bit, he'll still cry for the son he never had.

Like most Barese, Pop went into business for himself—he had to be his own boss. He came to this country when he was twelve years old, weighing all of eighty-five pounds. His older brother Joe met him at the dock and that same day took him on his delivery route. Uncle Joe delivered ice and coal in Brooklyn with a horse and wagon, and Pop was very quickly initiated by being told to deliver a fifty-pound piece of ice to a woman on the fifth floor, walk-up of course. Welcome to America!

Pop had no formal education, but IBM could envy him his computer brain. When it came to figuring money, he could run up and down the scales in English, Italian, or Jewish, and give us kids the answer while we were still trying to get the example down on paper.

We never really saw that much of Pop—he'd be gone by six in the morning and wouldn't be back until ten at night. But his figure dominated the house. We all waited and ate supper together at 10 P.M. There was never any question as to whether it was right or wrong. It was just a sign of respect. Now I know why I was so skinny. I was too tired to eat.

Not that food time was anything to brag about in those days. Breakfast was a chunk of Italian bread and hot cocoa. Lunch was easy—whatever happened to be left over from the previous night's supper; and if there wasn't any, maybe a bowl of farina or pastina.

But supper during those lean years looked like the farinaceous heading in one of today's menus. You could mix or match, but they'd run along like *pasta e piselli, pasta e fagioli, pasta e ceci, pasta e lentiche,* and like clockwork come Thursday and Sunday you could count on pasta with sauce. I must have made a thousand silent promises to myself in those days that I'd never eat pasta again.

We were poor, I mean house poor. It took every penny Pop

4

earned to pay the mortgage and run the four-family house in the Bronx, which, after pinching and hoarding every spare nickel and dime that came in their direction for years, the folks had bought. God, were they proud! Italian peasants who now were landlords. They owned land, and the old farmer instinct of owning a piece of their own dirt, at last, took firm hold.

From a gut memory deep within I can never forget being awakened at about five-thirty on a dark wintry morning, hearing Mom calling out to Pop as he left for work, "Mike, Mike, please leave me a nickel so I can buy a cake of soap," and Pop answering brusquely, "I don't have it, maybe tomorrow—ask me tomorrow."

During the many, many poor years I remember Aunt Anna and Aunt Paolina, who were then on welfare (we kids thought they were rich), coming over and bringing us their welfare surplus—butter, rice, those hideous welfare middy blouses and pleated skirts that we all hated and had to care for as if they were gold.

Mom and Pop couldn't get welfare because they had an "asset"—that damn albatross of a house that seemed to take precedence over everything. We were practically placed at the tenant's disposal by our bringing up: you just didn't refuse anything that an elder requested.

We would baby-sit, run errands, shut off the lights and then light candles for our Jewish tenants, walk their dogs, and if we ever took a penny we'd be killed.

Pop worked six and a half days, and Sunday dinner was the big occasion. He would ask about school and get all the reports from Mom on who did what to whom, and we'd wait for a nod of approval or a good blast.

Pop is a short man, about 5'5", and he weighed about 225 pounds then. But I never saw anybody step into him or try to cross him; they just knew better.

Mom was even tinier. She admits to 5 feet, but it's more like 5 feet going on 4'10". Mom is a real product of the small-town Italian culture. For years she sent us off to school with the same phrase ringing in our ears, "*Stat'attent, apri i occhi, guard' il vestito.*" (Be attentive, open your eyes, guard your skirt.) It just washed over me with repetition, like a litany, I heard it so often. I must have been at least fourteen before I finally realized what she was warning about. She was being the Italian mother guarding her daughter's "sole asset."

My vice was books. I'd run to the library on the way home from school, and stagger home with six or seven big fat books, all beautiful fantasies. I would have a book with me no matter what I did or where I went. I would eat with one propped alongside my dish, absentmindedly poking the spoon in my nose.

I always wanted to be the female Jack Armstrong, the all-American type. I would have loved sports, but Mom said everything from roller skates to bike riding was unfeminine. In fact, we could only play outside if it was in front of the house.

I guess raising four girls Italian style is pretty rough. Mom couldn't wait to get us married off and out so that her responsibility for keeping us virginal would end.

Of course we were completely prepared for marriage, by Mom's standards. We could cook and we could clean and that was it.

So we made Momma happy and got married. I think I got married because Mom said he was *simpatico* and *bello di facia,* which loosely translated means he was an attractive con man.

Momma made a novena of thanks that she had one less to worry about, and I was filled with brilliant thoughts like I'll never ever cook pasta again in my whole life. I can eat whatever I want now because I'm never ever going to be poor.

What a hell of a basis for a marriage.

Marriage was a hectic flurry of activity—working full-time, trying to fix and furnish our apartment, kept mind and hands too busy for introspection.

I was a Gal Friday for the Mason Tenders District Council of Greater New York affiliated with the International Hod Carriers, Building and Common Laborer's Union of America; no teatime outfit this. Some of those guys would just as soon stomp on your head with those big heavy work boots as step over you.

It was here that I received my baptism of sorts in learning to deal with all types of people. The literate builders who'd try to con the eyeballs out of your head would work men until they dropped in their tracks, if they thought they could get away with it, figuring they could buy their way out of any situation they couldn't talk themselves out of.

The laborers really ran the gamut. There was the newly arrived immigrant who couldn't speak English. These men had faced the fact that the only thing they had to offer was brute-force labor. They usually worked for a few years acquiring the language, the customs, and a case of the smarts, and went on to other things.

The American-born laborer was more often than not unskilled and illiterate. These men who'd move a bird's nest that was in the way of a bulldozer, and cry and curse over a dog accidentally run over by a piece of equipment, could as easily crush your head with a shovel because you spilled their container of coffee.

People, what made them tick—it was sociology in the raw.

My boss, the president of the Mason Tenders (bricklayer's apprentices), was one smart cookie. Very well educated in Europe, he spoke English with a fairly heavy accent. Every week or two he would take two of us out to luncheon at Luchow's, considered to be a very "class" restaurant. The pasta kid found out about lobster thermidor, wiener schnitzel, filet mignon, boiled beef with horseradish sauce, apple pancakes flambé, and shrimp cocktail. I never ordered the same thing twice as I tried to sample everything I had ever heard or read of.

The sampling came to an abrupt halt as I left with an advanced case of pregnancy. The few months of waiting didn't seem too long, however, as I was determined to make the entire layette by hand. The time went and Cindy came and she was great. Everything a baby is supposed to be and usually isn't.

After about four years of playing wife, I had become a different person. I was no longer interested in what was happening except in my own immediate surroundings. I felt stagnant and uncreative, and as time progressed, valueless. My marriage to a cop who'd acquired the nickname "Hollywood" was headed down the road to "Doomsville." Every once in a while I would weakly suggest I might get a job, but the reaction was bad and my motivation was poor and procrastination became the watchword to the Hapless Housewife Syndrome.

In 1955, on the Fourth of July, Mom had a barbecue, which meant a command performance, family reunion style—daughters, sons-in-law, and grandchildren.

My sister Ann, who works for the United Nations, provided

the day's excitement by bringing the physical requirement standards for the Policewoman Civil Service Examination. Neither I nor any of my sisters knew that such creatures existed. We were fascinated.

The day was taken up with attempting everything they listed. We broad-jumped and measured. We kept trying to find weights to press and ended up lifting flat irons and crowbars. We ran up and down the alley, simulating the agility test, to cheers and catcalls. Our attempts at sit-ups, even without weights, were really ludicrous.

It was great fun, except it made me realize what beastly shape I was in. Carried away with the generated interest, Ann, Lee, and I decided to apply for the test, just for laughs, and because my husband said, "Don't be ridiculous, what the hell makes you think you could ever pass the same kind of test I took?"

Frankly, I didn't have any sustained drive and didn't do a thing about it. Several months later I got a call from Lee. It was the last day for filing and that's what she was about to do. Ann had counted herself out because she didn't want to lose the eight years of seniority and pension she'd accumulated at the U.N.

"Well," I told Lee, "I'm not about to go downtown for filing so forget it, I'd probably make a jerk of myself anyway."

Lee lost patience with me. "Get off your behind and do something, get started before it's too late for you to ever do anything. I'm going to file for you and you're going to take it."

At eight o'clock on a miserably cold Monday morning, January 28, 1956, along with over 1,000 other eager, chatty females, Lee and I took the four-hour mental test. In the hall afterward, batteries of conversation surrounded us. It seems that many of the applicants had been taking special courses for periods ranging from six months to two years to prepare for this test.

Lee and I started to giggle. Over breakfast we talked about how idiotic we were to take this competitive test cold; you couldn't call it nerve, we didn't know any better.

Several weeks later a telegram arrived from Delehanty Institute. "Congratulations! You have placed number three on the recent policewoman's test. Will you be our guest at the annual Policewoman's Dance?"

The whole world changed. Suddenly I had some value in my

husband's eyes. He carried that telegram and bragged about it to anyone who'd listen. "That's my wife! Isn't she something!"

The physical test still had to be passed, which for me would be the rough one.

I'm probably the only female in the world who got barbells for Christmas, and was then enrolled in the Bronx Union YMCA, where I had the dubious distinction of being in their Policeman's Eligibles Preparedness Gym Class.

The set requirements issued by the Department of Personnel that became our Bible were really rough.

There were about fifty men in class and two women. How could you admit fatigue, aches, disgust, or dismay in front of a bunch of guys who felt the same way, but kept laughing and pushing each other along. So you got up and hurdled another wall. Camaraderie ran high with shared hopes. I've continued calisthenics to this day, vowing I'd never be a shlump like that again.

Lee placed ninth on the list, so the Panzarino girls really didn't do too badly—and saved themselves the price of the Delehanty course. In August 1956 we passed the physical tests and it was just a question of being called for the medical examination before being appointed.

Although I knew how slow-moving some of the Civil Service lists could be, I had to make some decisions as to the care of my young daughter. In order to work with a clear head I had to feel that Cindy was not being neglected. I enrolled her in a local nursery several months before being called, so that she wouldn't associate being sent to school with my going to work. When I did start work, my mother or sister Vera filled in by picking her up from school on the days when my hours conflicted. Happily they were kept to a minimum. This was one definite advantage this job had over a regular nine-to-five routine, in that I was able to maneuver my hours to fit my needs by volunteering for offbeat tours of duty and nights.

When Cindy was five we bought a house in the suburbs and also hired a live-in housekeeper. If a relative lives with you because you want them to, it's great, but if they live with you because you feel you must have them, it's a drag. The money spent on household help can be the greatest investment the working mother can indulge in. I wanted to establish fundamental habits and patterns that were to go on whether I was at home or not. I think that an ordered pattern gives children a form of security.

The first 5 women from the policewomen's list, as well as 540 men from the patrolmen's list, were called to take the medical examination on June 28, 1957. This was to be our official recruit class.

The 540 men received their medical examinations and were sworn in on June 28, 1957. The 5 gals sat and cooled their heels all afternoon waiting for their turn. It never came. The doctors apparently felt they couldn't cope with examining 5 women, after having examined 540 men, so our exams were postponed until after the Fourth of July weekend. We were examined and sworn in seven days later on July 5.

These seven days were to cost us five dearly, since a short time later they passed a law stating that the twenty-five-day yearly vacation previously given would now only be granted after having worked three years, and the effective date was July 1, 1957.

So the 540 men received twenty-five days' vacation and the 5 women received fifteen days.

Perhaps I should have been perceptive enough to realize that this more or less set the trend for the future, but I was so filled with a mixture of fear, apprehension, eagerness, and willingness that everything else seemed of little consequence.

After we were sworn in, and I paid the clerk my six cents for shield 349, I was officially assigned to Recruit Training School in the Police Academy on Hubert Street.

Recruit Training School

New York got around to building a new Police Academy several years ago. It was just in the nick of time since the old building at 7 Hubert Street, a glory to behold, was in danger of imminent collapse. This little five-story brick building had been condemned thirty years before when it was still being used as a neighborhood elementary school. What better use for a building considered unfit for youngsters than to turn it into a training school for New York's Finest.

The fact that our class survived the makeshift facilities was to their credit and a credit to the department, as it was then. Morale was high, we were all eager.

Perhaps that's the reason for the spanking new building they now have for rookies. With the present-day lack of motivation for police work in New York City, I can see the difficulty in attracting six hundred individuals and holding on to them if they were back in the old school building. The pendulum has swung full tilt in my seventeen years, going from an extreme gung-ho attitude previously prevalent to the present-day feeling that the only safe way to survive your twenty years is to see nothing, hear nothing, do nothing, think nothing, and above all say nothing, because you're wrong anyway.

Our little home away from home for almost five months had been designed for young children. The metal stairwells were narrow, the banisters affixed so low you had to stoop to reach them, and you had to kneel down to drink from the rusty fountains. There were no cloakrooms or lockers available. Whatever you had, and you had loads, had to be lugged about at all times. There were books galore, your gym gear, your gun, your coat, your purse, and your lunch. The men also had their baton, a fancy name for a nightstick.

You got thirty minutes for lunch but there was no lunch room, nor any facilities for eating. It took almost that long just to get down those narrow, overcrowded stairs.

The ladies' room was not really a ladies' room but a conversion job. It was a boys' room that now had a sign tacked on the door that said "Ladies." This was probably done deliberately as a fast breaking-in process to help us become aware of one of the most omnipresent problems for policewomen, the lack of toilet facilities.

Our bathroom's lovely orange-yellow-stained urinal seemed to dominate the room. It was not nicely hidden behind a partition or a door, but blatantly exposed. After a week or two of shaking our heads disgustedly, we did something about it. We changed it into a planter by filling it with plastic flowers in shades of orange and yellow.

We went down to order our uniforms feeling proud as peacocks, although the end results were pretty funny. The uniform makers used Police Department specifications which seemed to feel that if big is good, bigger is better.

The skirt had to be five inches below the knee. There had to be a two-inch allowance at the waistline of the jacket—it couldn't be fitted. The uniform purse must have been designed by some idiot who hated women altogether, and was completely unaware or uncaring of their habits and needs.

The shoulder-strap pocketbook consisted of two straight pieces of leather sewn together. There was no side piece or gusset inserted to provide width. On the front section, an additional small piece of leather, shaped to create a holster for your gun, had been sewn on. The whole thing measured eight and one-half inches by eight and one-half inches and you'd encounter difficulty inserting your empty hand into it.

But the very funniest item, although it wasn't very funny then, had to be the uniform overcoat. A self-respecting Russian Cossack would have turned his nose up at it. Made of coarse heavy blue wool, it had to fit over your uniform, and therefore had to be even longer and baggier. It weighed at least fifteen pounds. When I put it on, I sagged several inches. You'd think that this walking tent would have the redeeming vaue of keeping you warm; no such luck!

Within a day or two of being assigned to the academy we females became aware that we were "different." Although we were issued the same training manuals, the Penal Code of the City of New York, the Code of Criminal Procedure, the Administrative Code, the Vehicular Traffic Laws, the Health Code, etc., and attended the same classes with the same instructors and lecturers, took the same competitive tests, we weren't allowed to be entered into competition with the men for the trophies and awards issued to each graduating class. The reason given was that the women usually did better than the men academically, and if they were awarded the trophies, it would remove this incentive from the men.

This attitude really captured the basic feeling of the instructors, who reflected the feelings of the "brass." We women were tolerated, or worse yet treated as pets. This attitude carried over into the actual classroom. An instructor told the class, "I'd tell you what to do in this particular case, but there's a woman present." Thirty male heads turned to the lone female with annoyance clearly registered on their faces, feeling that they were now missing out on some important piece of advice because of that damn broad.

I found out through the grapevine what this tremendous piece of news was. According to law, a police officer must carry his weapon twenty-four hours a day, even off duty. Invariably the questions pop up, "Do I have to wear it if I'm mowing the lawn?" "If I'm at the beach and want to go swimming, what do I do with the gun?" The answer given in classes lucky enough not to be blessed with a woman was, "Shove it up your ass!"

I think my biggest disappointment was the omission of the policewomen from the physical training program. The men were assigned one half day to academic classes and the other half day to the gym.

We shared the half day of academic classes with the men and then were assigned to clerical duties in the recruit school offices for the remainder of the day. I had undergone months of gym work to condition myself for this job only to feel it deteriorating

13

before I even got out to work. This kind of work demands that you be in top shape, mentally and physically. Any cop who allows himself to fall apart is actually putting two strikes against himself in any encounter he may find himself involved in.

I firmly believe that the department should institute some form of compulsory physical fitness. It could be one half day a week at the academy or the range. Better still they should have a small workout gym in every precinct. Most of the men would take advantage of it. The ones who need it the most, won't. Keeping in peak condition should therefore be regulated in the same manner as range practice, only of course with much more frequency.

Some of those dropped chests, or beer-barrel bellies, or pots, are quivering last wills and testaments. You try to drag that lead weight of a stomach with you, and hop over that fence after an eighteen-year-old kid that just robbed the fruit man on the corner, and see how far you get.

A great detective friend in the Safe and Loft Squad, who was working long after he could have retired, suffered a heart attack chasing a thief in the garment section. Many friends have also been hurt and killed because they reacted too slowly. Being in good physical shape, and knowing it, adds to both your physical and your mental well-being.

But, back in the academy, no matter how much we asked or complained we got virtually nowhere. There were no gym classes for us, or calisthenics, or swimming, although I understand that recently the situation has improved.

They finally conceded to allow several gym instructors, on a voluntary basis, to coach us once a week in judo. We loved it, but it just wasn't enough. Perhaps the most important thing they taught us was how to fall. I remember some of the advice our mentors dished up, thank God! Because I've had cause to use it dozens of times during the years.

If someone comes at you, whether it be to rob, rape, or rap you on the head, *fall down!* In the first place, your attacker is surprised, so you've taken away his initial momentum. He knows he didn't knock you down, and he wonders just what the hell you're doing. He may decide he doesn't want to find out, and just run away. Score one.

In the second place, you present a much smaller target on the floor than you do standing up in the air. He can't stick a knife in your back, because your back is on the ground. He'll have to descend to your level to get at you, which means he'll have to kneel down and in so doing lose all the momentum of speed and drive that he could get by rushing at you.

In the third place, one has much more strength in the legs than in the arms. The legs contain the strongest muscles in the human body. If you draw your legs up and use them to kick out like a balky mule, you will in all probability seriously discourage your attacker.

It isn't very much like the judo you've seen in demonstrations and photographs but it's practical and it works and that is a lot more important to the average person afraid of walking down a street, as well as to the policewoman. They convinced us that studying the form of ritual judo was for us useless, that it must be practiced at least once or twice a week regularly in order to maintain the skill which they felt was mainly for visual effect. We were taught a goodly number of holds that could persuade someone to stay still, to come along, and even to stop breathing.

I've been asked so many times, particularly by women, what they could do if they were attacked on the streets. I have heard a dozen different kinds of advice, including carrying a police whistle and blowing it in their ears, giving them whatever they want quietly (including yourself) and hoping they go away, screaming loudly to get attention, or getting a large dog. There are of course other equally illuminating hints such as cross your fingers, don't walk alone, whistle a happy tune, offer a silent prayer, and make sure you've made arrangements for the disposition of your remains and property before venturing forth. Facetious? I'm afraid so.

There is no magic ritual or formula that will act as either a deterrent or an antidote in any and all given situations. The best advice I can offer is usually greeted with a look of inquiry and perhaps a look of disappointment. Keep your cool. Try to keep your composure and don't let your body or mind freeze up on you. Some people become zombies under pressure, riveted to the spot, unable to function in any capacity. When retelling the incident, they can give almost no details or descriptions.

With your mind operative, try to judge your attacker. Size

him up. If he was selling magazines at your doorstep, or your daughter brought him home for dinner, what would you think of him? When you are recounting the story, you will be able to convey not only a description but a clear impression of type, which is even more important.

Don't be afraid to talk quietly. This is not the time, however, for you to shout heroically, "You fucking son of a bitch, I work hard for this money and you're not going to get it!"

When I was seventeen, I talked someone out of raping me. A uniformed soldier followed me home one evening and literally jumped me, throwing me to the ground as we passed a vacant lot. I don't know where I got the presence of mind and the strength to talk for two and a half hours. But I did, like my life depended on it, which was so.

He pressed a knife under my throat so that I couldn't move, all I could do was sweat and talk.

Where do you come from? What kind of an accent is that? Where are you stationed? What are you assigned to do? What school did you go to? Do you like poetry? What kind? Do you remember your favorite? Will you recite it for me? Do you like books? Who is your favorite author? What kind of food do you like? Who is the best cook in the world? What was the last movie you saw? Who is your favorite actor? Do you have a girl friend? Do you have a sister? Is your mother living? What would your mother do if your sister got raped? What would you do? Do you know that it is considered a "disgrace" for an Italian girl to be "dishonored" and that she is then considered unmarriageable? Do you know that my mother will probably cripple me and tell me that somehow or other I'm to blame, or that she might even kill herself? Do you know that you are much too attractive to do something like this? Why don't you ask a girl for a date, I'm sure any girl would go out with you if you asked her. Are you feeling all right? Maybe you're a little upset about something; when did you eat last? What did you have? Where do you live? Can I call someone to help you or get you something?

Sounds ridiculous to talk this way with a knife digging in, but talk, talk, I talked until he was reduced to rubble. I left him hours later, with his face pressed in the dirt, crying passionately and asking his dead mother in heaven for forgiveness.

I stumbled off, weak-kneed and trembling. I staggered into the house and sought the safety of the bathroom, the only room with a lock, and then afforded myself the luxury of crying.

Since then I've talked my way in and out of many things, but that vivid first memory will always remain as the first shocker.

Keeping your wits functioning will help you know if you have any advantages going for you, or if discretion be the better part, etc. Your mouth and your brain are original issue equipment. Try 'em—they might work.

Our uniform gun was a 32-caliber revolver, with a two-inch barrel. We were given a "choice" between the Smith & Wesson and the Colt. I chose the Smith & Wesson because that's what the equipment bureau had in stock. The men were issued 38-caliber revolvers with a four-inch barrel.

Practice instruction at the ranges was superb. Those officers are a special breed. They know what they're doing and really go all out to convey it to you. They didn't care what sex we were; they just wanted us to know what to do with our weapons. I learned to respect the knowledge of the range officers and to acquire a healthy respect for this death-dealing tool in my possession.

We plugged along in school, absorbing all we could, until November 26, 1957, when we graduated with a kiss-off speech from Mayor Wagner and the then Commissioner Kennedy. The ceremonies were held in Hunter College and then we were assigned into our varied commands. The men were going to precincts throughout the five boroughs. There was no question as to where the women would go. Every female was automatically assigned to the Policewomen's Bureau.

Policewomen's Bureau

The new shining stars came into the Women's Bureau bursting with their fresh enthusiasm. In 1891 when the first women were appointed to the New York City Police Department as matrons, they were eager to perform their primary purpose, the searching and guarding of female prisoners.

Much to our chagrin we found that policewomen's duties were still basically the same as in the 1890s. Some of the more usual duties were:

1. *Matron duty:* Being assigned to various precincts with female detention cells, doing "matron duty," which was the strip-searching and guarding of all female prisoners. Every female arrested within your precinct area is brought to you to be searched for contraband, evidence, drugs, or anything which could be utilized to hurt herself or others. She removes her clothes and you have to scrutinize them piece by piece. You check the hems, pleats, waistbands, collars, etc., for razor blades, scissors, or drugs which may have been secreted. It is important to keep in mind what the prisoner was arrested for during the search. If it's an assault or murder charge you might look for a weapon, bloodstains, or powder burns. If there's a sex crime involved you might find semen stains.

On a busy Friday or Saturday you handle as many as twenty to thirty prisoners, and start to think you're running a blooming hotel. These temporary detention cells are ghastly bare cubicles measuring five by seven feet, containing a bare plank chained to the wall to serve as both bed and chair. There's no mattress, pillow, or blankets. There is a tiny sink in one corner and in the

18

other an open john. The toilet cannot be flushed from inside the cell, in order to prevent flushing down any evidence that might have escaped your search. The prisoner must ask for toilet paper, for sanitary napkins, and to flush the blasted toilet when they're done. The reason for this becomes obvious after you make your first mistake of handing an entire roll to some prisoner who has asked you two or three times previously for paper. What follows and usually in this order is:

1. Very gleeful prisoner
2. Entire roll jammed in clogged toilet
3. Cells flooded in whole corridor
4. Desk officer has to be notified for repairs
5. Prisoners have to be moved
6. Repairs being made by disgusted cop pressed into service
7. Prisoners having a ball at having a man in the cells, especially the pross who are verbally giving him the business
8. Cop leaves with some caustic comment about women
9. Very miserable policewoman

2. *Hospital prisoners:* Policewomen are assigned to guard female prisoners detained in hospitals. These prisoners might've been injured as a result of the crime, or during the arrest process; or they might have tried to commit suicide afterward.

Whatever the reason, they're usually in a ward of a city hospital with no provisions for guarding them. You're lucky to get a chair in a ward that may hold twenty patients. This is a difficult situation, as the other patients and the nurses are usually upset at the idea of a prisoner being there. If the prisoner patient is ambulatory you have to follow her about as she goes for X rays, treatments, or to the bathroom. Her phone calls must be intercepted and her visitors screened. This, in my opinion, had to be the most boring eight-hour tour you could catch.

3. *Guarding female material witnesses:* Material witnesses are a different breed of cat. Technically they're not prisoners, although they've often been brought to court and adjudged witnesses, if they were unco-operative and held in a special section in a jail usually reserved for alimony beats and other minor charges.

On the other hand, if she is volunteering information that aids a continuing investigation, the district attorney's office will put her up in a hotel room. If she has children they come to live with her. She receives a cash sum for each day that she is detained, plus meal allowances and whatever other expenses the DA's office feels may be necessary to keep her happy.

Some women seem to make a career out of being professional witnesses, milking it for all it's worth. When a female witness is guarded a male detective is always present as well. The policewoman is actually there to protect *him* from any charges that the witness might make that she was compelled, coerced, or otherwise taken advantage of sexually. Normal people who happened to witness a crime are often lodged and guarded in their own homes.

4. *Lost children:* Operating lost children's shelters at the various city beaches in the summertime was another "choice" assignment. A counselor or park attendant could handle it just as efficiently. Children are brought, dragged, and carried into the shelters by cops, lifeguards, men, women, and by themselves. If you can manage to extract a name from the child, you have it broadcast with his description and hope that someone will call for him. Some children seem to be purposely lost, with Mommy taking advantage of a free baby-sitting service.

5. *Varied uniform assignments:* These assignments often seem to have more value as public relations than law enforcement. The women in full uniform seem to attract more attention than they actually warrant, because they're so infrequently exposed to the public eye. In full-dress uniform they appear to be much more effective than they'll ever be given the opportunity to be.

Some of the uniform assignments covered: park dances and concerts, demonstrations, election tabulations, lecturing to citizen's groups, and guarding the appearances of dignitaries such as visiting royalty or heads of state, the Pope or the President. The policewomen often ended up being assigned to guard the hotel ladies' room even though the washroom might be ten floors or more away from the visitor. Nevertheless I would faithfully toss the bathroom looking for hidden bombs behind the plumbing and trying to flush out the "Bathroom Bomber."

6. *Searching DOA's* (dead on arrivals): A policewoman remained on standby at all times and would respond to any re-

ported female death that was suspicious in origin, accidental, or one in which the individual died while not under a doctor's care. Her duty was to search the body, removing jewelry and anything else needing to be safeguarded.

This was a particularly choice assignment since when you responded you had no idea if the DOA was found after being dead for a week or two, had been run over by seven subway cars, floated to the surface after being submerged for two months, had been brutally murdered in some maniacal fashion, had jumped ten or twenty floors, or had quietly committed suicide in lonely desperation.

As soon as the policewoman finishes her search, the body is bundled up and trundled off by the morgue men who strip and scrub it. The male medical examiner then performs an autopsy and the body is finally turned over to male undertakers who handle and embalm it. But the city fathers seem to think that the deceased's family would object if a male cop were to remove and safeguard any valuables. Sometimes the cop who caught the case might have to wait four to five hours before a policewoman became available to perform the search. What a wonderful use of manpower.

Those were the average assignments of the policewomen until the appointment, from the ranks, of a truly outstanding woman investigator as the new director of the Policewomen's Bureau in July 1952.

Utilization of Women

Theresa Melchionne, director of the Policewomen's Bureau, was my first boss on this job, and one of the best.

She really knew people. She was an excellent administrator with an unerring instinct for round pegs in round holes. Every policewoman, all 240 of them, she knew by name and assignment. Not only did she know her "girls," but she seemed to have her own pipeline of personal information on their families. It was not unusual to be called in and hear, "I understand your son is sick, how can I help you? Would working nights be of any value to you, or do you want to take a day or two off against your overtime?"

The women were divided into two camps. Those who thought her great and those who hated her. They could also be called the workers and the drones.

Director Melchionne had a haughty imperious look. But the coldness was in her bearing only. The person she was hardest on was herself. She was the first one in the office mornings and often had to be physically driven out the door by her aide-de-camp and chauffeur, Vera Braman. Lunchtime was a hasty container of black coffee and a package of oatmeal cookies.

She drove herself ruthlessly, and her aim was to establish women as an important investigative arm of the department. She had faith in our capabilities and was constantly seeking methods of acceptance and a chance to prove it.

Mrs. M slowly and painstakingly turned this varied group of women into an arresting unit. By dint of her own system of reward and punishment, she pushed toward her goal.

The boss would give two days off for an arrest, but by like token if she knew you were dogging it she would put you on DOA reserve for a week. That would sober you up.

She started with the few women that she had left after covering all the necessary details. Ordinarily these women would have remained on reserve duty. The reserve girls were now put on assignments to investigate illegal gypsies; then slowly there evolved the shoplifting detail, the Broadway Squad, the Degenerate Squad, and eventually the Abortion Squad. The girls with acquired experience eagerly shared it and relished a chance to display their prowess.

By the mid-1960s the Women's Bureau was responsible for six to eight hundred arrests a year, mostly cases that affected women and/or children.

There was also a constant demand then from the specialized squads for women to work as decoys and undercover investigators, now that their value was being recognized.

On October 28, 1963, Mrs. M was promoted to deputy commissioner, Youth Program, and left the Women's Bureau. Without a fighting dominant figure, the Police Department decentralized the unit. A number of girls were assigned to each precinct, and they went back to being matrons, making coffee, sewing on buttons, smiling and looking pleasant, and if they had a progressive-thinking desk officer, answering the switchboard or entering summonses. What a comedown. As new women were sworn in they were assigned directly to the precincts and never received any of this "on the job" or "street" experience. I couldn't understand how the city could justify nullifying a unit with that arrest record, with nothing to replace it.

I had my share of garbage the first six months on the job, and quickly looked for a way to rise above it. The fastest way was working for it—and work I did.

I was doing matron duty in the 14th Precinct, which covers the area between West Forty-second Street and West Twenty-seventh Street, from the Hudson River to Fifth Avenue. This takes in part of the Times Square area and the wholesale garment district. Most of the female prisoners detained there had been booked for shoplifting, junk, or prostitution, and often a combination of these. You lose your naïveté quickly in this atmosphere.

Of course they weren't all junkie pross. One call girl was brought in wearing a mink coat, with her long blond hair hanging loosely, and a tiny poodle still clutched in her arms. She seemed to be followed by a procession of oglers. I herded her inside for the usual search. But this one was a bit unusual, as she removed the mink and stood defiantly in absolutely nothing, and looked gorgeous. No wonder I had a half dozen or so guys gawking outside in the squad room.

One of the most hated details had to be matron duty in the 28th Precinct. This Harlem precinct is known for having the worst DOAs in the city. In the Two-Eight, I've had two subway suicides, untold jumpers, countless homicides, and my favorite, who actually died a normal death. Unfortunately this elderly woman lived alone and was washing the dishes when she had a heart attack. It wasn't until eight days later when the odor had penetrated the entire building that anyone thought to wonder about her, and to call the police.

The hot water had continued running during this entire period, and had turned that kitchen into a steam bath. The plaster was peeling off the walls from the heat and humidity. The body was in a state of advanced decomposition and she was completely distended with body gases.

When I walked into the hallway the stench hit so hard I felt flung back. The sergeant came out and offensively said, "What's the matter, you can't take it? She won't hurt you. She's dead, you know, ha-ha-ha. You get the same money as we do, so do your job."

I saw the two cops from the radio car that drove me there, looking angrily white. "I'll be back in five minutes, I don't have my DOA kit with me, since I was assigned to matron duty," I explained to mein herr sergeant. The fellas drove me to Harlem Hospital where I picked up a pair of rubber gloves, a scissors, and some smelling salts, meanwhile listening to them muttering, "The son of a bitch . . . the crummy sadistic son of a bitch, you can see that old woman only had a nightgown on, what could she have?"

Back we went. I opened the spirits of ammonia, hoping it would block my nostrils a bit, and dashed in with my gloves on. I cut the nightgown right up the middle—nothing, of course. A

24

hasty look at her hands for rings, her neck for a chain, her ears for earrings, and I was out the door. My lungs were bursting with my attempts not to inhale.

The fellas drove me back slowly; I felt sick. They wanted to get me some brandy, but I shook my head. I wanted to get back to the precinct and scrub, scrub, scrub. I vomited instead.

Two hours later I got a visit from my radio car friends. They were laughing, overtalking each other in an attempt to tell me about my "revenge." The morgue men had finally come, bringing the body bag to transport the corpse. When they reached over to pick it up, they recoiled almost automatically.

The sergeant blustered up, "For Chris' sakes . . . get the hell out of the way, let a man do it." He leaned over and wrenched the body to roll it into the bag. I guess that poor old lady had had the final indignity. The body gasses exploded and the sergeant was completely covered—head to toenails.

As any cop will tell you, the only thing you can do with that uniform is to take it out and bury it about two miles from your house, because you will never get the stink out. You also had better not go home for a couple of days.

Gypsy Squad

The very first introduction to anything resembling investigative work for policewomen had to be the Gypsy Squad.

Why gypsies? Well, pretending to foretell the future is in itself against the law, but it usually is just the opening gambit to bigger and better confidence and swindling games. Since gypsies usually rely more on cunning than physical violence, it seemed a natural tooth sharpener for the fledgling female investigators.

It was a simple matter to assign an unskilled woman to whatever team was working, since three women together seldom created any more attention than two; in fact often it was better. They could easily pass as fellow employees out on a lunch break or shopping expedition. You'd run into trouble, though, if they all looked like the popular conception of policewomen—truck drivers in drag.

Fortune-tellers, particularly gypsies, are really a class unto themselves. You had best check your gold fillings after a conversation with them, because they'll have them removed, melted down, and sold while you're still in the middle of a yawn.

Most people think gypsies are harmless, fortune-telling is a novelty to indulge in on a dull evening in order to retell at the next bridge session. To the normally well adjusted this is true, but there are a lot of unhappy, lonely, sick, impressionable people just hurting for someone to show them some interest and attention.

The gypsies seek out the weak, pander to their needs, and feed them what they want to hear. Actually this is their pin money operation. Their real scores result from their con games and flimflam swindles.

Gypsy women do not receive any schooling. This is how the men keep them in line. Marriages are still arranged by the families, and the women are purchased. The prices they bring depend on both their physical appearance, needed to lure customers, and their ability to tell fortunes and manipulate the con games.

The boys are sent to school, but usually get no more than a few years in because they are constantly on the move due to pressures from school truancy boards, pending court cases, pulling up stakes before a complaint is made, or just skipping out on the rent. But, whatever the reason, they are a nomad people, tied to no one spot but tightly bound to each other.

They do not buy real property or anything that might serve to restrict them, recognizing only gold and cash. In fact they are gold-happy freaks. I remember a custom-crafted gold belt buckle, three to four inches in diameter and about three inches high; a lion's head thrown back in a giant roar, its protruding tongue a mass of encrusted diamonds and fiery emeralds for eyes. It was a magnificent piece that literally jumped with life.

It graced the waist of the fattest, greasiest-looking male gypsy, whose eyeteeth were also capped in gold. His stomach was so pendulous, the weight of it forced his legs open, making him walk splay-footed. His white-on-white shirt, gray-rimmed at the collar, managed to stay unbuttoned just at the belly-button level, so that you were greeted by his hair-rimmed navel resting on top of that poor lion's head. Too much even for the King of Beasts.

Besides jewelry, gypsies surface their cash on cars. They love Cadillacs, particularly Coupes de Ville. They descend on a car dealer in wolf packs, ranging from the big fat old Queen, her husband, two or three male sons with their assorted wives, and a ragtag bag of children. If they leave without buying, that dealer had better check his stock. Chances are he is missing spare tires or hubcaps, and if he left any ignition keys in the cars they're gone. (And those cars will disappear within a few days also.)

A gypsy family was dickering price on a Sedan de Ville in a wholesale place on Jerome Avenue. Joey, the owner, was acting like a cat on a hot griddle. His 119-pound frame was poured into his Italian knit shirt, which was unbuttoned past his breastbone to display a heavy chain and pendant, his latest gift. Joey was his own character, and trying to find him or pin him down was like trying to feel a shadow or clutch a falling snowflake.

People were easy. Joey manipulated them with ease and a smile, but now he wasn't at ease and he wasn't smiling. The gypsies had spread out thousands of dollars in crisp hundred-dollar bills all across his desk, but he was mentally counting attendance to see if any of the others could be stripping the cars in the garage during the transaction.

He came out of his office to hear the old Queen trying to cajole two of the drivers to get their fortunes told, half price—only five dollars because she was just wasting time waiting for the men. It shouldn't be a total loss. Here they had seven thousand dollars laid out to buy a Caddy and old Queenie was already starting to make up for it.

Joey shook his head, returned to his office, and gathered up the money. "Okay, okay, it's yours, but do me a favor, don't wait here. Come back in two hours and I'll have all the papers waiting for you."

As they trailed out, Joey's usually fluid body collapsed into a deep chair as he said to the assemblage, waiting for their chance at a "hot bargain," "Jesus, those people make me nervous. But did you see that money? Always cash, always hundred-dollar bills, and always Cadillacs. Christ, how the hell do they come up with that kind of bread?"

Gypsy money is usually obtained through some type of swindle, the most common one being the evil-eye gambit. If after a routine reading the gypsy feels that she's hooked a live one, she'll suggest jealousy or the evil eye as the cause of some existing problem. If this is receptively received, the reader will have the victim return bringing items like an egg (the spirit is supposed to take form in the egg), a spool of thread (to help unravel the knotty problems), something touched by a loved one (a handkerchief or sock, in order to make contact), and ten to twenty dollars to purchase special candles for the reader to pray by.

If the mark goes this far, he or she is usually hooked. Naturally the egg confirms the presence of the evil spirit which only the gypsy can control or dispel. Inevitably the spell is narrowed down to the individual's bankbook. The money therein is said to be tainted and will have to be withdrawn and prayed over in order to cleanse it. Only in this way can the subject ever know happiness or good fortune again.

People have withdrawn life savings and then watched elaborate cleansing ceremonies. They've seen the money returned to them in a sealed box with orders not to open it for twenty-four hours or all the praying would be negated.

When they do open the package they are greeted with a stack of cut-up newspapers and it's the money that's gone, not the evil eye they were so anxious to put to rest. By the time the police get the report from the "sucker," they find an empty storefront.

Predicting the future is not limited solely to gypsies. Many experienced confidence workers operate out of their homes, offices, or tearooms.

The tearoom workers are the most innocuous, catering to the luncheon trade, groups of giggling office workers, women coming into the city for Wednesday's theater matinee, birthday and shower groups, and shy or eager young couples.

Everyone is looking for something to spark or titillate his interest. Harmless in itself, I usually categorized this type as entertainment, and never did much more than occasionally checking them out to see that they remained in the song-and-dance classification.

The lone reader who works out of her home is a different ball game. She survives on referrals, one client telling another. She makes sure her people keep coming back to her on a regular basis. Her power lies in creating a dependency on her as she weaves intricate webs of fear and hope enmeshing her helpless "flies," and consuming them at her pace and in her own way.

Because of this very closeness and dependency, complaints against this type of individual are rare indeed, and rarer still is finding a complainant.

Broadway Squad

When Mrs. M called me into her office and told me she was going to try me out with the Broadway Squad I knew I had my toe in the door.

The Broadway Squad was a pretty high sounding name for what we were, a pair of policewomen assigned to cover the Broadway movies. From the Paramount to the Strand, to the Roxy, to the Capitol, to Radio City Music Hall, and so on, and what we were particularly looking for were jostlers and exposures.

Jostling: Section 165.25 of the Penal Law reads: "in a public place, intentionally and unnecessarily places his hand in the proximity of person's pocket or handbag, or crowds another at a time when a third person's hand is in the proximity of such person's pocket or handbag."

Indecent exposure: Section 245 of the Penal Law reads: "A person who willfully and lewdly exposes his person or the private parts thereof, in any public place or in any place where others are present, or procures another so to expose himself."

Women would come into the movies, unaware of anything except enjoying the show. They'd take off their coats and whenever possible place them on empty seats next to them, usually together with their purses.

The jostler would change seats any number of times looking for the right situation. The very best possible setup was in the row behind a woman and directly behind the empty seat containing her things. He'd get in, throw his coat over the back of the seat in front of him, and then settle back. If this had attracted any attention at all it was because of the movement, and any suspicions were quickly allayed when she saw that he'd placed his coat there and seemed intent on the movie. The pick would make one or two preliminary moves, such as reaching for a hankie or cigarettes, but actually he'd be opening the purse, and locating and positioning the wallet beneath his coat. Fifteen minutes or so later he'd reach for his coat, taking the wallet out of the purse at the same time, wherever possible, and the entire bag if the wallet could not be located. This would remain under the coat slung over his arm. Quickly and smoothly he'd leave the theater by a side or rear door where the empty wallet and/or the purse would be discarded.

The exposures were a breed unto themselves. We referred to them as the sickies. These males would seat themselves near a female who appealed to them; she might be six, she might be sixty, and he would direct his sexual fantasy toward her. Some of them preferred to remain silent and some seemed to find it necessary to call attention to themselves to achieve the sexual excitement they required. I was often amazed at how some women could be so completely engrossed in the celluloid strips and so unaware of the drama in the next seat. I frequently had to call a woman into the manager's office after taking out an arrest, and point out to her that her clothing was full of semen stains.

My first experience with the squad was working with an "old-timer," Ann Gilchrist. Ann was a lovely-looking blue-eyed blonde, in her late thirties, who was a heck of a worker. I considered myself to be in luck and was more than eager to serve my apprenticeship.

Every policewoman had heard of the Gilchrist clutch. It was Ann's foolproof method for turning culprits into prisoners. "When Ann gets her hands on a guy, he doesn't stand a chance."

Sure enough, we were in the top balcony of the Strand Theater and we were seated near a woman who had her purse invitingly displayed. Perhaps someone else would find it as interesting as we did.

In about half an hour this 6'4", 225-pound hulk came and sat directly behind the purse, in the goody seat. The coat went over the top and he settled back. In a while he made a couple of posi-

tioning moves, meanwhile looking about and evaluating the rest
of the audience to spot any possible interference.

We knew he was going for it. Ann hastily said, "All you gotta
do is cuff him. I'll grab him and hold him and you put the cuffs on
his wrists."

"Gotcha."

I took out my cuffs and I was on the edge of my seat, which
was in the row behind him, one to the right. Ann was on my left,
directly behind him. When he leaned over again, Ann said "Now!"
and she put both her arms around his neck. I stood up with the
cuffs upraised ready to slap them on, except that he was now
standing up and Gilchrist looked like a fly hanging ineffectually
on his back. He shook her off like a wet dog sheds water.

We wrestled this thief every step of the way from the top balcony to the main lobby. One thing you could never use in a
theater, except under completely unusual circumstances, was a
gun. You couldn't risk harming so many innocent bystanders.

By the time we hit the main floor, I was shoeless, he was about
ten steps ahead of me, but in a lot worse shape. He was nude
from the waist up. When he hit the bottom of the steps he turned
from my view for a fraction of a second and I shouted to the
usher, who was standing there in his lovely fancy uniform, with
his arms folded across his chest, "Which way did he go?" "Who?"
came back the brilliant answer. With that I sat down on the steps
to catch my breath and was joined by Ann.

"How often does this moron see a guy who's six-four, nude
from the waist up, all scratched and bleeding, running out of the
theater in the middle of January? I give up," I said disgustedly.

Not one soul paid us any attention, much less tried to help.
Ann and I slowly and painfully picked our way back upstairs. We
had been pushed, punched, pummeled, and dragged over rows
of seats. Every few feet we picked up another item of his clothing which we had torn off in our attempts to stop him. We ended
up with a T-shirt, banlon sweater, a vest, and a sports jacket, all
in shreds.

We also ended up with the fanciest assortment of black-and-
blues and aches and pains. He didn't get the purse, though. In
fact the woman was still quietly viewing the movie and was filled

with disbelief when we asked her to come to the manager's office to check the contents of her bag.

My lesson for that day was simple. From that experience, I devised and used my own "movie mover" technique and it never failed me. When I was ready to make an apprehension I would lean over and firmly press my blackjack or billy directly into the back of his neck saying, "Don't move. . . . Police. . . . You're under arrest. . . . Now slowly place your hands in front of you," and my partner would then place the cuffs on him and we'd quietly move him out, often without anyone being aware of anything.

The only problem I had with this method was with the exposures. We'd march the character through the theater and into the manager's office and he'd be sitting there in handcuffs but still exposed in all his fallen splendor.

Johanna McFarland and I had just walked into Radio City Music Hall. Jo was a Broadway sharpie. She was black and moved so unobtrusively that people in the theater were completely unaware of her.

"I'll just pop down this aisle and see if anything is cooking," and Jo walked down the side aisle. I leaned over the back ledge waiting for her and as I glanced down at the back row, I started in disbelief. There, like eighteen inches from me, was a character, completely exposed, and manipulating himself like mad behind a tiny paper program. He was seated between two women who were engrossed in the film and unaware of what he was up to.

Jo came back. "Nothing's doing." I shook my head and she looked at me. I pointed down at the great masturbator right under our noses. She did a double take and we said, "Let's go!"

Into the aisle from one direction went Jo as I went in from the other. People were annoyed because there were no vacant seats and they wondered where we were going. We met in front of our exposure and I whipped the cuffs right on him before he was aware of anything, telling him we were police as we carted him out with us to the manager's office.

Once in the office, with the door secured, we turned to question our apprehension. Jo and I both looked at him and stared. Then we looked at each other and stared some more. A soft whisperlike "I don't believe it" came out of me to join Jo's "Oh no!"

Our exposure (who was still exposed) was sitting in the manager's big overstuffed chair, as calm as you please. His handcuffed hands were clasped in front of his chest, as if in prayer, and he was looking at us indignantly. He was also wearing clerical garb. I'd noticed the white collar when I first saw him, but assumed he was wearing a white turtleneck with a black sweater.

We made him empty out his pockets, and came up with an ID card and photos which unquestionably identified him as a Catholic priest. His reason for his actions? "I have a skin condition, and I had to scratch it." It was one we'd heard before.

He could have scratched himself through his clothing, or if it was so unusual, he could have gone to the men's room to seek relief. Of course the fallacy was in the fact that he was manipulating an erection, not scratching an itch.

"Jo," said I, all heart, "he's all yours. You're not Catholic, they can't do anything to you."

"Like hell, I wouldn't touch him with a ten-foot pole. You do what you want with him."

"But Jo, can you see me on the front page of the *Daily News*, hauling a priest into court, and for indecent exposure no less?"

We sat there mulling it over, knowing how deeply the church is enmeshed in police politics. I'd often commented that Police Headquarters ought to be located on Madison Avenue, because so many orders are issued from there. Discretion becomes the better part of valor.

We used our so-called discretionary powers and warned and admonished our apprehension. Which means I verbally reamed him, for whatever that's worth. He got a double barrel of cop, woman, and mother's fury, indignation, and outrage, and then I literally threw him out of the theater, warning him not to return.

34

Special Assignments

Policewomen are always on tap and subject to special assignments. I never minded them. They were often different and challenging. They also never lasted long enough for you to get disgusted or bored. You never knew what you'd be getting into when you were specially assigned to the such-and-such squad for one or two days or a week. Your orders would tell you where to report and how to dress and you'd be off.

On February 22 I was specially assigned to the Manhattan West Borough office and told to dress casually. I was still new on the job and looked like a young kid. On this assignment I wore my hair straight down and it reached my waist; and with pants and a sweater on I was taken for a teen-ager. This was my first taste of plainclothes work. The plainclothesman concentrates primarily on the enforcement of all laws governing gambling and vice. The fellas would use me to get in where they couldn't, either because they were too well known or the people were too sharp. I would try to make a "direct" play with either a bookmaker or a collector and then the fellas would swoop in and claim their collar.

Inspector Nods headed this outfit and the guys would tell you, he'd lock up his own mother. Nods was thrilled at getting some of his dirty work done for him. I made direct plays on February 20, 21, and 22 and the plainclothes team I was assigned to was going like gangbusters scooping up the numbers collectors after I'd placed my bets.

On the 22nd, George Washington's Birthday, Nods decided to lead his troops personally and made a big magilla out of it. He and Captain Barnett followed us in a car with walkie-talkies and binoculars. I placed my first bet at 9:30 A.M. at Broadway and 144th Street and Patsy Giarmino got busted for 974 PL, Collector.

Now Nods tasted blood and wanted more. So we rode downtown to Little Italy, where I was supposed to place a bet with a luncheonette counterman named Frankie. But Frankie was off that day, the tired blonde behind the counter said. He was either off or had gotten an off, that was for sure.

I left the restaurant wondering what to do next and still aware of the captain's car, a block away, and wondering what their reaction was as they peered at me through high-powered binoculars. As I paused, debating my next move, I was greeted by catcalls. "Hiyuh, sweetheart, you lookin' for me?" "Don't pay any attention to that wolf, honey, I'm the only guy here you can trust."

Four men, about twenty-one to twenty-three years old, were standing at the curbside. They looked like neighborhood smart-money guys—sharply dressed and strutting like bantam roosters, trying to outdo each other.

I figured if I played it cool, I could get them to steer me to whoever was taking the local action. "Don't bother me, I have enough problems. Frankie's not in and I don't know what to do. My father gave me this bet to put in with Frankie and they told me he's not here. I'm gonna get killed, my old man will think I didn't come in time to get it in. I don't know where I can find him. Do you know anyone else who can take it for me?"

A duded-up blond smarty-pants stepped forward and with twenty-three-year-old machismo said, "Sure, honey, give it to me. I'll take care of it for you, baby."

"Get lost, you're not a collector, I'm not giving you my money."

"Hey fellas, tell her I'm okay." A chorus of assurances floated around.

"Listen," I told him, "suppose he wins? Tomorrow where am I going to find you to get paid off? Why don't you guys tell me who's really taking the action?"

Blondie put out his hand and gestured for the slip. "C'mon, c'mon, honey, I told you, you can trust me. I'll tell you what. You come back tomorrow. If you win, I'll be here to pay off, and if you lose, I'll still be here and I'll buy you a cuppa coffee or somethin'."

I didn't really think this guy was a collector, but he was hollering for the action and I was being watched. If I didn't place the bet, I would be on the carpet and they'd want an explanation, and somehow I didn't think the truth would make it. So I gave him the policy slips and the money in marked bills and as he was making change, he was arrested. A more shocked, idiotic expression on a guy's face would have been hard to find. In Special Sessions court on March 28, Louis Faggile, no previous record, proved to be the neighborhood wise-ass. He was a lithographer, who was at home because of the holiday and was putting on this act to show his friends what a big man he was.

His lawyer asked for a dismissal of the charges because he would be inducted into the armed forces within the week if the pending charges were dismissed. He also stated that his client had been sufficiently punished by the ridicule of his cronies in this rough tough ghetto. Not only had he been taken in by a cop, but the cop was a woman.

Down on Mott Street that's pretty hard to live down, so the judge permitted him to change his address to the U. S. Army for the next two years.

Degenerate Squad

One of Mrs. M's more daring innovations was the creation, albeit unofficial, of the Degenerate Squad.

"No," we would answer our condescending male counterparts, who were forever jesting. "You don't have to be a degenerate to make the squad. Why, were you thinking of applying?"

We got more than our share of volunteers. The Degenerate Squad consisted of women who had a flair for investigative work and were attractive. Freckles, a beautiful face, a good set of legs, an oversized bust line or really sexy eyes, might be just the equipment necessary to work a particular case.

The number of complaints referring to acts of indecency climbed steadily year after year, as people became aware of the squad's existence and its successes.

Women complained of obscene phone callers, male neighbors who exposed themselves, children who were followed home from school; and there were accounts of molestations, in public and private. They weren't earthshaking cases of bizarre ritualistic horror, but things that affected and frightened the normal run-of-the-mill female. Then we received a case which seemed to open a Pandora's box of similar situations.

Twenty-year-old June called referring to a Help Wanted advertisement that had appeared in the New York *Times,* reading, "Part Time Receptionist, Upper 5th Ave., call TW 0-2002." She'd called and been given an appointment.

The address turned out to be a private apartment on Fifth Avenue. She was interviewed by a Mr. Todd, who asked her if she'd like to teach Spanish. He'd place an ad in the paper and they could split the income.

"What makes you think I can speak Spanish? I'm answering your ad for a receptionist."

"Receptionist? I wouldn't let you waste yourself on something like that. How about teaching dancing in Mexico?" queried Todd. As June hesitated, wondering what she'd gotten into, she heard, "I have a great idea, would you like to teach Greek?"

June was now thoroughly confused and upset. When Todd told her that she could save money by moving into his apartment since he had loads of room, June turned tail and ran.

Several hours and one phone call later, she became an official complainant. However, most of what she told us were impressions, fears, and intuition. You have to have a lot more than that to back you up in court.

So the "Degenerate Girls" were pressed into action, assigned to answer that employment ad and report all results. Other clerical policewomen busily checked his telephone application and his credit, and ran his name through BCI (Bureau of Criminal Identification) to see if he had a sheet, and otherwise tried to compose a profile.

The results were somewhat awesome. He had ten listings in the New York telephone directory, claimed membership in nine clubs, and claimed to be president of Todd Trust Company of Nassau, president of the Pan American Banking Company, president of the American Corporation of Lawyers Society, connected with Todd Shipyards, and related to Mike Todd.

When we made contact Policewoman Merry went to apply for the "clerical" job. Todd told her, "You're made for better things. As he looked her over appreciatively he asked, "Can you ride a horse?" He said he was making a movie on horsemanship that demonstrated proper riding technique and would like her to train for it by joining a class in session. Todd fetched a pair of tights and told Merry to change.

"I'll just watch the first time," Merry said. They entered a room where three girls about fourteen to sixteen years old were standing by a wooden chair with two pieces of string tied around it.

As they entered Todd approached the girls, touched their hair, ran his hand across a shoulder, patted one on the behind, saying,

39

"How're my favorite girls doing?" He told them he would demonstrate how he rode when he played polo in England.

With that he straddled the chair and showed them how to control a horse by using the reins. How to post was beautifully demonstrated as he slid up and down on the chair practically bringing himself to orgasm in the process.

Red-faced, he "dismounted" and had all the youngsters try it, watching them intently and "correcting" them by touching and holding them in what he stated was the rhythm they must achieve.

The lesson was abruptly over and two of the youngsters told to leave and call on Monday morning. The third was told to remain for a "special" lesson; but she wisely called her mother who told her to leave immediately. Todd then turned to Merry: "I want you to come back tomorow, I know I could use you in my movie. In the morning you can train with my riding class and then we can talk about your career. Don't disappoint me. I'm counting on you."

Merry later noted, in her report, that there was a large amount of photographic equipment in the apartment and that many men and women seemed to be entering and leaving various rooms.

On July 6 I was assigned to investigate William Todd. I went to Apartment 2A in this lovely apartment house on Fifth Avenue. A slovenly male white, about forty-five to forty-eight years of age, 5'11", about two hundred pounds, with wavy brown hair, receding hairline, fair complexion, watery blue eyes, and sporting a two- or three-day growth of beard, said, "Yes, I'm Mr. Todd. Come in, come in. Have you ever been here before?"

"No, no, I haven't," I answered as I followed him, my eyes quickly glancing into several sparsely furnished cubicle-sized rooms and thinking, "God, what a slobby-looking mess he is! He hasn't been out of that shirt for at least three days."

"Sit down," said Todd, pointing to a daybed, "and tell me how you heard about me." Aside from the bed, the only furniture the room contained was a table with a couple of rolled-up movie screens on it, some film cans and empty reels, and a glass cabinet that seemed to be full of different kinds of cameras and projectors.

"My friend Sandra answered your ad for a receptionist, and

says you offered her a job traveling. When she told her parents they had a fit. That's why she hasn't come back. She told me about it when I told her how bored I was with my job, and how I would love something that was different."

Well, Todd made them different, all right. First I was offered a job selling tours for the Hudson River Day Line. Then after a few questions he decided that I would work out much better in California, soliciting bookings for the Matson Lines on a commission basis. Could I leave with him this weekend? He'd personally break me in and test me out to see if I could handle these responsibilities.

I gave him my wide-eyed stare and said, "Gee, maybe I could. Do you really think I might be able to get the job?"

"Wait, I can do better than that for you. How would you like to have the penthouse suite on a cargo liner bound for Singapore? First-class all the way, just you and me." With this, he put his arm around my shoulders and gave it a squeeze. "You know what I mean, baby?"

I was starting to get the picture as he ranted on telling me that while we were traveling we could produce travel films. "There's really a demand for them." Todd drooled on about what a lucky day this was for us and urged me to consider the office as my home. "There are plenty of extra rooms, you can always find an empty bed in one of them. Why don't you go get your clothes now and come back?"

"My rent is paid for the month so I won't be wasting any more money," I alibied.

Todd appeared perturbed by my reluctance and then said that I'd need $105 as a deposit on a Bolex camera and a zoom lens that I would need for filming. "Now come back by two-thirty this afternoon so I can start making reservations, and don't disappoint me."

As usual the Women's Bureau couldn't get authorization to invest $105. So I returned to Apt. 2A at 10 A.M. the following morning. Todd opened the door and let me in. As I passed him in the hallway, he scooped me up and then dropped me on the daybed.

"Hey, what the heck are you doing? I came to talk about that job!"

"This is your job, baby. You're going to be assistant to the president of my travel film association, and since I'm the president you've got nothing to worry about." Todd was now in a "highly agitated" state. He grabbed my hand as I was trying to scramble off that daybed, and tried to make me touch his private parts. He pinned me against the cabinet with his body. He was sweating profusely and his speech was thick.

"Touch me. Damn you, touch me. Jesus, I can come so easy! Listen, stay still, damn you. I'll take longer the next time, but you've got to make me explode now." He was muscular and driving like a bull in heat.

"But I thought we were going to talk business," said I brilliantly, trying to extricate myself.

"Business? You lousy frigid bitch!" he shouted as I finally pulled away and bolted across the room. "What are you afraid of? I won't make you pregnant. I thought you wanted a job."

"I'll have to give this a lot of thought," I muttered. "You took me by surprise. I'll see you later." I sidled out the door.

This was the first case of this type and brought on a high-powered conference between the director and the Legal Bureau. I was told to make an arrest and charge Todd with assault in the third degree. I wanted to slap him with a vagrancy charge that had previously been used only on prostitutes. As defined under Section 887-4C of the Code of Criminal Procedure, a vagrant is a person who loiters in or near any thoroughfare or public or private place for the purpose of inducing, enticing, or procuring another to commit lewdness, fornication, unlawful sexual intercourse, or any other indecent act.

Disagreement ran high. You couldn't arrest a man on that charge. You could only charge a pross with vagrancy. They'd laugh you out of court.

Mrs. M, convinced of the merits of my argument, agreed to give her support and backing even if we had to go to the Supreme Court and make a test case of this. She felt that if we got a conviction on this charge we would have an effective tool that might prevent women from being used like pawns.

I asked one of the male detectives from the 23d Squad to back me up as I returned to the Todd apartment and informed Willie Boy that he was being placed under arrest for assault and for vagrancy. When the charges were spelled out to him, especially the vagrancy bit, bits of froth flew from between his teeth as he spit out invectives. "Fucking bitch. . . . Fuc—" He didn't get much further. I didn't have to smile anymore or give him the baby-browns. I gave him a good shot across that contorted face instead as I said, "Let's go, creep!"

In the follow-up to the investigation we discovered that Todd had been arrested previously at least six times, in Florida, Texas, California, Maryland, and New York City.

The organizations and clubs that he said he belonged to all disclaimed him. They had in fact been plagued by creditors and complaints. The firms he supposedly headed were nonexistent.

After a prolonged, involved trial, William Todd, bon vivant, horseback rider extraordinaire, and panderer of women, became a convicted vagrant as stipulated in Section 887-4C of the Code of Criminal Procedure.

The publicity attendant on the first arrest of this sort for vagrancy seemed to take the lid off a can of squiggling worms. New York, mecca of star-struck youngsters. Kids come here to make it but get made themselves instead.

At this time I was handling abortion investigations, because you can only do a certain amount of degenerate cases without reflecting, "Is the whole world a dirty old man?" When the boss had discussed the case with me, I begged off, saying, "I'm getting too old for that garbage. Let some of the younger kids handle it. I've been fighting for my honor so long I'm getting punchy. One of these days one of the jobs might start sounding "good." She conceded laughingly and I received a reprieve.

It lasted almost a week, until I got a "forthwith" call into the office. (Forthwith—that means move, baby, and you'd better not plead that the traffic was heavy!) I found the boss in her inner sanctum with four or five of the younger policewomen seated about. She was sipping her container of black coffee, and when I appeared in the doorway, her enigmatic Mona Lisa smile started to form. "Come in, dear, come in, we've been waiting for you."

I got the feeling I'm "it," and wondered if I had touched all the bases, made an error, or was about to sacrifice. I got the details, along with a mawkish container of coffee to wash them down.

The girls had struck out. The reasons given ranged from "He said I wasn't his type," or "Come back next week," to the defiant "He was never in when I went there!"

I thumbed them through my mind as I realized that there was more than ineptness here. It was another case of "Miss Goody Two-Shoes," unfortunately prevalent in our department. It was a condition sown and cultivated by the men, and adopted and nourished by certain of the women who basically disliked work and found this attitude the perfect answer to their goofing off.

My fictitious Miss Goody, so sweet, so prim, so proper, so ultra-feminine, would never appear publicly without white gloves, her purse, and a dainty flowered hat. She generated gentility and was venerated as a combined mother-wife-Virgin Mary figure.

From the time she entered the academy she heard, "Oh, you don't want to hear that, those details will make you sick; let the men handle it." "Oh, you don't have to bother studying that, you'll never have to worry your little head about it." The women soon learned to sit back, smile a lot, offer to type, listen to stories, and make like Miss Goody Two-Shoes; just don't make like a cop, or try to compete on the same level as a man.

My mind was churning with these thoughts; annoyance and disappointment in my fellow women vying with each other. I turned to the boss to see that the Mona Lisa smile had tightened somewhat.

"I'm afraid I'll have to ask my 'aging exotic' to help us out again." I realize now that Mrs. M hadn't wasted any of her psychology courses. At the time all I could reflect was dumbfounded shock. "Aging exotic?" Me? Christ! I sure didn't mind being called exotic, but goddamn, that aging part sure set my teeth on edge. So of course I fell right into the trap. "Okay, give me the dope on this quiff and I'll let you know if there's anything to it." Mona Lisa smiled and finally passed the sugar for the coffee, and I was off and running.

Abortions

Abortion . . . a three-syllable word guaranteed to be a controversial subject.

For three years I handled abortion investigations, under the old law, when abortion was allowed only if the life of the mother or her child was endangered. My feelings and attitudes on this subject underwent drastic changes as a result. Originally the idea of abortion was repugnant to me. But the tragedy in many of the cases weighed so heavily I've had to change my opinions.

Although the law now reads that women can be legally aborted as late as their twenty-fourth week or sixth month, I feel that any woman wanting an abortion should do it in the three to four months before the fetal heartbeat is heard. She's had more than enough time to think of all the ramifications of a pregnancy and to avoid the possibility of aborting a live fetus.

I was assigned in April 1960 to interview a seventeen-year-old girl who'd been admitted to Kings County Hospital in Brooklyn, suffering from a ruptured uterus and acute peritonitis caused by an abortion. I found her in intensive care, a pathetic little rag doll. I knew she was dying. She fluttered back and forth from consciousness as I tried to get a deathbed statement from her. A statement taken from a dying person is admissible in court if that person is aware of the fact that he or she is dying and it's made voluntarily.

I got her name and age and asked her who had aborted her and how. With difficulty and concentration she whispered, "Douche. . . she used a douche." "Who did it? What's her name?" I repeated it over and over, and she reopened her eyes and said,

45

"She made me promise . . . can't tell . . . ," and her eyes slowly crossed and then glazed and became rigid.

I shuffled to the nurses' station and asked for the patient's chart. She'd been brought in about four or five hours before by ambulance. Diagnosis: induced abortion—perforated uterus—hemorrhaging and blood poisoning caused by the introduction of a caustic solution into the womb. This was my baptism.

One thing I found out for sure: abortions, like gambling and prostitution, can't be stopped. Regardless of income, social standing, or education, a woman who wants an abortion can find someone to do it. You can get aborted with a piece of slippery elm for $15 or have a dilation and curettage for $1,500.

What kind of desperation would make a college professor's wife go to a basement apartment in Harlem where she let an unwashed slattern lead her into a cockroach-ridden bathroom? On instruction she took off her undergarments and lay down inside the dingy bathtub with her legs up on either side. The abortionist reached into her apron pocket and took out a catheter, poked a straightened-out wire clothes hanger into the tube to stiffen it, and then wiggled one end of it into an open jar of Vaseline. She inserted the tube and forced it into the womb. Handing her "patient" a sanitary napkin, she then gave instructions for the tube to remain in place for at least twenty-four hours. "You'll start to stain and then should pass the fetus; if you don't, come back in four or five days and we'll do it again. That's why I charge seventy-five dollars, because I guarantee my work."

This woman was one of the people who made me realize the shortcomings of the old abortion law. She certainly had a good reason in my book for wanting an AB. She had three boys, all of whom were retarded. The possibilities and the probabilities were more than she could take, but her doctor said his hands were tied since there was no danger to her life or the life of the newborn. So she resorted to the only alternative she'd heard of. In the process she lost her dignity, her composure, and almost her life.

A goodly percentage of abortionists had connections with hospitals or nursing homes. They either worked there or had friends or relatives who did, so they had access to medical supplies. The variety of types that became abortionists never ceased to amaze me. They ranged from unwashed individuals who signed their welfare checks with an X, to grandmothers who looked like they should be pouring at a tea party, to a practicing mortician, and then up the ladder to the pharmacists, nurses, and physicians, ranging up to Park Avenue gynecologists.

This heterogeneous group had one common characteristic—an insatiable desire for money. Greed, not altruism, was the motivating force.

The many complaints against doctors brought on a new phase of operations. A policewoman would pose as a patient seeking an abortion. If the doctor agreed to do it, or if he steered her to someone else, this became the basis for a court-ordered wiretap.

I became adept at pretending to be pregnant (my favorite role was a bookmaker's girl friend) and needing an abortion. I created the illusion of unlimited funds and a touch of snottiness, necessary to get me off the hook whenever the doctor decided that I had to have an internal examination to verify the pregnancy. Whenever the doctor would say, "Get up on the table and let me take a look," I knew I had a live one.

"Bullshit!" said I in my most classy manner. "Here's a report from the laboratory that the last doctor sent me to, that tells you I'm pregnant. I've been to four doctors already and everybody says they have to examine me. How many times do you think I have to be told I'm pregnant, and I'm getting damn tired of you guys sticking your fingers up there. You think I'm a goddamn fingerbowl or something? You either tell me you're gonna do it, or you tell me you're not gonna do it."

"Take it easy, don't get so excited. Okay, if you really want to go through with it, it's going to cost you. But after all, aren't you entitled to the best? Your boyfriend had the pleasure, now he's got to pay. I get twelve hundred dollars, in cash, before I touch you."

That was enough for me, so I left promising to return with Mr. Rich Bookie in tow, to complete the arrangements.

That firsthand conversation with the doctor formed the basis for a formal application to the court for a wiretap order. After testifying before a judge, outlining the formal complaint received by the bureau and the subsequent direct verification, permission to tap the doctor's telephone was invariably granted.

Thus began a full-scale investigation, which would consist of a three-pronged attack: monitoring of conversations on the wiretap equipment, direct visual observations, and tailing.

To hear some of these "men of medicine" converse in a casual unguarded fashion sometimes made me shake my head in fury and frustration. The back-and-forth referral garbage, plus the fortunes forked over for unnecessary laboratory fees, unnecessary hospital stays for tests, all freely admitted to each other as if laughing to see who pulled the biggest coup.

When they discussed abortions, some spoke all around the subject, but gave it no name. The monster remained unidentified, though present.

For foul experiences, my investigation of a homosexual, drug-using doctor who performed abortions ranked high. This guy was warped. Young, handsome, a member of a minority group that had made it: he should have been sitting high. But his personal life and involvements made him fritter away his practice and resort to the easy money of the ABs.

When pretty boy thought the girls were too far gone (past three months of pregnancy), he wouldn't touch them. Sounds good, right?—as if he had some scruples, knowing the dangers multiplied a hundredfold after this time period. No, he wouldn't touch them—he referred them to a nurse he had a working arrangement with. The nurse would go back to the old catheter method to induce the delivery. The doctor got his share, and if there was any problem the nurse called on him for medication and guidance.

One Monday morning I checked into our monitoring plant to review Sunday's calls on Dr. D. The bureau was working shorthanded and our girls were stretched out mighty thin across three boroughs, trying to cover the varied investigations. Sunday was our so-called day of rest. None of the doctors had hours, and things ground more or less to a standstill.

In Brooklyn, that Sunday, things had not stood still. Dr. D made an outgoing call to nurse White with a referral that was at least four and a half months' pregnant, too advanced for him to take a chance. The nurse said she'd use her judgment when the girl came, and the call ended.

That same evening Dr. D got a frantic call from nurse White.

48

Dr.: What is it? What's wrong?

Nurse: Doc, Doc, it's alive! Christ, I tell you, it's alive!

Dr.: Will you calm down and shut up. Tell me what happened, step by step.

Nurse: She came and I examined her. Doc, I knew she was no four months. I figgered her for five. But they wanted it so bad, and the grandmother begged me and promised an extra two hundred. Oh, Jesus, God, what are we going to do now, Doc?

Dr.: Damn you . . . tell me what you did and what happened.

Nurse: I put a catheter in and sent them home in a cab. I figured that was that. But I got a phone call a few minutes ago, and she passed it, and for Lord's sake, Doc, it's breathing, it's alive, they want to know what to do. They got the damn thing on the bed, and the cord is still attached and the chest is going up and down. . . . Oh, Jesus. Twenty-two years I been doing them. I've had some get sick, and I had some die, but I never had one borned live. They want me to tell them what to do. You tell me what to tell them.

Dr.: Tell them not to get so fuckin' excited, that's what you tell them. They going to let a little thing like that frighten them? You tell them to cut the cord, but make sure you tell them to only tie it on the girl's side, not the other. After they tie it off and cut it, tell them to take a pillow and put it over the face for a few minutes and that'll take care of the whole problem. Then make sure you give her some penicillin tabs and you're riding easy.

Nurse: You really think it will be all right?

Dr.: Hell, they don't want it, do they? So what's the big deal. Let them do something about it.

The machine droned on with personal calls between the doctor and two gay friends about who was better in bed, and then another call from nurse White.

Nurse: Doc . . . Doc! They wrapped it up and brought it here. They cut the cord . . . it's not tied, but it's still breathing. Jesus, it's a goddamn boy and it won't stop breathing. They said they put a pillow over its face, but nothing happened. I don't want this thing here, Christ, we're in big trouble. Can't I bring it to you?

49

Dr.: You know something, I used to think you were pretty smart, but you're dumb as shit. Now I'm gonna tell you what to do, for the last time. You just wrap that damn thing up in newspapers. Don't give me any shit about its breathing, I don't want to hear it. Wrap it good, plenty of thick paper and string. Then take the fuckin' bundle outside and go for a walk. Just walk, away from your house, and away from her house and just dump it in a litter can and walk away. That's all there is to it. When those sanitation men empty those cans tomorrow night, they aren't gonna be picking around the garbage.

Nurse: Oh, God, Jesus . . . Doc, if you say so, we'll have to do it."

A much later phone call told the doctor that his instructions had been carried out.

Dr.: Where did you dump the bundle?

Nurse: I don't know. I walked and walked and there were always people around. When I saw a basket with nobody there, I dumped it in and kept walking, 'cause I was afraid someone would stop me.

Dr.: That's just fine. Believe me, you've got nothing to worry about. Just take a sleeping pill and by tomorrow you'll have forgotten all about it.

The tape ground to a finish. As the two reels spun drunkenly on, it was my turn to sit back in anger, muttering, "Oh, shit! . . . that poor thing."

I whipped off the reel and brought it in to the powers that be. The only way we could prove an abortion homicide, despite the incriminating tapes, which were inadmissible in court as evidence, was if we could find the tiny corpse. Sanitation was contacted and we got the sad news that all the garbage pickups in that section of Brooklyn had already been to the incinerator. The homicide case literally went up in ashes.

The nurse was arrested and agreed to testify against the doctor. She named the girl, who turned out to be fifteen years old, and her grandmother. They were also picked up, and turned state's witnesses. In a grand raid we managed to catch the doctor in the midst of performing an abortion on a seventeen-year-old.

Our raiding party had a police surgeon with us who was prepared to step in and finish the operation when the good Dr. D was led away. It's one of the two AB cases that really set my teeth on edge, so I always push them into the back of my mind.

I was riding pretty high in the bureau at this time, considered more or less the expert. At one point we had separate wiretaps going on three doctors, and I ran around from one to the other trying to keep them all functional, operative, and productive.

If any monitored calls sounded like an AB was going to come off, I'd scoot over to that tap to try to cover it and to make the necessary tail.

Tailing was necessary to establish our Who's Who of abortees. We had to get names and addresses so that when the abortionist was arrested we could have everyone he had aborted brought in to give statements.

There'd be about three or four policewomen assigned on each tap. Since an influx of women into a residential neighborhood was always cause for gossip, we'd try to get an apartment and blend into the neighborhood. The frustrated actress in me would come out as I directed the various tableaus. In a lower-class tenement neighborhood, the policewomen would sit around on stoops wearing jeans and housedresses. They'd push baby carriages containing drink and wet dolls that never drank and, thank God, never wet. In the posher areas, the housewives became nursemaids in white uniforms and pushed the same baby carriages.

My personal favorite was dressing as an old crone. Who the hell looks twice at an old woman hobbling down the street or sitting down to rest just about anywhere. I started with a longhaired gray wig, combed into a bun, and makeup applied so that it aged me thirty-five to forty years; gray eyebrows, putty wrinkles, and purple lips to simulate a heart condition. A trip to the Salvation Army and seventy-five cents made me the proud owner of a suit ten years old and six sizes too big. I wrapped both of my legs up with Ace bandages and wore my uniform oxford shoes, which completed the aging process beautifully.

Another ploy I used was taking my dog to work with me. You had to walk your dog, right?

This fun-and-games was great for summer, spring, and fall, but when old man Freezo came nipping, things got pretty sad. We had no alternative but to make observations from our cars. There's something to be said for spending eight to ten hours in a car, but nothing that's good. If the heater's on, you get too hot, kill your battery, and attract attention with the running engine. If you don't run it, you freeze to death. That numbing cold starts in your toes and keeps going up. I don't care how you dress either, you can look like a blasted Eskimo and still end up like a block of ice because of the inactivity.

Food usually began the day's conversation. In summer you hoped for a hot dog vendor, ice cream man, or someone pushing custard. In winter's deadsville we stalked the neighborhood for a grocery man who'd make a sandwich or a friendly hamburger or pizza joint. We'd draw straws to see who was the day's gopher. (In every precinct the brass had someone assigned who became their Go For, their official flunky.)

But what had to rank as our No. 1 problem was trying to find a bathroom. I christened us the Broken Bladder Brigade. We used to think it was a drag getting a cup of hot coffee. Well, that was nothing compared to getting rid of it. I've seen men I worked with wander off between cars or go into a doorway and knew they were relieving themselves. What the hell was a woman supposed to do—squat in the street? I swear I'll always be able to spot a female officer, even off duty. The giveaway: she'll never pass a ladies' room without leaving a tinkle behind. After all, you never know where your next bathroom is going to be.

Dr. M in the Bronx was a steerer for a Park Avenue doctor. When Dr. Park Avenue was arrested and the witnesses were picked up, their stories were all basically the same except one.

Helen Wander and her boyfriend Benny Korn went to see Dr. M. Their problem—an unwanted pregnancy. Dr. M gave her a slip of paper with a doctor's name and address on it and told her to be there the following morning with five hundred dollars. Helen stopped at the bank and withdrew money for the AB.

Bright and early next morning, February 27, 1962, Benny and Helen were in the waiting room on East Sixtieth Street, waiting. They were seen, briefly, by a male with a heavy accent who asked them how much Dr. M had told them to bring and for Mrs. Wander's phone number. "Go home and wait. In exactly one hour you will receive a phone call. Leave now, go right home and then wait!"

At ten minutes after eleven the phone call came through. A female directed them to an address on Union Turnpike in Queens, at 7 P.M. Helen quickly interjected that she and Benny had taken the day off from work and were anxious to have it done in the afternoon. "Well, be there at two o'clock, but he's not going to like it," and the female voice hung up abruptly.

The address proved to be a private house with the doctor's shingle out on the lawn. It was one-thirty when they went into the office. A male, in dungarees and T-shirt and obviously agitated, came out. "You're much too early . . . that's not good. The cleaning woman is still here, you're just going to have to wait." And he stalked out.

After almost a half hour Dr. Harvey Lothringer returned. He called Helen into the examining room and asked for the money. When she gave it to him, he gave her several injections for pain. Then he asked her to lie with her feet in the stirrups. He brusquely told her that he autoclaved (steam sterilized) everything, as he inserted the speculum into her vagina. "You're about six weeks pregnant." She felt him insert other instruments into her private parts, but felt no pain; she heard a sound which she described as "gurgling" that went on and on.

After the procedure, she received sleeping pills, antibiotics, and instructions. The doctor then asked Benny what kind of car he had and what his plate number was. He wrote down the information and directed Benny to a spot about six blocks away. "Just wait there, I'll drive her out to join you."

Helen and Benny looked at each other uncomprehendingly, but sheeplike they obeyed. Dr. Lothringer directed Helen into the back seat of a large white station wagon, and pushed her down until she was lying flat. "Stay that way," he snapped, "until I tell you it's okay to get up." Then Helen heard a motor hum and knew that he'd opened the automatic garage doors at the same time as he'd started his engine. The wagon shot out onto busy Union Turnpike. When they came to an abrupt halt, she remained in position until the doctor opened her door and said, "Okay, get out." She did, and looked blankly about until the doctor said,

"That's him, behind you," and pointed at the VW parked about a thousand feet down the street.

She made her way to a startled Benny. They were both pretty quiet and subdued on the trip back to the Bronx.

After getting Helen's story I knew this abortionist must be going like gangbusters. I didn't have to try to make direct contact since I already had two beautiful witnesses, complete with testimony and bankbook withdrawals that verified the money transaction. As a dental hygienist, Helen was even able to identify the instruments used. It seemed almost too good to be true. I conferred with Mrs. M, gave her résumés of the statements, my feelings, and observations reports. She was very interested and impressed. "Work it for a few days, find out whatever you can, and let me know."

After a few days out there on Union Turnpike I came to the conclusion that this man had covered every conceivable angle that might be used against him. His corner house, a two-and-a-half-story red brick building, was in an upper-class area. There were two entrances, one on Union Turnpike and the other on the right-hand side. This side entrance opened into a large adjoining private parking lot which was enclosed by a seven-foot-high plastic fence.

One could enter the building through either door, the parking lot, or the garage. When the doctor's station wagon pulled into the lot, he'd open the electric eye garage doors automatically, his wagon would slide into the building, and the door would close quickly behind him.

In other investigations it was a simple matter to follow suspected patients to their cars and then maintain a tail until they reached their destination. In this case there was no warning before that wagon would shoot out into the street and be off. My amazement grew with each day. There was no one coming to see him, but every once in a while that wagon would whip out, the doctor at the wheel.

I took my notes and sketches and hied back to the office for another conference. Mrs. M suggested going to the Bronx district attorney's office, since our information had originated from a Bronx wiretap, with the thought of augmenting that tap to include the Queens doctor. Unfortunately they said it was out of their jurisdiction, but suggested the Queens district attorney's office since the actual crime took place there.

On May 11, 1962, I kept an appointment with Assistant District Attorney Bernard Patten, who was in charge of the investigations unit and homicide investigations in the Queens district attorney's office. With me I brought my two witnesses and the policewoman with whom I was then working. The lieutenant in charge of the DA's squad was present, as was the official stenographer.

From two-thirty until five-thirty that afternoon, Helen and Benny recounted their stories in detail. They were sworn in and their statements taken officially.

Then they were told they could go home. I was startled, as I thought they would be needed to sign the wiretap application, so I asked them to wait for me outside.

The ADA started to thank me, which was tantamount to a dismissal. "We'd like permission to obtain a wiretap order, with your sanction, Mr. Patten," I quickly interjected. "We have them in the Bronx, Brooklyn, and Manhattan, all with the co-operation of the district attorney's offices there, and we've had terrific success. We have our own personnel to man the wires, so we won't drain your squad, but we'll give you copies of all the reports as they come in and keep you completely apprized. When we have sufficient information to make a raid or an arrest, we'll work it as a joint effort, so that it will come out as being under your aegis."

Having shot off my mouth and loosed my most powerful ammo, I was told to cool my heels and wait outside. What the hell was this bit? I wondered. Every other DA's office had eagerly grabbed our cases when we presented them, because they were all super publicity conscious, and knew that when our cases broke, they usually garnered headlines. Since the district attorney is an elected official, he thrives on getting into the papers as often as possible. He needs favorable publicity that shows his effectiveness to help insure his next election.

As I sat there tasting sour grapes, Mr. Patten's secretary asked me to go back in. After a lot of throat clearing, I was told that they would keep the statements on file. Period. I asked if they would go along with the tap and our working the case. Mr. Patten stated, "We don't work on doctors in Queens."

"You don't what?" I was aghast.

"It is our policy not to get involved with physicians. If the Women's Bureau wants to try to get a tap on their own, we won't interfere, but we won't apply for it through our office."

"But you know the bureau is not a full-fledged squad. If we got the material on a doctor, the indictments and the prosecutions would have to stem from your office."

"That's our policy, that's all I can say. Thank you for coming."

The next morning I was in the boss's office, ranting and raving. "*They* don't work on doctors. I showed them my sketches; I told them that this guy had the most perfect abortion setup I'd ever seen; I brought in my witnesses; and they tell me they don't work on doctors. What are we going to do now?"

"Nothing," she said quietly.

"You're telling me to do nothing?"

"No, I'm telling you that we can do nothing. If they don't want us working there, we have nothing. No case, no indictments. You can't fight them. Besides, look at this folder full of cases that other offices want us to work for them. We'll work where we're wanted and have co-operation." She got up and came and put her arm around me. "Don't take it so hard, I know how you feel."

"Okay . . . okay! It's the same old story . . . don't make waves. I guess I just learn hard. Let them protect their goddamn doctors, then when the bastard kills somebody, I'll want to see what they'll have to say. So, where do we go from here?"

"Turn in your report, take the rest of the day off, and simmer down," she said.

On a dreary Thursday morning, June 7, 1962, three weeks after my interview in Queens, I began my usual pilgrimage to work. Driving past Bronxville Lake, I snapped on the radio and caught an excited announcer's voice. "Appalling discovery, pieces of a girl's body found clogging the waste disposal drain in a Queens house. The area has been roped off, and there is frantic activity as attempts are made to retrieve the bits of bone and flesh. It is believed that the victim may be a nineteen-year-old Westchester girl who has been missing since Sunday when she went to the doctor's home for an abortion." My ears pricked up. "An alarm has been issued for the alleged abortionist and suspected butcher, Dr. Harvey Lothringer of 185-01 Union Turnpike."

I pulled off the road and sat there stunned. Cold perspiration flooded. I had rivulets running down between my breasts. I tried to push away what I had heard. Gesu . . . Gesu . . . could I have saved her? Too shaken to go to work, I turned the car around and went home to change my clothes, which were completely sodden. I was chilled, despite the fact that it was a June day.

My hands were still cold, my face ashen, as I changed, listening to another newscaster repeat the gruesome story. The New York *Daily News* carried it this way:

Parts of a young woman's body were found choking the sewer line leading from the $85,000 brick ranch home and office of a well-to-do physician in the fashionable Jamaica Estates North section of Queens.

Police suspected that the presumed victim is Barbara Lofrumento, who has been missing since she went to the doctor's home for an abortion on Sunday, according to her mother.

The physician, Dr. Harvey Lothringer, 41, was also missing and listed as a suspect, and an alarm issued for him.

The victim was last seen alive by her mother about 2:30 A.M. Sunday, when the two of them arrived at the plush house and office at the corner of 185th Street.

The pieces of her body began turning up yesterday after the doctor ordered a sewer cleaning service to clear out the traps in his home.

On Monday morning, Mr. & Mrs. Lofrumento had showed up at the Queens DA's office to make an official complaint that their daughter was missing. Somewhat reluctantly they told the story.

On Thursday, Barbara had come to them with the news that she was pregnant. Lofrumento, who was a pharmacist, had through a friend's intercession made arrangements to meet Dr. Lothringer at 2 A.M. in Grand Central Terminal.

There, on schedule, the girl and her parents were met by the doctor and a female friend. The price of the operation, set in advance, was $1000. Mrs. Lofrumento paid the money and accompanied her daughter to the doctor's home and office, but Mr. Lofrumento was sent home.

The mother sat in the waiting room for hours. At 7:30 Monday morning the doctor came and told her everything would be all right. "You can go home and come back for her later in the day." When she returned, the house was locked and dark and there was no answer to her many phone calls.

On Tuesday the doctor called a friend and asked him to have a sewer service clean out the traps in his house. He obtained the key from Lothringer's parents who lived nearby and let the sewer cleaner into the house.

As the work was being done, pieces of human flesh and other organs began coming out of the choked sewer lines. The cleaner called the police.

Besides Dr. Lothringer, police were seeking the woman who was with him at the Grand Central rendezvous.

I heavy-footed it into work. There were no smiles in the inner sanctum this morning, as the boss's grim face met mine. "I guess you know?" I just stood there nodding. Then she told me to turn in all my reports and files on the case immediately, never to discuss the case outside of that office, never to mention Dr. Lothringer to anyone, and if there was any leak, (guess who) would be left holding the bag.

"But we might have saved that girl! I told them . . ."

"There will be no further discussion—this is an order. I get orders and have to take them. The phone has been ringing all morning. The district attorney himself has called me on this. I have no say in the matter; my hands are tied. Do you understand?"

"Of course I understand. We caught them with their pants down, and now we have to pretend like it never happened. They didn't want any part of us before, but now they want my notes and reports and everything, right? Well, it's not right! In fact, it stinks."

I paced the office with frenetic strides, filled with the livid fury of futility. The old "Don't make waves" syndrome, or how to break a good cop in ten or fifteen frustrating minutes. I threw the papers on the desk and ran across to the ladies' room where I vented my rage with scalding tears.

Sidelined, I followed newspaper accounts of the case. The *Daily News* on June 8 stated, in part:

As the hunt for Lothringer and his runaway-companion became international in scope, the Queens District Attorney's office began lining up evidence against the doctor to prove he was the mainspring of an abortion ring. The extent of Lothringer's operations was indicated by District Attorney Frank D. O'Connor.

"My men moved in to pick Lothringer up on Monday in connection with two other abortions," said O'Connor. "We were just a day too late. His home had been under surveillance for three weeks. He was part of a full-blown abortion ring, with steerers and referrers, operating citywide and throughout the state. Because of the present confusion over the legality of wiretaps, we did not wiretap the house. If we had used wiretaps, this poor girl would have been alive today."

DA O'Connor would have to disclaim any knowledge of the case, but he made statements that his men had been working on it. These statements were untrue. They were made to obviate pinpointing the responsibility.

If it became public knowledge that there had been previous complaints against Dr. Lothringer, which were turned away, the onus of the death and dismemberment would fall smack upon the district attorney—and elections were coming up.

Assistant Medical Examiner Richard Grimes said that never before had he encountered such a minute dissection. The body was diced into two-inch cubes, obviously with some sort of power saw. Even the skull had been cubed. The ME's office estimated it must have taken nearly twenty-four hours to cut up the body. The fragments were washed down a toilet bowl. The teeth were compared with a chart of Barbara's teeth. This established, without a doubt, that the dismembered body was Barbara's.

The hunt for Lothringer and his girl friend, Teresa Carillo, spread from the United States to Canada where his father had a hunting lodge, to Miami, Cuba, and Mexico, where they were known to have friends.

Finally on September 10, three months after they had fled, they were tracked to a tiny republic called Andorra, population 6,439,

59

on the French-Spanish border, where Lothringer and Teresa were living as "Mr. and Mrs. Victor Rey." Andorra, a charming tourist spot high in the Pyrenees Mountains, has the added attraction of having no extradition treaty with the United States.

The French police stepped in and made the arrest when Mr. and Mrs. Rey crossed the border into France. Since Lothringer had been arrested on French soil, he was extraditable. His girl friend was not taken into custody.

On the heels of the capture Queens Assistant District Attorney Chetta sped to Kennedy Airport bound for France and carrying a warrant for Lothringer based on the charge that the physician committed a criminal abortion on May 11, 1962.

Lothringer's lawyer questioned Lothringer in Perpignan, France, and got an oral confession. Because Barbara was five months pregnant, he was chary about an operation and tried to talk her parents out of it by boosting his fee to $1,000. They "crossed him up" by agreeing to pay it.

An air bubble developed in Barbara's bloodstream at the very start of the operation, and she expired. He admitted the dismemberment and indicated he did it to avoid involving Teresa.

Lothringer was eventually extradited and brought back to face trial. Two years and twelve adjournments later, he interrupted the picking of a jury and agreed to plead to the lesser charge of second-degree manslaughter, to cover all counts in the indictment. That meant he faced a maximum prison term of fifteen years.

On July 23, 1964, he was sentenced. He received from two to eight years in Sing Sing . . . which made him eligible for parole in thirteen months. Mrs. Lofrumento, who was in court, fainted and had to be removed. Mr. Lofrumento shouted angrily, calling it "discount justice."

Manhattan South
Burglary Squad

Ringing in on January 16, 1963, I got what seemed like my two thousand four hundred and fifty-seventh forthwith into Mrs. M's office. Something was up. I could see her face. She was trying to stay composed but would fall into a big grin every time she stopped concentrating. Something good for a change? "What's up, boss? You look like you just inherited a fortune. Share the wealth."

She looked at me and her face softened. "Sit down. I can tell you now that it's all okayed. Marie, I know your work, what you've put into this job. Nobody knows it like I do, and you know that I always try to promote my best workers into the Detective Division even though I may be cutting my own throat. I can't always manage it, but when I do, it makes me proud to reward one of my girls.

"I have a brand-new slot for you. They've never used women before. You'll be one of the first to be detailed to a burglary squad. You're being transferred to the Detective Division, but you'll be working on the policewoman's shield." (Meaning: You have the job, but not the money.)

"You're being officially transferred to Manhattan South Borough Detectives, but will work out of the Manhattan South Burglary Squad. Just remember I vouched for you and never make me feel ashamed, and you'll never have to thank me."

She seemed to realize that I was about to drool in happiness, so she passed the coffee to keep me from making an absolute idiot of myself.

"Keep in touch. Drop in and give us the latest news from the big outside world. Now, get outta here and let me get some work done."

I hugged her.

I approached this new assignment never imagining that these years would prove to be the most diversified, challenging, and therefore interesting ones in a varied, hectic career.

My first plunge was right into a glamour bath. New York's finest hotels had been hit by a rash of hotel burglaries. The information had been kept under wraps, in an effort to keep the guests from being alarmed, but the thefts had reached epidemic proportions. The Police Department created a special assignment, the Hotel Detail, to work out of the Burglary Squad.

In interviewing past victims, as well as current ones, a pattern seemed to evolve. Virtually everyone burglarized was either wealthy and well known or well known and presumed to be wealthy. They had come into New York for a short stay, and had received some publicity in connection with their arrival. Many of them were movie personalities, foreign dignitaries, or "society."

It seemed we had some literate burglars who had taken to reading the columns, making life a lot simpler for them. So here I was, knee deep in "names" from Zsa Zsa Gabor, Pearl Bailey, Shirley MacLaine, Deborah Kerr, Judy Garland, Merle Oberon, Helena Rubinstein, Irene Selznick, Joseph Cotten, Henry Fonda, Cary Grant, Hope Lange, to General MacArthur.

Confirming my fondest suspicions, I found that glamorous women didn't look much better in the morning than anyone else, and that glamour boys look pretty raunchy when they've had a snootful and haven't shaved: the big difference was that most of the women tried to hide to keep anyone from seeing them looking below par, while the men would strut around bare-chested thinking they oozed manliness.

The hardest part of this detail was deciding who might be burglarized. The system we evolved was to interview those we felt might become victims, explain the situation, and ask for their co-operation. If they agreed, a team of detectives would be moved into an adjoining room. A wired mat would be installed under the rug, outside of their doorway. Our plant would notify us if they were going out and the alarm mat would then be activated. When anyone stepped on it prior to gaining access to the room, the detectives in the adjoining room would be alerted. We were aware of the comings and goings of the floor maids and they weren't pounced upon every time they went in to turn down a bed.

Reactions from the people interviewed were strange and varied. Some became so upset at the thought of being burglarized that they checked out immediately. Others became indignant . . . invasion of privacy . . . police state . . . Big Brother . . . preferring to take their chances rather than get involved with the police. Then there were the truly grateful, surprised at the interest taken before a crime was even committed. They'd ask a million questions, offer you a drink, volunteer their help, or try to have dinner sent up to your room. I even remember being asked if they could come and sit in our room and watch in case someone broke into their room.

Several weeks later, the squad got what seemed to be a possible break in one of the largest outstanding cases, $400,000 in jewelry stolen from the Hotel Pierre suite of Irene Selznick, the former wife of David O. Selznick and the daughter of Louis B. Mayer.

A stoolie in the Tombs, the men's detention facility, awaiting trial and hoping for some sort of leniency, sent word that an inmate, "Bobby Hooks," had bragged that he knew who had pulled the Selznick job. Several of the men went down to talk to Hooks, who boasted that he was the best Negro burglar in the country. "These white cats got it made, nobody looks twice at them when they walk into one of these classy hotels, but it takes smarts for a black dude to work." He talked about his various disguises—wrapping a turban around his head and painting a caste mark on his forehead, purporting to be a U.N. representative; hiring a chauffeur's livery and leaving a parked limousine at the curb; or coming in wearing a tuxedo and carrying an instrument case. Nervy and pretty effective.

Hooks admitted that "Al" had done the Selznick job. "Al told me he took the stuff and gave it to 'Phil Di' to get rid of, but Philly beat him out of the money. Then he had Al's bail picked up so he couldn't do anything." The detectives asked

Hooks if he knew what type of property Al had taken. A Tiffany diamond ring that was supposed to be as big as a wristwatch and a charm bracelet with wedding bands inscribed with the dates and places were the things he remembered.

This bracelet hadn't been listed in the original loss report, which further corroborated Hooks's story.

"Al" turned out to be Alfred Modson, a twenty-one-year-old, curly-haired, baby-faced thief, who was angrily languishing in jail because his bail had been revoked. The timing was great. Al was doing a big burn. He had heard that Philly had spent $10,000 to have his bail rescinded because he'd lost Al's share of the jewelry proceeds playing craps. We asked for, and got, Al's permission to interview him in the Manhattan district attorney's office.

When Al was convinced that we already knew everything that had occurred, he admitted not only to this burglary, but to other large burglaries in the midtown area totaling over *one million dollars* in less than one year.

Eventually he was to pick out forty-two individual burglaries that he could identify not only by hotel, but by a complete description of the property he took from each place. He said that the burglaries he committed while he operated in New York were too numerous for him to remember, since he couldn't recall a first- or good second-class hotel that he hadn't operated in.

Al was a pro . . . just barely out of pimples and still too physically immature to be called handsome. The girls would say he was "adorable." At twenty-one Al knew how to get around. His suits and shoes were custom-made and he could spend five or six hundred a day with ease. Although he lived with his girl friend on the West Side, he would think nothing of sending three dozen roses to a nightclub entertainer if he thought she had smiled at him. Al used to list his occupation as "welder," but when he was arraigned in court and questioned by the judge as to what he did for a living, he said simply, "I'm a thief."

He was a loid man, which means his specialty was to use celluloid strips to force open a door lock. The very best loids seem to be generously provided by the hotels themselves: the Do Not Disturb signs that are found hanging conveniently on so many doors. The loid is seesawed until it catches the bolt, where just a

64

bit of the right leverage will spring it open. A good loid man can get inside in about thirty seconds.

Al was good, but his story of the Selznick job made us shake our heads. This guy had them like an elephant. Sandy, his girl, was taking a relaxing bubble bath while Al impatiently paced the room. Impulsively he left and took a cab to the Great Northern and then a second cab to the Hotel Pierre, where the scoring was better. He loided two rooms on the ninth floor but found nothing he considered worth taking. Then he walked up the exit stairs to the tenth floor and his favorite pickings, the corner suite. After knocking four times and ringing the bell without response, Al quickly loided the door going straight into the dressing room and to the dressing table. He opened the top drawer and found jewels. He opened the second drawer and found jewels. Wrapping them in handkerchiefs, he put them in his pocket and left as he had come, walking down to the ninth floor and taking the elevator down. The doorman called a cab for him, and as it pulled up Al sweated for the first time. He was afraid to withdraw his hand from his pocket, in the fear of spilling the jewels, and couldn't tip the doorman. This bothered him as he mumbled an excuse about not having change of a twenty. When they had pulled away he sank back in his seat for the short ride home.

Time gone? Thirty-five minutes. The haul? Four hundred thousand dollars' worth of jewelry . . . and Sandy was still in the tub.

She hopped out in a hurry, though, when Al dangled the goodies. There were fifty-four pieces in all. Sandy was dumbstruck at the beauty. Al had to shake her and tell her to get a move on. They had to go out and make some noise, get seen, establish an alibi.

Al wrapped the jewels in a towel and then flushed the handkerchiefs, also taken from the Pierre suite, down the toilet. Then going down to the basement he buried the loot under a pile of dirt and debris and he and Sandy went dancing.

The following afternoon he brought the jewelry to Philly's girl friend Louise's house. A little while later a man Phil introduced as Eddie the Jeweler arrived and examined the stuff. He was excited but worked meticulously as he louped each piece to determine its worth. "This is the meat right here," he said as he examined the ring. He gave Al $500 and agreed to give him $10,000 on

Monday, $20,000 on Wednesday, and $14,000 on Friday for the three big pieces, and to discuss the prices for the remaining pieces the next time they met. The money was to be delivered to Al by Philly.

Eddie set right to work taking the stones out of their settings to make identification difficult. In fact, Al stated, Eddie had shaved two and a half carats off the top of the Tiffany diamond, and later complained that he'd cut his hands to ribbons removing the settings. I guess one must suffer for one's art.

Three days later Al had received a total of only $7,100. He was supposed to go pick up $20,000 but he got picked up and remanded instead. Al held Phil accountable as he was the one who had put up his bail. When he did get out again he sought Phil to find him with $9 in his pocket, big holes in his shoes, and a story that he'd lost $22,000 shooting crap.

The only thing Al had left to show for this particular fling into high finance was the suit on his back and the seventy-five-dollar pair of shoes on his feet. But we were able to mark as solved burglaries totaling about a million dollars. This didn't eliminate hotel burglaries, but it put a hell of a crimp in the activity, and turned a lot of thieves into other channels.

In our revolving-door system of justice today, the punishment, if any, that's meted out is not in itself a deterrent. To a thief the occasional sentence is taken in stride and accepted as the dues one pays to belong to that particular trade union. It's part of the game, they'll say.

This is one reason for my belief in specialized detective units. The members of the Burglary Squad, as an example, get to know most of the thieves in the area they cover. They know when one is coming out of the "can" and have informants that can tell them if the guy is going straight or going straight to his next heist. After a crime is committed, and they are at the scene, they can spot MO's (modus operandi, or style of operation) that will often spell out a particular individual. These squads are invaluable, not only in the apprehension of criminals, but as a deterrent to crime as well. (In much the same way, the Women's Bureau, under the old structure and through their varied types of investigations, not only served the community but was also the only controlling force to check crimes affecting women and children.

Since the abolition of the Women's Bureau in New York City, trafficking in these areas has been largely unchecked.)

For the squad it meant the elimination of steady "plants" in the hotels and a chance to return to street patrol. There were about thirteen of us assigned to the office, with a Lieutenant Mackin in charge, and we were responsible for the prevention and/or investigation of any burglaries committed anywhere from the Battery to Fifty-ninth Street in Manhattan, from the East River to the Hudson River. This takes in a lot of people and places.

Before the emphasis on the hotel plants the squad had steady teams of working partners. My appearance created a new problem. The lieutenant, a genius at decision making, stammered that he didn't quite know what to do with me. His six-foot-two-inch, 220-pound hulk draped around a doorjamb as he shifted from foot to foot. Every sentence started with "Uh . . ." and was interrupted while he probed and explored every cavity and crevice in his mouth with a large wooden toothpick, making sucking noises that sounded like a kid slurping in a long piece of spaghetti.

He finally suggested that I ask the various teams if they would be willing to accept me as an additional member, because he didn't want to listen to them complain if he arbitrarily told them they had to work with a woman.

"How do you work it when you get a new guy in the squad?"

"Oh, that's different, I assign him to work as the third man in a team, until we get to know how he works. By that time, he's usually made friends in the squad and then there may be a little shifting around of partners with people trying out different combinations."

"Well, why can't you do the same thing?"

"'Cause"—pick, pick, *slurp, slurp*—"you're a woman, and the guys just aren't going to buy it. Listen"—*sluuurp*—"if you want to you can ride around with me." I turned to look into his vapid blue eyes, to find them slowly making the trip down my size 9 with the dullness slowly giving way to lechery and the toothpick applied with more intensity.

"No, no, Loo, I wouldn't dream of asking for any special privileges. I don't want the guys to resent me because I'm a woman, but I don't want them to accept me just for that reason either. Give me a chance to work it out."

Damned if he wasn't almost right. The first team I approached with confidence, because we'd worked together on an aspect of the Modsen case. Tailing suspects on foot and by car, we'd sat for hours and days making observations and I felt that we'd gotten to know each other. Joe, whom we always teased, was quiet, somber, a sort of older, gray-haired Montgomery Clift. He constantly had a pipe in his mouth, which he would try unsuccessfully to light. The reason for the failure and the nature of all the kidding was that Joe probably never put more than a half teaspoon of tobacco into his pipe at any one time. He couldn't afford it, with the flock of kids he had home that looked like a stepladder when they lined up side by side. So Joe smoked matches.

Nick was the boisterous one, eager to please, but quick to anger. He'd make the quick decisions and Joe would usually accept them—with exceptions.

I approached this team without trepidation, telling them about this fantastic opportunity to work with me on a permanent basis. They looked at each other, then away—at the ceiling, the desk, the floor, anything but me. "Hey, I'd appreciate it if you'd just level with me." In a nutshell, it turned out that Nick was afraid of his wife's reaction to his working permanently with a female. He couldn't bear the thought of listening to her every time he happened to come home late, whether he happened to be working or not. Joe said it was okay with him, but that he and Nick had worked together for over a year and he couldn't see splitting up.

I smiled weakly. "Sure, I understand." I understood, but it didn't make it any easier to accept. The next team I considered asking I knew mostly by reputation. They were supposed to be pretty rough and tough, but good workers. When I finally cornered them they giggled like fourth-grade schoolboys. "Ho . . . ha . . . you want to work with us? Hey that's great, we've been telling them for years they should give each team its own woman. Baby, that's just what we need . . . we'll have a ball." There was a lot of elbow digging and looks exchanged between them. "What a shame they disbanded the hotel plants . . . man, we would have had it made!"

Another team I mentally dismissed because of the "Farmer." He was about six-foot-one or two, had a beer-barrel belly, and always looked like his clothes were full of cow shit. He was also Lieutenant Mackin's gopher—which automatically made him the office stool pigeon. This could be a very uncomfortable person to do business with, since his commitments and obligations certainly weren't to his partners.

I was feeling as blue as Kelsey's equipment. I felt that if I didn't solve this dilemma myself, I'd most likely end up doing clerical work. The very thought filled me with renewed determination.

A man everyone seemed to have a nice word about was a first-grader named Ed Lehane. One of the top men, he'd been on the job about sixteen years. His partner was a tall skinny drink of water who looked like a weed blowing in a windstorm. This six-foot-two-inch, 150-pound weed smoked black gnarled malodorous guinea stinker cigars. He seemed to walk around surrounded by his own portable cloud. Jimmy Capano had straight black hair that shone like an Indian's; sad brown eyes that seemed to bring out the mother instinct in the girls; and a nose that looked like it had been broken several times. Jim was a comparative newcomer and had undergone, to a much smaller degree, the reluctance to accept that I was suffering. Ed had finally said, "Give the kid to me, I'll break him in. Everybody's got to start someplace!"

The hangup with this team was that the leader was in the hospital after having a severe attack of what later turned out to be the typical detective's ailment—gastric ulcers. No one seemed to know when he was coming back. Jim was a third wheel, just filling in with other teams and marking time until the Master's return. I grabbed him and asked him if he would work with me, for both our sakes.

As a third or extra man, Jim was susceptible to every special detail or extra assignment that came up, since he was most obviously able to be spared. As a third man, even if he participated in an arrest with another team he wouldn't be credited with it. So Jim agreed to work with me until Ed came back. "Well," I thought to myself, "it's a beginning."

We worked together for a few weeks getting in and out of a couple of minor scrapes and getting to know each other. Jimmy didn't drive, which was a severe handicap in this type of squad where you operate out of your own car, while you do patrol. Most teams would alternate, a day apiece at the wheel—eight hours of maneuvering in city traffic while trying to make observations can leave you pretty limp.

Jimmy'd call Ed regularly at the hospital reporting all our exploits and the job gossip. Naturally, Ed was curious and, by now, he was asking a million questions. Jim told him that they ought to keep me as a full partner when he came back. After a few weeks, when he knew he was getting out, Ed agreed. Perhaps he was too weak to fight it, or maybe he needed someone to share the driving chores. At that point I didn't care, I just wanted to get my foot in the door.

I was filled with stories of his exploits long before he came back. He had captured the Mad Bomber; the United Parcel stickup murderers had fallen to him; the acid blinding of Victor Reisel had been his case. I was looking forward to meeting him with a mixture of fear and anticipation.

Ed was Irish, but he was a left-footer. This is a Protestant Irishman. In the New York City Police Department, dominated by Irish Catholics, and taking its orders from Madison Avenue (New York Archdiocese), this put him one step below a black on their sliding scale of worth. After all, they reasoned, a black can't help being born that way, but you can always change your religion. This probably helped make him a hell of a fighter.

I remembered seeing him for the first time, officiating at a department function when he was president of the St. George Association. What had impressed me was his facile mind, glib tongue, and the way he seemed to have the crowd in the palm of his hand. About 5'9", he was slim and wiry, with hair that was dark brown but thinning, and blue eyes that reflected the trigger-fast mind that never stopped thinking or scheming. His complexion ranged from flush pink to raucous red depending on his mood, which could run the spectrum from Irish ire to Gaelic gaiety.

Seeing him when he returned to work was a shocker. Ed exuded weariness. The hospital had discharged him with a full battery of prescriptions. One pill twenty minutes before meals; one twenty minutes after, to be swallowed down with Maalox or Mylanta or some other product to alleviate gastric distress.

His blue eyes still managed to smile, though his face was gray. "They turned me into a washrag . . . three weeks on milk and

Maalox and nothing else. I've lost twenty pounds. But don't worry, I'm coming back strong. It's going to take a lot more than that for them to turn a spade over me."

"Ed, do you have any objections to working with a woman?"

"Yes, as a matter of fact, I do. I don't want to work with a woman, I want to work with another cop, and from what I hear that's what you are. So, when I work with you, I'm working with another cop. Remember we're a three-man team, and you're one of the boys."

I heaved a sigh of relief, "Thank God, that's over," and then looked over my two partners and laughed wryly to myself. Jim had turned out to be a devout hypochondriac. What he didn't have, he thought he did, and he already had more than his share. I started to laugh, "Oh, God, we're gonna be beautiful. What a team. Listen, we're perfect for each other. We'll call ourselves the ruptured ducks, because we all have our own cross to bear, and we'll go out there and kill them, we'll knock them dead. Ed, you've got to get back on your feet, and Jimmy . . . God, you're a regular canvasback, you spend more time stretched out than up, and me . . . well, just being a woman seems to be a handicap around here. It's a winning hand—three of a kind!"

What they didn't know, and what they weren't about to find out for a good while, was my real reason for laughing so loudly. Not only were they going to work with a woman, but with one who was just a little bit pregnant.

The next two or three months together changed us from people assigned to work together to "partners." A real "partner," on this job, is better than a paid-up life insurance policy. A partner is:

Someone whose loyalty is so intrinsic that you never have to ask yourself, "Is he?"

Someone who when you take the lead in a situation and head in, you don't have to look over your shoulder to see if he's with you . . . you know it.

Someone who knows what you're going to do, before you do it; and knows that you know that he knows.

So our three-man team of partners hit the streets. Most of our work was actual patrol which resulted in pickup arrests as opposed to complaints. In pickup cases, it was just a question of using your eyes, ears, and antennae to observe anything that looked out of the ordinary. If something was afoot, then you jumped in and took whatever action was warranted. Complaint cases were investigating crimes that had already been reported.

Our arrests covered a gamut of crimes. If we had reason to think someone was pushing junk, we weren't about to turn our backs on it because it wasn't a burglary case. Which was exactly what happened one particular night when the three of us were strolling around Times Square. After walking down Forty-third Street, off Seventh Avenue, we just sort of stopped and looked at each other.

"You too, huh?" said Ed.

"Yeah," I nodded. "That's an awful lot of bad-shape junkies spread out on that block. They're keeping away from each other, but they're here."

"Okay, okay, I know," said Jim, backing off to find a dark spot to cover us.

We had noticed that whenever a new junkie came into the block he went into a particular hallway, but when he came out he would lounge and loiter, walk off a bit, but never leave the block. Now we knew the spot, we just had to hold on and try to keep it cool until the man with the stash made the shape.

We adopted the next entranceway, as obvious as you please. I had my back to the door and Ed faced me, with his arms around me. In Times Square, this attracted no attention at all. I could look right out, over his shoulder, and give him a running commentary on what was happening. "Wake me up when it's time to move," Ed teased as he drooped his head onto my shoulder.

"You fink. Uh-oh, there's an old guy coming up the street. I never would have figured him, but I swear I can feel vibes from every one of these slobs." Ed's body was tensed for action as he whispered, "Keep talking, tell me everything."

"He's coming slow, but his eyeballs are going like crazy, he's taken us in, he's almost to the next doorway now and he's not taking his eyes off us. Haa-haaa-haa," I giggled out loud, for his benefit, I knew he was taking it all in. "Oh, man, you're too much . . . too much . . . listen, why don't you be a nice guy and spring for a room, huh? I'm freezing my ass off out here!" It worked, you could almost see him mentally dismissing us. "Okay," I whispered into Ed's ear, "he's standing in the doorway, looking up and down the block. He's into the hallway. Hey, Jesus, the block is alive, but they must have a number system like a goddamn bakery. They've all moved closer, but only one guy is coming forward, the rest are jockeying for position. Here he comes. He went in!"

We sprang apart, two minds working together, and dove for the doorway, screaming our usual, "Police, don't move!" Grandpa didn't like it one bit and ran for the cellar steps but was persuaded that it really wasn't too polite. We turned to find Jimmy standing in the doorway, grinning his lopsided grin. His reaction: "Next time, how about my getting a turn doing the doorway bit?"

"Oh . . . you idiot," I said in exasperation, "help us search these guys. The old man put the stash in his coat pocket." We got ourselves a batch of pure cocaine and a couple of prisoners to take in.

In the precinct, during the booking process, we came up with a few unusual details. Our peddler was fifty-nine years old, ancient for a pusher. His first arrest, at the age of fifteen, was for possession of cocaine. He hadn't been arrested at all in at least sixteen years because he had such an excellent cover. He was employed as a lithographer for the New York *Times* in their Times Square plant and peddled the stuff on his meal hour and during breaks.

His last vehement curse echoed in our ears as we left him in the detention cell. "Just wait, you bastards, I'll fix you. You're dead in Times Square. By tomorrow everybody will know about the red-faced Irishman and the skinny blonde. You're dead." We shrugged unconcernedly as we left, until we were out in the hallway, then Jimmy mimicked in a whining falsetto, "Everybody will recognize the red-faced Irishman and the blonde." He whooped and dove down and whipped the wig off my head, bobbypins and all. "Ouch, you bum, give me back my head and let's go get some coffee." And arm in arm we left.

We ended up making an awful lot of junk collars because of the close affinity of junk to burglars. The largest percentage of house burglars were all on junk. They had to operate every day of the week to keep themselves in stuff. Sometimes we'd spot one of our known burglars and we'd tail him to get him right. Unfortunately sometimes he'd make a junk buy instead and we'd step into him figuring, well, it's one way to get him off the streets; and we'd lock him up for possession.

That's what happened one day when we planted on Mick Burns. We spotted him and stayed with him for over two hours until he made his move. Then into a hallway he went, we gave him a minute, figuring he might be breaking into an apartment and we'd catch him in the act. Then we tiptoed in. All was quiet. We spread out to see if we could spot anything. As I approached the fire stairs I heard a faint movement. Moving in to see if it was a mouse or our pigeon, I saw Mick with his sleeve rolled up and a hypodermic needle plunged into his vein, giving himself a shot.

"Cops. Freeze!" I hollered. Ed came flying down the stairs. Mick flung the hypo and took off like a bird. Ed shouted to Jimmy to grab the stuff as he and I were flying out the door. Mick was almost bent double and going like a gazelle. We gave him about half a block's chase before I decided this was bird feed. We weren't gaining, we were just getting our constitutional.

"Micky Burns," I bellowed, "I'm shooting!" Nothing happened except that Ed and I were starting to huff and puff, so I let one off into the air. Mick put his brakes on and came to a screaming halt, so that we almost ran over him as he shouted, "Don't shoot, don't shoot!"

"You crummy bastard, I'll remember how you made us sweat," Ed said as he threw cuffs on him.

I signaled a passing cab to take us to the precinct, and we tossed Mick in before the startled driver could change his mind about driving us.

The routine paperwork was made a little more pleasant because Georgy Barrett was on duty in the squad room and he greeted us with, "Hey, you picked up that scum bag? Good for you."

When we finished, he said, "I may as well go down with you, I have to check out this telephone complaint. I know it's a crock, but the woman left her name so I'll go talk to her and see if she had too much to drink."

"What was it?"

"Oh, she's been watching too many movies. She said a couple kidnapped some guy at gunpoint and drove off in a cab. The woman was wearing brown boots and a green suede coat." His voice dropped off as he saw me get out from behind the desk, wearing brown boots, and then reach over and fling on my green suede coat. "You're kidding . . . it was you guys?" Barrett said.

"Listen," Ed said, "you solved it without even leaving the squad room. Just mark it 'Case Closed with Results.'" Even Broadway Barrett just shook his head.

Things didn't always work out. Sometimes days of work went down the drain. But when something got blown out of sheer stupidity, it was something else.

We were back in one of our favorite cesspools, Times Square, with information that a connection was being made right in Father Duffy Square for junk in exchange for swag (stolen merchandise). We decided to saturate the area for a couple of days making observations.

I was in my black leather pants suit, black short boots with rhinestones all over the front, and a little black leather pea cap. I decorated the front of Whalen's Drugstore, like so many of "the girls."

Ed was wearing his tourist's special. He had a large oversize green suede cap and a green suburban coat with a suede front and lots of furry stuff sticking out. It was enough green to turn you bilious.

Jim was in one of his better outfits. He had an unironed shirt, about three sizes too small. He said that he had taken it out of the ironing basket that morning because he didn't want to wake up his wife.

We were in and around for about four days and things were shaping up pretty well. We could tell the players without a scorecard and were waiting now for a big coup.

Jimmy was sitting on one of the park benches with some of our "people" and Ed and I were draped on the plate-glass window of Whalen's, when the burglar alarm went off from inside the store. A black body came hurtling out and into the intersection with someone screaming after him, "Stop, thief. Help . . . police . . . robber!" The alarm wailed.

We had to blow our cover. From the park bench, from the window front, we emerged with drawn guns. Our fleeing felon hit the pavement and rolled himself under a taxi that was waiting for a light. The startled cabby seemed to have a stroke as three bodies hurled themselves over his hood yelling, "Police! Don't move the car, there's someone underneath!" We knelt down and extracted our suspect, with a little persuasion. It was a trembling sixteen-year-old that we dragged back to the store, noting meanwhile that Broadway and Duffy Square were very, very empty indeed.

"Okay, what happened?" we asked the manager after we were all in his office.

"Well, well, uh . . ."

"What did he take, goddammit?"

"I didn't take nothin', man, nothin'. He lies, he say I took somethin'." The kid was regaining his composure, as the manager's face seemed to get whiter.

Ed grabbed the manager by the tie, and said slowly and distinctly, between clenched teeth, "What . . . did . . . he . . . take!"

The fat white face turned red as he whispered, "He tried to take some candy bars, but he dropped them when I saw him."

"Candy bars? Candy bars? You're joking. You put on the alarm, you came out screaming. We could have shot this kid, we could have killed him for you, you fat son of a bitch!" I screamed. Ed's normally red face was pinched white; he hissed, "Fuckin' son of a bitchin' bastard."

The kid was crying as Jimmy took the cuffs off him, handed him a batch of candy bars, and told him to take off and stay out of trouble.

Sure the case we worked on was shot, but what had us bugged all day was how close we came to getting really loused up. Carrying a mistake like that on your conscience the rest of your life wouldn't be the easiest load in the world.

Every team, at Lieutenant Mackin's discretion, got their share of special assignments. Some were more desirable than others. The easy ones that looked like they'd culminate quickly and easily in an arrest were called grounders. A complainant might call in and say her former boyfriend just forced his way into her home and stole her furs and jewelry and she wanted him arrested. This was a real grounder.

That, of course, was assigned to the Farmer and his partner. They'd interview the woman, get the boyfriend's address, and arrest him. Case Closed with Results. So the Farmer was "fed." This kept him free, timewise, to take care of the boss's varied needs, and still kept his arrest record up high enough to warrant promotion.

A lot we cared. No matter what kind of garbage he gave us we came up smelling like roses. It drove him up a wall. We were clicking like gangbusters, and ranked number one, two, three in the squad for activity. Mackin didn't like this one bit. We used to smile, when the inspector would insist that we handle a particular thing, or the FBI would come looking for us to assist them, to see how much it rankled him.

During December we got specially assigned to work the Diamond Exchange block. We had Forty-sixth Street between Fifth and Sixth avenues. One short city block to cover from 10 A.M. to 6 P.M. Ostensibly the purpose of this was to protect the merchants during the hectic Christmas shopping rush. We felt it was to keep us pinned down. By limiting our area, the percentage of incidents must, of course, be fewer. Also, he could pop in and out, at will, for a month and make sure we were where he had put us.

As usual, he was wrong. In the first place, imagine sticking a woman on a block chock full of diamonds. Who could leave? Who wanted to leave? This one little block had everything a thief could yearn for. In our one month we made a lot of friends, a lot of enemies, and five collars.

The one that stays with me was the cutie that pulled the diamond switch. This type of theft is based on deception rather than force. The crook, a combination con man and sleight-of-hand specialist, goes into a jeweler and asks to see diamond engagement rings. He'll usually specify a type, emerald cut, pear-shaped, or round. Regardless of what he's shown, he'll request something larger. Out of this batch, he will zero in and pick one out saying, "This is more like what I had in mind." He'll hold this in his hand and examine it carefully and ask, "Do you have something like this only maybe a little bigger, I don't want her to think I'm cheap." The jeweler starts getting excited, thinking he's got a real live one. In his eagerness he won't ask him for the diamond back, as he burrows in the safe to bring out the larger stones.

The thief quickly substitutes a similar-styled ring for the real one, puts it on the counter top, and walks out. When the jeweler turns, his feelings seesaw up and down. First, fear. He thinks the ring was stolen. Second, he sees the ring on the counter and feels relief. He picks up the ring, sees it's a phony, and feels sick. By then the thief has had enough time to blend with the crowded street scene.

One cold snowy morning we saw an excited jeweler bursting through his doorway yelling on the run, "Police. Help. My ring. Thiiiieeeeffff!!!" As soon as we saw him, we stopped looking at him, but turned instead to watch the street panorama. Most people stop in their tracks and stare when witnessing something. The ones that keep moving are the ones to watch. We saw what we knew was our boy about twenty-five feet ahead trying to make tracks in the mush and slush of the new snow. We gave chase with our siren call, "Police. Stop." Stop, hell, he manufactured adrenaline and double-timed it. We started to gain on him as people started clearing a way for us, when he darted into a building and tried to get into an elevator. But he had Ed, Jimmy, and me on his back dragging him out.

"We got 'im, we got 'im, Marie," so I stepped back, figuring there was only one of him and three people on him could be confusing. I ended up witnessing a combination adagio dance and wrestling match as they tried to cuff him. Our diamond switcher had flipped his wig and we had a full-bloom psycho on our hands. He was fighting like a veritable madman, hysterically shouting, "No cuffs, no cuffs."

What made it funny was that not one of the three of them could get any footing or traction. There was about a half inch of wet gook on the marble lobby floor from the snow and wet boots tracked in all morning. They fell and twisted, and squirmed as they tried to turn him over on his stomach so that they could cuff his hands behind him. He was as strong as a mule. After about five minutes they succeeded in getting one cuff on him. They looked like they had taken a mud bath.

"Enough of this bullshit." I stalked over to the bodies, stepped over our "almost" prisoner and straddled him, sitting on his shoulders. I dug my hands into his scalp and practically pulled him off the ground by the hair. He howled in sudden pain as my fingernails dug in unmercifully. It worked, though. The sudden shock relaxed him long enough for the guys to close the handcuffs on him.

Our team was acquiring a reputation through the job. When

we made an arrest in a precinct we didn't use regularly, the desk officer would say something like, "Oh, you're the hotshots from the Burglary Squad, we know all about you guys."

I had found true acceptance from my partners, and this attitude was contagious. Suddenly people, meaning men, wanted to work with me. Since my team thought of and accepted me as an equal, and I had a public record to back me up, I was now openly a part of their world.

A different type of special assignment came about when we got a forthwith to meet the lieutenant at a particular place. When he arrived, he drew back and looked us over, as if he were appraising stock on the hoof at butchering time. "Now, what the devil?" I thought to myself.

"Jimmy, you're out . . . but, uh, what about you two? You got nighttime clothes?"

"It depends on what you mean by nighttime clothes, Loo. If you mean evening gowns, yes, I have a number of them. What kind did you have in mind? I warn you though, you'll never fit into them." We all laughed . . . he didn't . . . *c'est la vie*.

"Okay, then you have to go home and get changed. Ed, you gotta get a tux someplace. President Kennedy is having his hundred-dollar-a-plate Birthday Ball and the Secret Service wants an extra thirty-five detectives assigned, besides the uniform men. They always have these details, but the President says he doesn't want his guests to feel strange or intimidated by having 'obvious-looking' cops around, and has asked that only detectives with appropriate clothing be assigned. You report to Lieutenant Kelly, Room 1214, at the hotel at six-thirty, so you better get a move on."

I dashed off to change, with of course the big question, "What shall I wear," uppermost in my mind.

The Birthday Ball was a ball. Nothing but the best, first-class all the way. The President shook hands with all his important guests, and unknowingly with about thirty-five detectives, all of whom he greeted and thanked for coming, with his famous infectious grin. I was assigned a particular section of the ballroom, and blended like mad. Things went very well, and there were no unpleasant incidents.

A lineup of big names was there as special entertainment. Jimmy Durante excelled himself and Ann-Margret really came

79

on. She played up to the President, so that for a moment I felt that I was watching the harem girl perform for her sheik. She looked magnificently animal as she tossed her long red mane and kicked up her heels. A detective later bragged about observing the Secret Service men as they spirited Ann-Margret to an impromptu departure via the fire escape.

After all the guests had gone and everything simmered down, the staff had a lobster thermidor buffet for the newsmen and the police officers. I often wondered if this constituted receiving a gratuity from the President, in the eyes of the department. You never know what Big Brother is thinking. The pendulum swung with a telephone message from the Homicide Squad. The Homicide boss said, "Do you know a flat burglar named Shep?" (A flat burglar is one who specializes in residences as opposed to stores or places of business.)

"Sure do. I've locked him up. Twice, as a matter of fact. Why?"

"Do you know where he hangs out, or who his friends are? Do you think you could come up with him?"

"My answer is yes, but could you tell me what it's all about? This is a bad-news guy, you know, really bad. . . ."

"I've already cleared it, you're specially assigned to Homicide for the next few weeks. C'mon down, fill in on the background, and pick out whoever you want to work with. Your job is just to get Shep and bring him in to us."

"Gotcha. If you've no objections I'd like to work with Ed Lehane, one of my regular partners." (Jim was on vacation.)

We read the complaint, the autopsy report, and looked at the pictures of the crime scene. Then we went to the apartment house of occurrence and interviewed the employees and the neighbors and came up with the background picture of a little old lady.

She was eighty-five years old. She could pass for seventy-five but felt she looked more like sixty-five. She took obvious pains with her appearance; her long silver hair was always in a meticulous French knot. Although slightly bent, she was proud she hadn't gone to live with her children. She was happy in her own apartment, surrounded by her beautiful things and friendly people. When she came down for her afternoon walk the doorman would watch her leave and he'd mutter, "That old gal's all right, not afraid of nothin'!"

The previous day, when she came back, she found her door unlocked. An afternoon burglar, surprised at the interruption, panicked and thrust a two-pronged carving fork into her chest with such force it was imbedded in her breastbone.

The Homicide Bureau had come up with "Shep" as a possible suspect for the murder. They pulled his yellow sheet from the nickname file and saw that I'd given him his last collar. Therefore I got the assignment: "Get Shep."

Shep is Rodney Shepherd, M W 27 years, 5'11", sallow with bad junkie acne and a skinny 145 pounds. His clothing is usually dark and nondistinctive, except for an accessible pocket to hold the knife which is his trademark.

Shep is a junkie burglar, who steals because he shoots maybe forty-five to sixty-five dollars a day. It's a heavy habit and he has to hustle to clear enough to stay ahead.

After the gut-shaking experience of the theft, the burglar is only half done . . . now he has to peddle what he's stolen. Junkie burglars are a dime a dozen, but fences aren't that easy to come by. This is how we played Shep. We made the rounds looking for the floating fence.

The guy we were looking for was Three-finger Jack. Jack worked out of the Horn and Hardart automats. He made rounds like a doctor with visiting hours. Ed and I looked almost like regular people. I was wearing blue jeans, sneakers; my reddish-brown waist-length hair was in one long braid down my back and my gun was in its usual inside-the-waist holster. If I attracted any second looks at all, it was probably due to the tight dungarees.

Ed was sporting his green corduroys, green banlon sweater, and green hushpuppies that helped him acquire one of his many nicknames, "The Green Hornet." And so we looked for Shep.

By the third Horn and Hardart we were both pretty well awash with coffee, but we went through the motions anyway. We carried our cups toward a table which allowed a clear view of the revolving door. A young rookie cop, looking like he had stepped out of a police academy bandbox, strolled past the doorway, shakily trying to twirl his nightstick. Ed and I exchanged smiles as we set our coffee down.

Then we saw Shep coming toward the door, head down but

eyes searching. We made a beeline for the entrance, getting there so fast Shep hadn't even completed the turn in the revolving door. As it opened to let him out, we quickly jammed into the same section of the door and propelled it to keep turning so we were once more facing the street and talking quietly all the time.

"Okay, Shep, let's keep it quiet so no one gets hurt . . . just keep moving." Ed and I were jammed up against him. Our guns were drawn but our bodies hid them as we pressed up tightly against him. We each had an outside arm gripping one of his.

We took him out without any commotion and now we were "talking him in" as we walked to the car. We walked and talked, without attracting any attention . . . and were only a few hundred feet from the car when I caught a glimpse of our rookie, across the street, standing on the park ledge surveying his territory.

"Shep, you're doing fine, let's get you to the car . . . nice and easy and you won't get hurt . . . keep walking and . . ." A few seconds later a blinding pain enveloped my right elbow. My fist clenched and my fingers trembled as I tried to keep control of the gun. Blinding tears of pain blurred my eyes as I saw the uniformed cop holding his nightstick raised high to strike again.

Ed hollered (he couldn't whirl around with the gun in his hand, this moron might shoot), "We're on the job!! You son of a bitch, we're on the job!!! My shield is in my back pants pocket. Take it out!" The kid did, and of course things were different now.

Meanwhile, Shep had fainted, thinking he'd been shot. He had an obsession that I'd be the one to shoot him someday, and now his fears overcame reality.

My right arm was hanging uselessly like a bowl of unset Jell-O and I tried to figure out how I managed to keep from squeezing off a shot, even as a reflex action. I was so mad I was going to rip into this rookie and chew him out, except that the red-faced Irishman beat me to it, with one of his better blasts which included all the words that end with "itch," "ick," "uck," or "ucker"!!

The young cop explained that he saw the sun glinting down on the gun metal while he was standing on the rise across the street. Figuring we were kidnapping Shep, he'd come to the rescue.

Why he didn't get the drop on us and just ask a few questions, he couldn't answer. Perhaps it was partly because he'd been a cop less than a year. I never could get a logical reason for why he picked on me instead of Ed.

Every rainy day when my elbow hurts I remember how I didn't bother reporting it to the Medical Bureau because there was just too much work to be done. I also think of Shep stretched out on the pavement, and of how surprised he was when he woke up in the 6th Squad office.

I'd been doing an awful lot of soul-searching and decided that I had to level with my partners. I was in my seventh month of pregnancy and feeling fine, but I had the horrid dread of something happening that I might not be able to cope with because of my condition, and I couldn't chance that happening.

The seven months had been a challenge, both physically and mentally. I recalled an article in *Reader's Digest* about the Trapp Family Singers, who'd fled Nazi occupation during World War II.

Arriving here as impoverished refugees, they were pleased to secure short bookings throughout the country. Mrs. Trapp, however, was visibly pregnant and felt this would deter future bookings. So the ingenious momma went out and bought herself a flock of brassieres in escalating sizes.

As her stomach got larger, she would slip into the next size bra, which she would stuff with towels or what have you. Since her top was in proportion to her bottom, it didn't attract attention . . . until one evening when she almost had the baby onstage.

Mrs. Trapp, let me tell you . . . it worked like a charm. Of course I kept my weight under control, in fact I gained just nine pounds during the pregnancy. But a nine-pound football in your belly isn't all that easy to hide. I used the larger size bra gimmick with astounding results. The best I got, usually from someone I hadn't seen in some time, was, "Hey, Marie, putting on a little weight, aren't you? You'd better cut down on the spaghetti." I'd laugh and agree that I'd go on a diet soon.

Physically was something else again. During the first two months I had tremendous pressure on my bladder. Of course I pleaded a kidney infection, which became a big joke after a while. We'd be following someone on foot, and I would dive into a restaurant, shouting to them, "Keep going, I'll catch up." After a while they shook their heads and called me a leaky faucet.

I didn't want to go out on maternity leave, we had too many things going. But I knew that if my concern for my partners wasn't enough of an incentive, the department regulations stating that a policewoman couldn't work beyond the fifth month were.

I told the boys that fateful October 24, 1963, and the noise was like Christmas and New Year's Eve put together. "Is that why you were in and out of every ladies' room in New York?" "Hey, Marie, don't bother putting me down for an assist on this case!" "Mackin will say you should have gotten permission first." "Oh, you miserable bum, you know we're going to look like horses' asses. We took enough ribbing working with a woman, what the hell are they going to say when she leaves us pregnant?"

We all sort of simmered down and took a run down to Chinatown to one of our trustworthy dives. Since I was throwing in my leave papers this was to be our last lunch and we made the most of it. We ate like overstuffed walruses, practically staggering out of the place, filled almost as much with fellowship as with good food.

"Thank God you're driving," Ed said. "I'm so full I can hardly move. Just drive around, let's not get involved in anything on your last day—and don't spot any of your specials either."

"Funny, very funny. No respect for an almost mother, I can see."

When I first started patrolling with the squad, I learned to be aware of people's movements. The eyes were the biggest giveaway. When someone was overly alert to people around him or observing him, you could see the eyeballs darting to and fro, taking everything in. This type of person was "eyeballing" and usually up to something.

The first step in an attempted crime usually starts with eyeballing, followed by some furtive motion. My specialty was pointing out a character walking along with his head swiveling in all directions. Stopping in front of a padlocked store he'd look up and down the street and then turn and bend over making frantic motions. At this point we'd swoop down, tell him to freeze, raise his hands, and turn very slowly. Instead of a burglar we'd often get a poor shnook taking a pee in a doorway.

I decided to loop around the Village and say ciao to friends like Mamma and Petie in Monte's and Ed Henry, and tell them that their food had not been responsible for my weight gain.

As I was driving west on Tenth Street, a block of lovely residential brownstones, I saw something that immediately struck me as questionable. A male light-skinned black was standing at the base of the flight of stairs leading to the house, and was very, very busy eyeballing the street. At the doorway was another male, about thirty-five, curly-haired with a moustache, who could pass for Puerto Rican or mulatto. He was just turning away from the door and shook his head at the fellow down below.

I drove past them and started to circle the block again.

"Fellas, hey, wake up, you overfed horses. I think we got a couple of movers. These guys look like good daytime flat burglars." I told them exactly what I observed and by this time they were alert although still slumped down to avoid easy detectability.

We were back in the block again, and they were three houses away from the first one—in the same positions. I drove on past them, dropping Jimmy off on the corner to keep them under observation, while I swung around once more. At the top of the block I dropped Ed off, so that the two men were now in between Jim and Ed. I stayed in the car and gave them a loose tail.

These guys were so anxious to score they were practically frothing at the mouth, but they couldn't seem to connect. Whenever they picked a building, there was either someone home, or someone passing by spooked them, or a neighbor leaned out a window and asked who they were looking for.

They had walked blocks meanwhile. By this time I was praying they'd do something right and score so that we could end this cat-and-mouse game. On Broadway now, they saw a parked truck with a padlocked back and quickly inserted a tire iron through the lock to force it open. At that point the driver came flying out of the building. "What the hell do you guys think you're doing!!" he bellowed. Our birds flew.

They slowed down about Fourteenth Street. Meanwhile I had picked up my overweight friends, who agreed that these guys were becoming more and more desperate. At this point the two cut through the park at Union Square and Sixteenth Street. I followed and we saw the same thing our suspects saw, at the same time, and knew that they'd go for it.

A shiny new Pontiac, packed to take some folks away on a trip. Four or five suitcases were on the back seat and a fur coat was slung over the front one. Those two guys never even broke their stride. They were on either side of that car and the side vent windows were jimmied open. They were inside in less time than it takes to tell it.

"This one is ours, Momma . . . you stay in the car, that's an order," said my newly concerned partners as they jumped out with drawn guns. The mustachioed cat, later identified as Theodore Oliver, had removed a suitcase, which he had in his right hand, and the fur coat, which was slung over his left shoulder. James Stranee had one suitcase in each hand, as they both made hasty tracks away from the car.

They were blocked by Jim and Ed with drawn guns. Oliver threw the fur coat at Lehane, and then as he struggled free, swung the suitcase, like a club, down onto his head. Lehane went down and I thought he was done for. Simultaneously Stranee had flung a suitcase at Jim which sent his gun flying, and the two of them were on the floor wrestling for possession of it.

I was out of the car, gun in hand, racing over. I let fly a warning shot that made Oliver swing to attention. He bolted with me in hot pursuit after a glance showed me that Capano had finally subdued Stranee. It didn't take more than a few hundred feet for me to realize that I could never hope to keep up with him on foot. I ran back to the car, thinking to myself, "That bastard killed my partner."

Oliver ran through the parking lot, making sharp turns and cutting through the metered sections to try to throw me off. The car took a good bruising, but if I had to use it as a battering ram I was going to. I was steering with my left hand. My gun was in the right and I was looking for a good shot.

I pegged another one off, my right hand across my chest and the gun pointed out the window, and he knew this was it. He ran out of the park and onto Broadway, doubled down to make a small target and taking advantage of the parked cars and trucks

86

as cover. He kept going and so did I. At Eighteenth Street, which is an eastbound street, he ran in going west. "This is it, kiddo, here goes nothing." I put the gun on the seat between my legs and used my hand to keep the horn blasting away to warn the garment area trucks that I was coming through, wrong way or no wrong way. The brake squeals filled the air as the traffic burned rubber with their sudden stops. A cacophony of sound filled the air as all the trucks and cars hooted at the same time. Truckers stood on their dashboards yelling, "Hey, lady, you crazy or somethin'? You wanta get killed?"

People on the sidewalks were aghast, frantically waving their hands, gesticulating that it was a one-way street. Everyone and everything came to a screeching halt except Oliver, still running, and me, still trying to run him down.

He was bent over and running close to the building line, counting on the people to shield him. I finally saw a clear spot about ten feet ahead of him. I gunned the car and veered sharply to the right, on and over the curb and straight to the wall, cutting off his flight with about three thousand pounds of steel.

As I jumped out of my car, gun in hand, Oliver tried to duck away and I wrestled him to the wall by dancing a tattoo on his skull with my gun butt. Suddenly a new gun butt appeared and the flight was over. I glanced up to see a very, very white-faced, haggard Irishman, puffed out but not down.

He put cuffs on Oliver as I stared. "I thought you were dead."

"Do I look dead, you crazy broad? I saw the whole thing. When you took the car, I was behind him on foot, but you'd never take your eyes off him long enough to notice anything else. I threw a couple at him, but it didn't slow him down any. I kept pace but I couldn't overtake him until you cut him off with the car."

Sirens were blaring and bleating as radio cars and unmarked cars converged on us. We were swamped by bosses, chiefs, and Indians trying to help. "Just take our prisoner into the house for us, we have another partner in the park holding a second prisoner."

"Don't worry, we got them, they're on their way in."

An inspector said, "You feeling okay? You sure you can drive? You can come in with us, we'll have someone bring your car in and park it by the precinct for you."

"She can drive, Inspector, don't you worry about her. She's okay!" This was Ed's indirect accolade. "You can go on in, we'll be there in a few minutes. Thanks for everything."

On the short ride over I heard otherwise. "You crazy stupid son of a bitch, we told you to stay in the car. Suppose something happened. . . ."

"Suppose something happened?" I interrupted. "Oh, brother, if that isn't an understatement." At that the tension was broken and we could laugh again, laugh in relief that we were still able to laugh.

"Boy, you sure know how to go out on maternity leave. Most of the other girls get a nice baby shower."

We got to the house and had to fight our way through the squad room full of reporters and TV cameramen setting up their lighting and other equipment. They seemed to surround us and I felt a momentary drowning sensation. I felt an arm go around my shoulder, and an authoritative voice said, "Nobody talks to them before I do. Come inside." We were shepherded into Lieutenant Thomas Kissane's office. He was the boss of that local squad, and therefore bore some of the responsibility for reporting what had occurred in his confines. I had never met him before, but was to work for him in later years and get to know that he was a stand-up boss, the highest accolade the troops confer on a ranking officer. It meant that the boss had the guts and "stand-up" integrity to do and say what he thought was right and not just politically expedient. It also meant standing up for your men, when you were being indirectly pressured to offer them up as whipping boys.

"Shut the door and sit down." When we had, he just looked at us, then quietly said, "How are you? Marie, you okay? Eddie, geez, I haven't seen you since Charley's dinner. Hey, Joe, would you run down to the liquor store and bring back a pint of brandy." He had turned and pressed a bill into one of his detectives' hands, saying, "Hurry it, will you, I think these guys could use a drink while we wait for the ambulance for Oliver."

"Ambulance? For Oliver? For what?" we chorused.

"What are you kidding, he's got a slug in his shoulder."

"Oh, brother, I thought I missed him. Nothing slowed him

down, and there wasn't any blood on him when we cuffed him."

"I threw a couple at him too, but the bastard ran like a gazelle," said Ed.

The social amenities were next, we went through our interviews, photographs, and television appearances, and then had to start in with the mundane clerical procedures attendant upon the arrest for grand larceny, possession of burglar's tools, and felonious assault on an officer.

The department rules state that a policewoman must remain out on maternity leave a minimum of 180 days from the day she gives birth. She may stay out longer, if she prefers, but she cannot return earlier.

The reasoning behind it is simple. While on leave you don't get paid. If by returning earlier your "weakened" condition caused some complications, you'd have to go on sick report and be entitled to sick pay. Therefore it behooves them (in the pocketbook) to keep you on a nonsalary basis for as long as possible.

James Michael made his proud debut on January 9, 1964. But, in my own way, I had to attract a little attention even here. I was isolated with the first case of childbed fever in posh Harkness Pavilion in about fifteen years. When I got flowers from the guys in the squad, the card read, "Hey, tiger, can't you ever do anything like anyone else? P.S. We knew you had it in you! Ha-ha." Signed, "Your Boys."

One hundred eighty days from January 9 made my target date June 5. I had, for months, been negotiating with the Immigration Department to bring over a British girl whose praises had been highly sung to act as my aide-de-camp, alter ego, and general stand-in, so that I could return to work with a clear head. Mary Cole got into Kennedy Airport when Jim was three months old.

This worked out beautifully. We had three months to all get used to each other. I have very decided feelings about child-rearing and on that score I was adamant. I couldn't care less about how a floor is washed, or furniture polished, but how and what a child eats or is treated or feels, that is important.

Mary, my lovely British doll, was the greatest. She had been a blitz baby in London in World War II, and hadn't had a particularly happy upbringing, so she left home and joined the Royal

Navy, where she probably was responsible for breaking a number of hearts. Mary was bright, clever, and undaunted.

Cindy and she became fast buddies and she cared for Jim like a newborn pup. I watched and let the feelings get strong and true. Now I could go back to work.

Safe, Loft, and Truck

It was payday and everyone was in. We all went out to lunch and snickered over the fact that the activity figures for the month were way off because the lieutenant had us serving penance. He disliked us mainly because we weren't subservient to him; polite yes, obedient yes, grovel . . . nyet. His house didn't get painted by us, we didn't do his gardening, carpentry, or other chores. Most bosses in these special squads handpick each one of their men, and they're usually all special contracts. We three were not. We were just workers, and he resented this. When we'd really had it up to here with some illogical move, we'd get him where he lived, with, "Gee, Loo, am I glad all those stories I heard about you taking everything but a hot stove are phony. I was worried for a while. But, tell me, what are you going to do with that dozen pair of asbestos gloves?" That was usually good for another couple of weeks of clerical duty.

The whole world had changed when we returned from our meal. Orders from downtown—all the burglary squads were transferred into the Safe, Loft, and Truck Squad. That meant the burglary squads from all the different boroughs would now be a part of SLATS. It seemed unbelievable. Conversation and conjecture ran rampant.

"The Safety Lock Boys," as we burglary folk called the SLATS members, always operated on a level somewhat removed from the norm. They had members who hadn't made an arrest in years, and were first-graders. These men were always involved in some sort of ultra high secrecy case and accountable to no one but the inspector. After I was with them awhile, I was to realize that these big cases usually stemmed from Madison Avenue and entailed keeping a nun, or a priest, that was suspected of some violation of vows, under observation; and of reporting.

They were also the only squad I knew of that had members that'd been promoted from third-grade detective to first-grade, bypassing second.

Aside from this, they had a coterie of the best hardworking, *real* cops assembled in one unit. In this job of nicknames, I was to award them by calling them the "realies," which name took hold and was used by all the Burglary Boys when they referred to the SLATS.

The Safe, Loft, and Truck Squad specialized mainly in just those things. Any burglary or robbery involving a safe; any burglary of a warehouse or business loft; and any and all types of theft from trucks, such as hijacking, were their special domain. Now Burglary was being assimilated into them, and we were all wondering at the possible changes that might ensue.

There were virtually none, to begin with. The transfer had come with such suddenness that there was no preparation. The office was thronged as the SLATS captain made what was supposed to be a welcome speech. He had close to a hundred men, and was suddenly inundated with about sixty or so more, four or five more lieutenants, and a sergeant or two. He solved it very quickly by telling everyone to continue doing exactly what they had done before, in their same areas and under their former bosses, until further notice.

About the only silver lining I could see for Captain Meeghan was an eventual promotion to inspector. There wasn't a captain in the job with that many men in his command.

With this transfer the safety lock people inherited problems they'd never entertained before. They now had eight women on their hands—a major disaster, to hear the captain tell it. After the meeting, he called us into the office and told us in no uncertain terms, "I do not want women in my squad. I have never tolerated a woman here and do not intend to start now. I have called you in to tell you that if you have any preferences as to where you're assigned, then I suggest that you take whatever action you can to achieve that goal, because I intend to get you transferred out forthwith. I want you to realize that this is nothing personal."

The girls stared in disbelief, too shocked to say anything. He continued, "I don't want my men distracted. I have good men and I don't want them to get in trouble." (Shades of Adam and Eve, I thought.) "Do you understand what I mean? I'm going over now to see the chief of detectives and request your transfer from my command. I know he'll understand. I'll tell him that my men just are not equipped to work with women."

I said through lips tightened with anger, "Just what kind of equipment do you think they need, Captain?" A brisk "har-umph" as he cleared his throat. "You're dismissed," and he turned his back.

"What happened?" all the guys clamored when we emerged from the lair. "That quiff seems to think we're going to corrupt his sainted angels," I said, frothing at the mouth. "He's going across the street now to get us transferred right out again!"

"Don't feel so bad. I'm sure he's going to talk to them about more than just you girls. That's probably why he's all up in the air. Stop and think. There's never been anything but Irish-Catholic in this squad. There are no Jews or blacks. A few months ago, he let in the first Italian, but I think he makes him sing 'When Irish Eyes Are Smiling' every morning at roll call as a pledge of allegiance.

"Anyone 'lucky' enough to have problems at home that ended in separation, or you should pardon the expression, divorce, became doubly blessed by being dumped from the squad. It's just not allowed in the Holy Roller Good Book. Now all of a sudden he gets a load of you dropped on him—women, and to add insult to injury, two of you girls are black. And you guys, what a mess —Jews, Protestants, and Italians. Let me assure you that this man is fingering his prayer beads on the way over, across the street, wondering what God hath wrought."

Luckily, there's usually someone with a friend, and this time was no exception. "I know someone in the chief's office, I think I'll give a buzz and see if I can figure out what's cooking," was greeted by loud cheers. The cheers got louder when he said that a study was being made as to where the burglary squads would act more efficiently, on their own or under an over-all command, and there'd be no changes for at least two or three months. "Whew . . . that was close. Well, it's always good to be working where the boss doesn't want you. But I'll make him eat his words. You'll see, we'll dance rings around 'em," I said confidently. "I'll have his men asking to work with me."

"Okay starbright, simmer down, you sound like you're planning a major invasion. You've only met the captain, wait until you see the inspector. He says 'woman' like someone else says 'venereal disease.'"

Then I met Inspector Dooley. He seemed harmless enough— pale, see-through skin, washed-out blue eyes, looked a lot older than he was. He had pictures of a young man and a large framed photo of a daughter, as I presumed. How could anyone surrounded by photos of their children be bad?

"Sit down, sit . . . so you're in one of my squads, eh? What did you say your name was? What's that again? Spell it. C–I–R–I–L– E. Oh, what kind of a name is that? Oh, it must be a marriage name. Are you married? What church were you married in? Oh, what parish do you live in? How many children do you have? That's all? What was your maiden name? What? Is that one of those Italian names? What school do you send your daughter to? Why isn't she in parochial school, you are a Catholic, aren't you?"

I found myself starting to bristle so I tried to divert the questioning. "Is that your son? What an attractive boy, you must be very proud of him."

"Yeah, that's him all right. I used to have great faith in him, but he let me down."

"Oh, I'm terribly sorry for you, perhaps it was something he couldn't help."

"Oh, he could help it all right, no one forced him, or made him, but he went and married a guinea."

I shook my head, thinking I had heard wrong. Then I laughed —of course, he was pulling my leg. Boy, I thought, it's a good thing I realized it before I said something wrong. I kept smiling as I said something inane. "She must be a lovely girl for him to have picked her."

But he ran right over my remark as he continued with, "And now to add insult to injury they've got a half-breed son." I saw the veins sticking out alongside his eyes and I knew that he was not making pleasantries, that this was where he lived. "I never

94

even let one in the squad before, and now I have one in my own family."

"That's your grandson you're talking about?" I queried.

"He's no grandson, he's a goddamned half-breed."

"Inspector," I spewed out, "that's probably the best blood your family line has seen in generations!" I got up. "My partners are waiting for me, I'm sure you'll excuse me. Ciao, gentilissimo Inspettore."

We tried to stay away from the office as much as possible, and yet top everybody in activity. We were knocking them dead with grounders. They were the fast pickup collars that we'd see and take action on. We got car bangers (larceny from vehicles), car thieves (where they stole the cars), flat burglars walking away with shopping bags full of stuff. We wanted numbers, and they were coming our way.

They still kept the burglary squads lumped together, but they were separate and apart from SLATS. Our "Sweetheart Team" still ranked as No. 1–2–3 among all the burglary squads in New York.

The hotels were starting to get clobbered again and had requested the department to allow the squads to include them in the regular patrol. So we were now free to come and go in our finer institutions. One of my favorite spots for "observing" was a corner table in the Palm Court of the Plaza. The window walls faced two directions and gave you a clear sweep of the floor, a really ideal position.

The palm-filled room was a veritable oasis of tranquillity compared with the bustle outside. You could sit and observe in an almost offhand detached fashion, as you drank the *Kaffee schlag* and listened to the strolling violinist. Class, that was class.

Toby, the squad kibitzer, and his partner John joined us one night with word of a possible hotel stickup that evening. Toby took in the musician strolling from table to table as he sought the adulation of the fawning women, with a fatuous smile slathered across his face.

As the violinist started in our direction, Toby made furtive beckoning gestures. The musician's smile became puzzled as he noticed Toby's frantically insistent gestures. Toby motioned him closer, then whispered in a loud stage whisper, "Your fly is open!" The violinist blanched, but the song went on; his wild pirouettes became ever widening circles until he reached the security of the piano and the song climaxed in a wild crescendo.

As the crowd applauded, he bent, checked his zipper and took a bow. We howled with pity and laughter. "Why did you do that, Toby? The only thing that guy had showing was his ego."

"That's why I did it. C'mon, Handsome," he turned to John, "we have to tell the team at the Americana."

Our unofficial alert was called off when we heard that a flea-bag hotel over near Ninth Avenue had been hit to the tune of twenty-eight dollars. So Jimmy, Ed, and I resumed street patrol. We were riding around when the police radio crackled a forth-with: "Meet Lieutenant Mackin on Thirty-second Street and Sixth Avenue." Around we spun wondering what that was all about. It was 10:50 P.M. and we were due to go off duty at 11. "It can't be good, I know that much," drawled Jim. "He gives away snowballs in January."

It took us six and a half minutes to collect our basket of snow-balls. The Farmer and his partner were with the lieutenant, but their shamefaced looks let us know they were about to give us the business. "Oh, hey lissen, glad you guys got over so fast. Lemme explain, uh, *sluuurrpp*. We got a teletype from the Miami Police Department today with information that a Caddy with Florida plates was coming to New York to pull a hotel burglary."

"That's some piece of news. How come we got it so late? Well, anyway we'll cover as many hotels as we can and see if we can spot it, even though we're supposed to be going off," said Ed.

"Wait a minute now, you don't have the picture. I had a team assigned to this information since this morning," said he glancing at the Farmer who was chewing at a cuticle on the side of his index finger. "The FBI spotted the car for us at one o'clock this afternoon, and I've had the boys sitting on it since then. As a mat-ter of fact, I've been here most of the time myself."

We looked at each other, and then at them. Reading between the lines, we knew what they were doing. This was a really good piece of information, and it'd been funneled just to one team, instead of having every working team in New York on the lookout. They were so hungry for this case that they'd planted on the car for nine hours, but now they figured the car had been abandoned and they wanted to drop it and go have a couple of balls.

"Lissen, you guys, I, uh, know you're off duty, but I expect the men from Photo and Prints and we can't leave the car unattended . . . you know . . . it can't take long. Listen, I'll tell you what, if nobody shows by twelve you can call the twelve-to-eight guys and tell them I said they should relieve you. Okay? Lissen, it's the Caddy with Florida plates in the middle of the block, near the Statler Hilton." *Tch—cchh—urp.* "See ya."

"That creep sticks us on a dead horse, and I miss my train again, one of these days Helen is going to stop believing me," Jim beefed. "Make up your mind, Jimmy, have we got a basket of snowballs or a dead horse?" I asked. "C'mon, let's find out."

We clambered over that Caddy comparing notes. "The car's locked, all four doors, would they bother if they were abandoning it?" I asked. "Maybe they were having trouble with it. I see the muffler's knocked off," Jim chimed in. "Yeah," Ed nodded, "but that resonator muffler was picked up and is on the floor in the back—that's not the actions of someone giving up on a car." We agreed and decided to "work the car."

We pulled into the block and parked across from the Caddy. Jimmy stretched out in the back and Ed slumped down in the front, so that to all appearances I was alone. We spent an hour this way with the conversation sporadic, but revolving on the same thought: "Wouldn't it be something if they showed!! He'd have a fit! Jesus, he'd send us to Siberia for sure! Oh, please . . . make something happen!"

"Fellas, a white Chevy just pulled in right behind our Caddy." I could feel them tense. "There's three women and two men in it. They're just sitting there, but I can see them eyeballing. One of the guys is getting out and . . . yahoo, he's opening the trunk on the Caddy. He's looking all around and now he's nodding okay. The other guy is out. He opened the trunk of the Chevy. He's carrying a big black case over and is putting it in the Caddy trunk. The trunks are staying open, looks like he's going back for more. You know if these guys didn't score yet, we're killing a good bet. Let's try the old Auto Squad bit."

"Good thinking," Ed threw out. "I like your footwork, kid. Fancy stepping . . . let's move it."

In about fifteen seconds we appeared, shields in hand around the Caddy trunk with its two loaders. Jimmy had fallen back about ten paces to cover both us and the females in the car, although there weren't any guns in evidence anywhere.

"I'm Sergeant Quinby from the Auto Squad, can I see your license and registration?"

"What's wrong, officer?" asked the short stocky one wearing black horn-rimmed glasses.

"We have a complaint from the hotel that this car has been parked illegally all day."

The relief clearly visible in Michael Pell's face, he repeated, "Auto Squad . . . oh well, no problem. Hey, Nancy, can I have the registration, these good people just have to check our papers. Here you are, officer, no trouble at all."

Ed went to our car and pretended to call the plate in on the radio, but we'd inherited the original teletype when we inherited the assignment. "I'm sorry, but you'll have to come into the station with me. I'm sure it can be cleared up, but your registration is for a two-door Coupe de Ville, not a four-door."

Pell, the talker of the two males, became expansive. ". . . terrible misunderstanding . . . officer . . . Sergeant . . . don't want to embarrass the girls . . . straighten this out man to man . . . take a hundred." And he pressed something into Ed's pocket.

As if by signal, three guns emerged in three hands. "You're under arrest for attempted bribery, mister," Ed said to the astonished group as we made the men assume the search position. In the tall good-looking one's pocket I found a beautiful set of picks and screwdrivers. "We got the right ones, Eddie, he's even got a set of hand tools." The Kirk Douglas look-alike spun around and said, "They're not from any Auto Squad."

"You so right, baby . . . oh by the way, what did you say was in those five cases you put in the Caddy?"

We took the whole kit and kaboodle in to the 14th Precinct and called Mackin at home to give him the happy news, but his wife said that he wasn't in. We left a message to call us immediately, that we'd made an arrest.

It took us hours to sort out evidence. What we had was five

jeweler's sample cases that contained sixty-three watches, every type and style, encrusted with diamonds and other stones, gold, and platinum. What we didn't have was a complainant, someone who had reported sixty-three watches stolen. A little thinking and some phone calls later, and we did. The salesman didn't even know he'd been robbed. These guys had come from Florida headed for big pickings: the National Retail Jewelers' Convention, at the New York Hilton Hotel.

When I woke the Benrus representative at 4 A.M., he sleepily denied anything having been taken.

"Mr. Jones, will you get yourself out of bed and go and see if it's there. . . ."

"Oh my God, I've been robbed. All my sample cases are missing, my whole line. . . ."

"Mr. Jones! Will you listen, we have all your samples, that's what I'm trying to tell you. We arrested five people. You just be in court in the morning and we'll tell you the whole story, okay?"

Meanwhile the fellas had been working on the big bag originally put into the Caddy. They called me over and I whistled in awe. It was the most extensive, best-looking set of burglar's tools I'd ever seen. There were over four hundred keys to fit hotel rooms all over New York City as well as other major cities in the country. There were lock cylinders that could be used to change locks, master keys, jimmys, shims, lock molds to create keys, screwdrivers, picks, and even celluloid strips. It was the works and represented a fortune in not only money but the time necessary to accumulate this type of kit. "Wow . . . would you call these guys professionals?" I laughed.

Pell had ulcers and he and Ed discussed their favorite antacids. When he started giving Ed advice I said, "He sounds like a blasted doctor, in fact he looks like a doctor. "Dr." Pell started to laugh and admitted passing himself off in just this way, registering in the best hotels as Dr. Pell.

Frank Lerner dressed and looked like a prosperous executive. I couldn't visualize them being stopped anywhere. We didn't find out what role the women played, but knew that Pell and Turner had driven up from Florida with them, and one of them owned the Cadillac.

Mackin finally called about four-thirty in the morning. Do you think he was thrilled at our accomplishments? In a pig's ear. We told him it was a shame he hadn't called earlier, that he could've gotten in on some publicity.

"You mean they were there and gone already?" he grunted.

"Well, Loo, we've been here four hours already."

"Yeah, yeah, well, I guess that's that."

"Listen, Loo, please notify the captain in the morning, and the inspector, 'cause we'll be going all night and have court in the morning. After court, we'll come into the office."

"Sure . . . sure."

We couldn't charge them with the actual theft, but with the possession: criminally receiving, possession of burglar's tools, and attempted bribery. Hours later, as we were turning them over to the Department of Corrections for their court appearance, one of the guards searching Pell came up with a bit of glassine with two tablets encased in it. He whooped like he'd discovered the Kimberley diamond, "Aha . . . what's this!" Ed and I looked up slightly glassy-eyed from fatigue and hunger. (You couldn't get anything all night in the house, except coffee which had already produced a massive heartburn.) Our eyes lit up and both hands reached up and snatched it away from the astonished officer. Ed peeled them. "Here's one for you and one for me," and he popped one into his mouth as I did the same. "Hey, 'Doctor,' you were holding out on us!" Ed laughed and turned to the guard, "Relax, Charlie, they're only Mylanta, an antacid tablet. Marie and I finished ours hours ago, and then we went through the doctor's supply with him. You don't know it, but you saved our lives."

We knew we'd captured some good-sized fish by noon of the next day, although it's a wonder we still had our wits about us. We'd been working twenty continuous hours, and the end was nowhere in sight. Somehow or other you seem to build up an immunity to fatigue after you've been through this routine a number of times. Perhaps it's because all of the work is the type done under pressure, where time is of the essence, and then there's always the next step to go to that keeps you rolling along. I found I could do without the sleep, but not without eating.

Our prisoners were big. They'd had lawyers flown up from Miami to appear for them, and bail was made immediately. The

FBI sent their agents around to take a look at our people and to request copies of the photos we'd taken. It seems that agents all over the country had worked on them, but had never been able to tie them in with a hotel burglary, which they felt was their main enterprise. They congratulated us, which felt fine.

We swaggered into the office about 4:30 P.M. after running the gauntlet on the way in. Cops, outside, on the way in, waiting for the elevator, even the elevator operator, had comments and words of praise. This job had some grapevine. What happened in a back room of a Bronx precinct was being repeated with embellishments in the front room of a Staten Island house within hours.

"You did it again, huh? They oughta call you the Three Musketeers," said one of the porters, who happened to be one of the nicest guys in the building. We smiled and waved to him as we went in. The silence was deafening. Everything seemed to stop as we went in. Even the phone dared not ring. Just six or seven sets of eyeballs looking at us solemnly.

"I must be in the wrong place," said Ed. I clapped my hands a few times. "All right, kiddies, the fairy princess is here—you may awake from the frightful spell cast upon you!" Jimmy just said in his nasal way, "Just what the hell is going on around here anyway?"

J.J. was the clerical man. He had a steel plate in his head as a result of a line-of-duty injury. The department in its usual spirit of magnanimity had broken him to clerical work. The clerical work and the pain had driven him to drink. J.J. figured that there wasn't anything else they could do to him, which made him one of the rarities, someone who spoke his own mind . . . when he could be bothered tuning in.

J.J. broke the silence and without any preliminaries. "Why didn't you call the office? How come the bosses weren't notified? The inspector is up the wall. He says forthwith to his office as soon as you show your faces. He's been like an animal all day. I'm telling you, he's made life hell here. You'd better get in there, 'cause if he walks in here . . . If you called me, I coulda covered for you. Couldn't you let me know? I would have helped you, you know that."

"Thank you, J.J." I patted him on the head, "Don't worry, baby, we're okay. We'll talk to you later. Okay?" I turned to go, and saw Ed punching his closed fist into his palm muttering, "It should be the son of a bitch's head!"

We bearded the lion in his den, which was the office adjoining SLATS. The inspector's clerical man went in to tell him that we were out there, and we saw him come storming out in three directions at once. "Come in here! Get in here now!" We all started toward the office, and he seemed taken aback. "Not you," he pointed at me, as he strode back to his office. "I don't need a woman around when I talk," and he slammed the door behind them.

It really didn't make much difference, I could hear all the four-letter words, the five-letter ones, as well as the six-letter specials, right through the door. The walls vibrated as his voice rose and fell, mostly rose.

The inspector had been caught off base and was embarrassed. He was right. He had standing orders to be notified of anything out of the ordinary that took place. A special report called an "unusual" had to be in the chief of detectives' office within twenty-four hours of occurrence, and it hadn't been done. When he came into the building and the elevator operator congratulated him on the squad's arrests, he was caught flatfooted. He had to read about it in the papers.

"You guys think you're running your own fucking department? I'll have your ass out on the street so fast you won't know what happened to you. I got called for information from the chief and I had nothing to tell him. Do you realize what that makes me look like, you stupid bastards?"

Finally the voice started to ease up, as the bile got spewed out. "Well, goddammit, say something. Don't just sit there, like fuckin' idiots without a brain in your head, why did you do it?"

"We didn't," Ed said incisively. "If you want to listen to what happened, we'd like to tell you . . . just the way it happened."

"Don't give me no bullshit stories, 'cause I'll find out anyway, and then it'll be worse . . . understand that!"

"Jimmy and I will tell you now, and you can ask Marie later what happened, and you'll hear the same thing. Besides that, I don't think certain people will have the nerve to deny what took place. You see, last night . . ."

About fifteen minutes later I got called in. "Young woman, I'm going to ask you one question and you'd better tell the truth." (I was going to ask him if it was on pain of excommunication, but I failed to see him appreciating it.) "Was a notification made concerning this arrest to your superior officer, last night?"

"Certainly, Inspector, we called the lieutenant's wife at home about twelve-thirty and told her that we made an arrest on the plant he had left us at, and to have him call us, since he wasn't at home.

"And he did call, somewhere about four-thirty in the morning. We told him we had five and that the papers had been here and the whole bit. We told him we had sixty-three watches to voucher and asked him for help. He passed right over that, so then we asked him to make the office notifications, because we'd be hung up in court all day.

"Inspector, why don't you call him in? We've no objections to your asking him . . . in fact we want you to. Let's get this thing out in the open. We're out there trying to do a job for you, but every time we do anything this guy gives us the shaft."

The inspector was strangely silent, sitting back in his chair with his head in his cupped fist. Jimmy uncoiled himself, "I'll go get him for you, okay?"

"No use," he said quietly. "He called in this morning and took the day off against some old overtime."

We looked at each other, and now we all knew.

"Okay, men, go back to work. That was a good collar you made, I like it. I wish to hell I'd known about it. Now, you're going to have to make out all the clerical reports that are overdue. When you finish them you can leave." I felt like an old-time laborer, standing hat in hand, as I bobbed my head and said, "Thank you, sir."

I called up Tony Blue Eyes, who had a place I called the Sawdust Trail, right across the street from both Headquarters and the Annex. It was strictly primitive—sawdust on the floor, belly up to the bar, no butter with the bread, and, needless to say, no menus. Just good food. Tony's "Hey . . . uh . . . what're you gonna have? You better take the shrimp today," constituted both greeting and menu. I told him, "Tony, they're killing me, *Io muoro di fama*, Tony. *Fame mangiare*. I know your kitchen is closed, send up anything, Tony, we've got hours of work yet. Oh, you're beautiful, next time I see you I'll pinch you on the cheek."

My cohorts were laughing. "Keep laughing, go ahead, I won't share anything that comes up, then." They shut up in a hurry. In just about fifteen minutes, Tony's nephew brought up the loveliest-looking chopped steak with big, fat home-fried potatoes, a big slab of Italian bread, and of course, no butter. It was enough to make you cry with happiness.

When we finished all the essential reports that couldn't wait until the next day, we'd worked close to thirty straight hours. I know that I had been up nine or ten hours before that, which meant that I hadn't slept in about forty hours. This presented no problem all day, in fact it usually never entered our minds. Going home was another story altogether. I'd open all the car windows so that the draft would blow my hair all over the place and annoy me no end. Sometimes it wasn't enough; the insidious drone of the wheels as they covered the twenty-five miles to Crestwood would act as a metronome, and I'd find my head start to droop with fatigue.

I'd give myself a smart slap and reach for my Wash 'n' Dri's to wash my face, put another one around my neck like a kerchief, and stick one down into my bra. Then I'd blast the radio and start to sing along with it. Boy, have I gotten some weird looks from passing cars. Who cared? I'd do anything to avoid what really woke me up—the impact of your wheels hitting the curb or the median divider that jarred you awake like a plunge into a bath of ice when you momentarily dozed off.

When I pulled into that driveway, I'd have to sit for a few minutes to collect myself. . . . "Thank you, God." Then I'd gather up my stay-awake paraphernalia and be home.

The Safe and Loft people tolerated the Burglary folk but had swallowed the pill of integration hoping that if properly ignored for a stipulated period of time, they'd just sort of blow away. The feeling was more than returned by most of the BS boys, who felt they were being patronized. We told both sides that they were acting like a bunch of prima donnas. What difference does it make where you work, as long as they let you work?

We were more than happy to pitch in with another team, and the Safety Lock Company was pleased with the way things had worked out. We found ourselves in demand as other teams asked us to assist them in various ways. The captain called Ed in and told him that the burglary squads would be going back soon, and he'd like to keep our team in Safe and Loft and wanted to know if that interested him. Ed did a fast weighing of pros and cons. He knew how we felt, God knows we'd discussed it often enough. We'd be working where they requested and respected us; we'd get rid of the lieutenant; so far, two pluses. We'd be working with a really bigoted inspector, and a captain who was a religious fanatic; that's two minuses. The inspector truly respected good work, which was the plus factor that tipped the scales.

"Will you keep our team together?" he queried. "You told Marie you were looking to transfer all the women."

"I'm going to talk to her now." So I took Ed's hot seat in the office and was shaken out of ten years' growth.

"Harumph, sit down, Marie . . . hmm. Uh, this is totally new to me, I've never had to say anything like this." All I could do was to look at him inquiringly. "I want to tell you that I've been watching you and I've had to agree with all the things people have told me about you. I didn't want to. It was a lot easier to just lump you with all the rest, but I can't in honesty do that. I like not only your work, but the fact that the men respect as well as like you. Nobody has had one bad word to say about you, they all say you're a real lady. I just want to say that I'd like you to stay on in our office, I think you'd be an asset, and when the other girls get transferred out, I'm requesting you stay behind with us. Oh, by the way, I've already spoken to your partners about the same thing—we can use your team."

What does one say when you feel you've been handed an accolade that always seemed just beyond your reach. Just a very sniffly quiet, "Thank you . . . thank you, Captain."

"Don't thank me, young lady, you earned it."

Our scope broadened. We sat on stickup plants when the Loft candy stores, and later on a series of wig stores, were being robbed. We included the garment area and the warehouse district in our patrols as we explored the hijacker's pattern of operation.

Each week was different, in that you never knew what type of work you'd be assigned. If we were given Patrol, we could more or less name our territory. This would give us an opportunity to dress "down" and put on our shuffling clothes. If we pulled Hotel Patrol, on the other hand, it gave us a chance to come on like gangbusters and dress "up." Every day I'd try to outdo my outfit of the previous day and come on like Mrs. Astor's pet horse. There weren't too many opportunities in this job to really "dress," and when the occasion arose, I gloried in it.

When it came to dressing up, Ed wasn't bothered the least bit. He loved to dress up like a banty rooster and strut around. On the other hand, there was Jimmy. You had to strangle him to get him into a tie. I'd come in looking like the President of the Tuesday afternoon Literary Society; Ed like he was the visiting speaker; and Jim like he was delivering a telegram.

The hotels were thrilled to have us around; we gave them protection but the place didn't look like it was crawling with cops. Tom Clinton at the Plaza approached us: "We've got ourselves quite a problem here, you know. Our security people have been working on it for months, we didn't want any word to get out, but they just haven't been able to come up with anything."

"Shame on you, Tomaso, we've been around; you've been keeping secrets."

"Well, Mr. Salamone wanted to keep it an internal affair at first, but now we agree that we need help."

"Here we are, baby."

"Our guests are being systematically burglarized. There's no sign of entry, nothing's disturbed . . . just one or two pieces of jewelry in each theft and cash if it's around. Sometimes the people have checked out and returned to their homes before they notice the loss. It's got to be an inside job, but so far we're batting zero. I told Salamone that I'd try to get you people interested enough to give us a hand. How about it?"

"Our pleasure," said the dashing Mr. Lehane in his black mohair suit, red-and-white-striped shirt, and black tie.

"Darling, you know you can depend on us," I said, elegantly secure in my Italian knit three-piece suit, powder blue with dark blue piping, royal blue plush felt fedora with a feathered band, and matching blue leather shoes and bag.

"Oh my God, you mean we're going to hang around this place for a few days, maybe a week?" said the panicked Mr. Capano in what must have been his son's old Cub Scout uniform.

We dragged him protesting into the security office. We wanted information: any leads, cases, lists of stolen property. Then we wanted a listing of every date they'd suffered a loss, and a listing of what employees worked on those particular days. The flustered security fellow's files were a floperoo.

I pulled out a drawer at random, when he protested that they didn't keep much in the way of records, saying, "Well, you must have something in these files!" The only bulky file seemed to be under the initial O, so I dove in there. When my hand closed over something, I started, looked, and said, "You're not going to believe this . . . nobody will." I pulled out a nice, large, juicy-looking orange. The guard mumbled, "I wonder how that got in here; well, I better get out on the floor, somebody might be looking for me," and flew out of there as if he had been stung. We roared. "Listen, it's not all that bad," I said, "at least he filed it under O."

When we finished our homework, we'd narrowed the field down to five maids as suspects and decided to set a trap and nab our culprit right in the act. The management had the housekeeping department assign all the suspected women to one designated section on the sixth floor. They also reserved a hundred-dollar-a-day suite there for Mr. and Mrs. Joseph Edwards, plus an adjoining room for a Marie Sorrell. Jimmy, faced with the idea of wearing a tie for a week, put in a request for overtime leave—and got it.

We did a lot of planning, and a lot of borrowing, but on Sunday afternoon Mr. and Mrs. Edwards, an obviously affluent couple, arrived at the Plaza in a chauffeur-driven limousine and checked into their suite.

As the New York *Daily News* later printed, "Mrs. Edwards, a chic, trim brunette, was elegant in a mink stole, and much jewelry. The couple's luggage was matched—and expensive. They got the full VIP treatment. The management sent flowers and candy to the suite."

It's pretty hard to fool a maid. They've seen too many rooms to be taken in by a setup. They know what a used room looks like . . . they've had to pull them back together often enough. We had to bring clothing, underwear, toilet articles, makeup, the whole bit, and make it look good.

The maids were working the eight-to-four shift, so we had to be in our suite by 7 A.M. to make it look like we'd been there. We'd hang up the Do Not Disturb sign and go through the paces. Draw the tub, wet the floor, mess up the towels, use the glasses, leave out the toothpaste, wet the toothbrushes, hang up a pair of drying stockings, leave the nightclothes hanging in the bathroom, change the order of things on the furniture tops, throw a garment over a chair, leave a bathrobe on the bed, melt down the cake of soap in both the sink and the shower, and on and on. Wet the razor, leave the top off the deodorant, and lest it be forgotten, wreck the bed.

By the time we got through, we'd order breakfast sent up to the room and then be ready for phase two. I had with me a rather elaborate two-tier traveling jewel case which held some of the nicest pieces I could gather. We'd treated each piece, and the case itself, with a chemical powder that had to be brushed on with a feather. This special compound from the Police Laboratory is invisible to the eye, but turns a brilliant orange when it's subjected to water or a black light. We also dusted a billfold and each of the bills we were using as marked money.

When the scene was set, we'd switch the sign so that it would ask the maid to clean, and go into the adjoining room registered under Sorrell. Now in here, we had a completely different operation. This guest was supposed to be a call girl, and her room a bit of a mess. She was supposed to be out all night, and sleeping most of the day, so that she'd chase the maid away when she came to clean up. I had the maid shaking her finger at me and laughing understandingly when I'd say, "Will you get out of here, I've only been home for two hours."

When the suite was cleaned, we'd tiptoe back in and check for losses. On the fourth day, we said, "Something's wrong, but what?" We were sure our identity was good, so why wasn't there a nibble? Could it be that she was intimidated by us and the fact that we were supposed to be known to the management? Maybe she wouldn't rip off a friend of her boss's. We had to give her an edge, a security blanket.

The next morning, when we could hear the maid's cart outside, I, as Mrs. Edwards, all gussied up and with an overnight case, opened the door. I could see the maid as I said, "I hate to go, darling, will you miss me? But you needn't worry, it's only until tomorrow. I'll give Mother your best. Ciao, dear," and then Ed said, "I'll walk you to the elevator, now be a dear, and don't worry about me, I'll be fine." I boarded the elevator and he returned to his room.

I went down to the security office and changed to Marie Sorrell, nighttime entrepreneur, with the blond wig, my knit slacks and sweater, and my swinging hatbox. I waited about an hour and a half and then I called Ed and asked if she was still up on the floor. She was, and just across from the extra room. "I'm on my way."

When I stepped off the elevator I could feel her eyes boring into me, as I went directly to the door of the Edwards suite. As I put my hatbox down, she stepped out. "You got the wrong room, that's Mr. Edwards' room, you belong next door."

"Not today, sugar," I said, knocking at the door. "You know, when the cat's away, and all that jazz. Ha-ha." The door opened a few inches, and Ed peered out.

"Hiyah honey . . . here I am. Aren't you going to let me in?" Ed reached out with one hand and hastily pulled me into the room as if trying to keep the maid from seeing him. We turned on the radio, and he called room service to send up a bottle of champagne.

After about an hour, I very conspicuously took my leave for the long trek to the adjoining room, where I now hung up a Do Not Disturb sign. Ed put up the Maid Please Clean sign on his room and slipped into the room with me, but not before he slipped five twenty-dollar bills (all treated of course) under an ashtray on the dresser top. He hoped that it looked as if I had forgotten to take my money when I left.

We waited. So much of this job is waiting. As a rookie, when impatience tore at you there was always an old hair bag that would tell you, "Listen, kid, get used to it, this whole job is 'Hurry up and wait.'"

Time hung heavy. It wasn't until about three o'clock that we heard the now familiar noises that meant the maid was cleaning the suite—the sink and tub running, the toilet flushing, the vacuum running. Finally it stopped, and the door snapped shut. Another minute to clear the corridor, and then we flew in to check.

The jewel box was there and seemed intact, the furs were there . . . and then we both stared: the money was gone from under the ashtray. She took the pross' money figuring nobody was going to beef about that.

We called Tommy Clinton, told him we had a hit and to assemble all the maids with access to the sixth floor for an interview. There were seven women lined up when we walked in, and one of them must have been a nervous wreck.

"Okay, girls, first of all I want you to know that this young lady and I are detectives with the Police Department." We showed our shields and Ed continued, "Secondly, we know that one of you just stole money from Room 643. Now, does anybody want to tell me what happened? No one has anything to say? You think we can't prove it? My friends, we can. Nothing, eh? Okay, will all you innocent women be good enough to dip your hands in this bucket of plain water." I rinsed my own hands and dried them on a towel. "Now, I want you all to do the same thing."

One by one they stepped up, nervous, worried, giggling. As the fourth woman dipped her hands the chemical changes began, but we made them all finish. "Okay, ladies, hold up your hands for everyone to see."

One pair of hands was a lovely orange-yellow-brown; almost a brilliant brash iodine stain. Everyone "oooohed" and "aaaahed" and said, "Lord, have mercy."

We arrested Marie Goddard for burglary and possession of burglar's tools. It seems she wasn't even assigned to that room, but had a master key that got her into any room on three particular floors of the hotel. Marie Goddard, alias Marie White, alias Marie Crussen, admitted that she'd systematically ripped off guests for the two years she'd been employed there, and in doing our homework we found that she had stolen over $120,000 in that period.

"Ree," as she was known, was a better thief than she was a salesperson. She'd gotten $175 for a watch worth $10,000, and $75 for a ring worth $7,000. When we located the ring in a pawnshop, I looked with skepticism at the proprietor. "You gave seventy-five dollars on a rock this size? You're kidding me. How come you didn't question the authenticity, get identification and so on as required? She said it was hers? The ring can't be a size five and that woman has hands that could double as ham hocks. Okay, we're putting an official police stop on it, and it'll be held as evidence."

Your friendly smiling maid, Ree, had previous arrests for prostitution and homicide by stabbing. I understand that the hotel industry had often appealed to the city in an effort to have their personnel fingerprinted and their backgrounds checked out, but that their requests had been denied.

The Plaza was thrilled, Mr. Salamone wrote a letter of praise to the commissioner, and Ed and I got dispossessed and thrown back out on the streets.

We were out there, beating the bushes and shaking the trees, but it was one of those late fall days that rightfully belonged to August, and the sudden heat and oppressive humidity seemed to have dulled New York into a torpor.

Nothing was cooking in the Village or the Lower East Side. Herald Square and Broadway seemed to be dressed for church, so we made our way northwest just a-lookin' and a-lurkin'. On Eighth Avenue and Fiftieth Street we came to a screeching halt in front of the automat cafeteria, to assess the situation.

"I'll tell you one thing, fellas, there's not much moving on these streets today, and my feet are starting to feel like cans of stewed tomatoes."

"You know," said Jim, "we can watch the city from a sitting-down position too. Let's drop into H&H. We can have an iced tea and see if any of our Broadway crowd drifts into this shop once in a while. At least it's air-conditioned." We nodded in agreement as a well-dressed man in his late thirties left the cafeteria and approached us. We watched him, out of habit, but nothing registered. He came closer and seemed to occupy the center of our horseshoe standing arrangement. We all looked at him as he stood there with a large-sized grin on his face that indicated he recognized someone.

He was a stocky, well-built, light-complexioned black, clean-shaven, good skin, clear eyes, dressed in a suit and tie, but he

111

was batting zero, as far as recognition goes. He stood there smiling ingratiatingly, trying to force recognition, glancing first to one, then to the other, and then the third. "Man, don't you know me? I spotted you from inside. I figured I better come out here and say hello to you people. Man, man, I'm Oliver . . . you shot me last year!"

"Jeezuz H. Keerist," exploded Jim.

"Of course, we knew you, Oliver, we were on something, and besides we didn't want to embarrass you," Ed explained hastily.

I shook my head in disbelief. "What happened to you, Oliver? You look beautiful."

"Hello, pretty lady, did you have your baby? I read about it in the hospital the next day. I felt like a fat cat; everybody came to see who got shot by the pregnant policewoman. I was famous. I want to thank you, 'cause they really helped me up there. I just got out a few weeks ago, and I feel new. I'm off the stuff and straightened out."

"Well, let me tell you, it's some heck of a difference. I'll bet you put on thirty pounds. You look like a Hollywood movie star," I ladled praise as I would a hearty stew. You never knew when you might strike pay dirt, it might keep the guy straight a while longer, if lack of motivation or feelings of unworthiness were the root of his problem.

"Your baby, did you have a boy?"

"I sure did, a real tiger."

"I knew it, I said to myself, that officer, she's gonna have a real boy. I'm glad everything was okay."

"Thanks, Oliver, I appreciate that, really do. Now will you take care of yourself and keep up the good work."

"Lissen, keep your nose clean, stay out of trouble, and keep away from pregnant women," Ed shot out, "and you'll be all right."

We watched him walk off down the street before we went in for our tea. Then we dove inside and cracked up.

Jim made a routine call to the office to report where we were. When he returned he said, "Marie, they want you in the inspector's office tomorrow at three. They wouldn't tell me what it was about, just said that you'll be working with a couple of the

(Reprinted by permission of the New York *Daily News*.)

The "old lady" checks out her handbag as a patrolman cuffs the narcotics suspect she captured at gunpoint. (New York *Daily News* photo. Reprinted by permission of the New York *Daily News*.)

Marie Cirile and Robert Volpe on an Art Squad stake-out on Central Park South. (Photo by *Newsday*, Long Island. © 1972.)

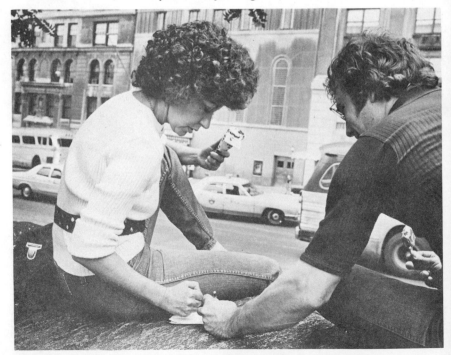

Yankee catcher Jake Gibbs congratulates the only woman ever to win a *Daily News* Hero Award. Looking on is daughter Cindy. (New York *Daily News* photo. Reprinted by permission of the New York *Daily News*.)

Det. Cirile's parents and daughter are proud witnesses as she receives the *Journal-American* Public Protector Award from First Deputy Commissioner John F. Walsh. (Deputy Commissioner Community Relations, Police Department, City of New York.)

Det. Cirile looking over some of the award[s] garnered while with the N.Y.P.D.

Det. Cirile displays a Dürer print, part of th[e] $200,000 stolen art haul recovered by th[e] Art Squad. (Reprinted by permission of th[e] New York *Post*. © 1972, New York Po[st] Corporation.)

Det. Cirile in "full-dress" regalia.

Some of the guises utilized
in various investigations.

More disguises for more cases.

Communion Day.

Marie Cirile with her husband,
Patrick Spagnuolo.

"Cin," alias Cynthia Anne.

"Jim," alias James Michael.

(*Daily News* articles reprinted by permission of the New York *Daily News*.)

Realies, and that they didn't need Ed or me. Whatever it is, they said it was gonna be for a few days at least."

Our conjecturing was to no avail. We had nothing to go on. But I felt mollified at the concern they showed by saying, "They better give you somebody decent to work with, not some stiffs that'll leave you hung up somewhere."

"I'll survive, remember our motto. We gotta come up smelling like roses! Well, I'll see you around. Try not to lock up everybody while I'm gone, will you?"

The next morning Tim, one of the inspector's super-favorite first-graders, called me at home. He wouldn't go into any details on the phone except to tell me that it involved hotels and to please dress up. "Thanks, Tim, that takes a load off my mind. There's nothing worse than showing up in heels and a fur coat, and then told to blend on some dock. See you in a while."

Tim, his partner—Casper—and I discussed the case as the inspector sat in and listened. Their information, which I assumed came from a wiretap or the FBI, was that a trio was headed up from Florida and would be checking into the St. Moritz Hotel that evening to commit a burglary or burglaries. They needed the money to winter in Florida where they could follow the dog races, as would anyone of good taste.

Tim and Casper already had the co-operation from the hotel's management, and had gotten us a suite on the sixth floor. The hotel was to assign the suite across the hall to our suspects when they checked in. Considering the time, Tim said, "I think we'd better get over there, we don't know when they'll show up. I'll try to fill you in on the way."

I was told that there were two women and one male, all young and attractive. They had a photo for Victor Borrato, twenty-five, dark brown hair and eyes, 5'10", 175 pounds, who claimed to be a model. "He certainly won't be hard to spot."

Casper, who was as quiet as the friendly ghost, just nodded his head and said, "He's really good-looking and always works with women. They travel first-class." We got to our hotel suite shortly after four and checked the vantage point of our door to the door of the suite they would occupy. It was perfect, except that you can't see through a door, and we had to know who was leaving and/or coming back.

After getting a somewhat reluctant okay from the manager, Tim drilled a hole through the door and we were in business. We split to await the new arrivals, Tim outside the hotel, Casper near the elevators, and me near the front desk. We didn't even have time to get restless.

A big yellow Cadillac convertible pulled right up to the front door of the St. Moritz. Two stunningly attractive, suntanned girls hopped out of the car, stopping only long enough to press the car keys into the doorman's hand and say, "Have someone bring in our luggage, we're checking in."

They were both tall, slender, and leggy. Susan, twenty-five, with shoulder-length blond hair, had a fur coat tossed casually about her shoulders; Linda, twenty-four, had black hair piled high on her head in startling contrast to her blue-green eyes, and a leather coat slung over her arm. They seemed to ooze vitality, and eyes seemed to follow them, consciously or not.

As they approached the registration desk, Tim came in and said that was Victor's car, but he wasn't with them. He caught the manager's eye, nodded, and the girls were given the suite of honor. The bellhop started bringing in the luggage and piling it up. Six, seven, eight, nine . . . ten suitcases. Tim and I looked at each other. "They're getting ready for a siege," I said. "This doesn't look like a hit-or-miss proposition."

"They look like they might slip the hotel itself into one of those bags," Tim laughed. "I think we're in for a long one."

We borrowed a maid's outfit from the housekeeping department, just in case, and went upstairs to see that our girls had settled in. Our peephole worked fine, we found out, when at six o'clock Victor lightly knocked and was whisked inside.

Almost within minutes the team was in operation. Victor took one of the girls and went to another floor, where he'd have her knock on the door. If the room was occupied, the guest would open the door to find a very attractive, apologetic, and apparently confused guest who said, "Oh dear, I must have made a mistake." But if no one was in, Victor would select one of twenty-five celluloid strips he carried and use it to slip the lock. The girl would act as the lookout, while he'd steal whatever had any value. Then, back to their suite via the fire stairway, to unload. Victor then switched girls, went to another floor, and repeated the process. They worked almost continuously from 6 to 11 P.M. that evening hitting suites, returning, unloading, and so on.

What they didn't see was me, the omnipresent maid down the end of the corridor with her dust mop or can of spray polish. They didn't see me either as just another elegant guest waiting for the elevator, or striding across the floor, key in hand. But I saw them and couldn't believe what I saw. These people didn't stop, they were carried away with getting into as many rooms as possible.

At eleven o'clock they called it an evening and went out to dinner. At this point we had to figure it as an all-night job, and possibly going into tomorrow, since we had no idea if they'd check out when they came back or stay over and take their sweet time.

We all made whatever phone calls we had to make and prepared for a longie. At 3 A.M. our happy guests returned, but there was no outside action, and they had apparently bedded down. We tried to take turns relaxing on the sofa, but it didn't work out too well. "Fellas, tomorrow you'll be seeing a lot more of the maid than you will of the 'elegant' guest, from the shape I'll be in, and I hope you guys will be able to see. I think you're getting windburn in your eye from that peephole."

The next day seemed to last forever. There was no movement all morning from the late sleepers. At three o'clock they were back in action, with the very same system. The only change was their clothing; the girls wore smashing outfits.

At eight o'clock they called the garage for their car. The yellow Caddy was pulled up to the front door and the ten suitcases were loaded into it. The three passengers never made it. We scooped up our trio of models and asked them to act like model prisoners and not give us a hassle as we returned them and the luggage to the suite they'd occupied on the sixth floor.

When the luggage was opened, we found a soup-to-nuts collection: a white full-length mink coat, mink stoles, mink coats, tape recorders, traveler's checks, credit cards, rings, cuff links, watches, bracelets, other jewelry, and odds and ends.

While we were assembling and itemizing the stolen property, the hotel was canvassing the guests to see who had suffered losses and to assure them that the hotel had been co-operating and thereby saved their property. They confirmed what my fallen arches had been saying. Our trio had broken into thirty-nine suites since their check-in the previous day. They had indeed been busy bees.

Charged with grand larceny, burglary, and possession of burglar's tools, the only complaint came from the dark brunette. "Why couldn't you have arrested us after we had supper?" One of the hotel officials overheard, and probably feeling magnanimous in that everything had come out all right, smiled and ordered room service to send up a posh dinner. Then it was off to the less than posh stationhouse where they were booked.

Everybody was happy but the bad guys. We were pooped but grinning; the captain was thrilled; the inspector was overjoyed; the hotel was ecstatic; the newspapers taking pictures of these three really attractive thieves had a field day; and thirty-nine guests at the St. Moritz were breathing a sigh of relief at having their valuables returned. Things just couldn't have been too much better, job-wise, except for my constantly frustrated efforts at getting the detective's shield.

I'd been a policewoman for five and a half years, during which time I had been recommended for the Detective Division many times. Finally after five and a half years I was assigned to the Detective Division, but still operating on a policewoman's shield. This means you get paid a patrolman's salary despite the fact that you might be working side by side with a first-grade detective who is receiving a lieutenant's salary.

It was over two years now that I'd been in the Detective Division without receiving compensation for it. Every six months your superior officer evaluates your performance and submits his recommendations to the chief of detectives' office. I had received "recommend advancement in grade" until the melody became a lament in frustration.

The system the department had for promoting females was archaic as well as unjust. There are four first-grade shields, nine second-grade shields, and thirty-seven third-grade shields set apart for females. If these shields are given out, that's it. In other words, as a policewoman bucking for a third-grade shield, I had to wait for some third-grader to drop dead or retire. If by some chance a second-grader retired, a third-grader would have an opportunity to go to second, leaving a vacancy in the third-grade slot.

The competition would be fierce, like vultures feasting on carrion. When the word was out that someone was thinking of retiring, the contracts would fly. Every eligible (for whatever godforsaken reason) female would contact her rabbi (an important person of influence) and start the ball rolling.

All of us seemed to have our own ideas as to how to achieve this goal. We had the certain percentage of women known as the "boss's girls." These girls attended each and every Police Line Organization affair, learned to drink like fish, dance like eels, sing "Mother Macree," and left with one of the bosses.

Of course they weren't all that way. We had the ones that just had steady affairs with a big shot, and he didn't always have to be in the Police Department, he might be in a labor union, or be a politician; someone with enough influence to extend into the Police Department either through the mayor's office or sometimes even higher.

I had more than my share of opportunities to short-circuit the system, but if there was one thing my sister Lee and I agreed on it was that we would get our shields "standing up," thank you! —and not earn them on our backs.

Man, it took a hell of a lot longer that way, I'll tell you. I had gotten numerous citations from the department lauding my work, and every time I went before the Honor Board, I would hear, "You're bound to get the money on this one." Only to hear, when the next opening was filled, that it went to somebody's secretary who had never worked out on the streets one day of her life. These were the seeds of discontent that sprouted into the "Why bother?" attitude that was becoming more and more in evidence among the women.

I was determined to do it the other way, by killing them with quality work. How long could they ignore the "unusuals" that flowed into the chief of detectives' office bearing my name and title, "Policewoman"? How long could they ignore the newspaper stories, and the reporters asking for personal interviews? How long could they justify not issuing a shield based on job performance alone, when the papers were watching?

Two weeks later, as a Christmas present on December 24, 1964,

I got my detective's shield—standing up—and almost fell down with shock. It was a long time coming—seven and a half years of working and scrambling and fighting and sweating and praying.

What no one could realize was how much getting the shield meant to me, in so many ways. It meant an actual achievement that I had gotten strictly on my own. I needed this desperately because my private world was disintegrating and becoming insupportable. I'd made up my mind to get a divorce and needed the salary increase to be able to go it alone.

For years I had immersed myself in my work, using it as a protective device. I always had a case to think about, to keep me from things I wouldn't acknowledge or care to see. At home the children were my outlet and my energies diverted to heavy gardening, painting the house, wallpapering, making drapes: I had to keep busy to keep from thinking.

For several months, I'd been feeling physically miserable. I went to see a doctor who diagnosed it as pleurisy and was giving me diathermy treatments. After several weeks, I was feeling steadily worse and getting weaker. I'd lost about ten pounds which I could ill afford to lose, and was starting to drag myself around.

While at a regular checkup at my dentist's he expressed concern. "Marie, you look awful, what's wrong?" I told the story. "That doesn't look like any pleurisy I ever saw. Look, I've known you fifteen years, I'm not letting you out of this office without doing something. Now you sit there." He reached over and called a doctor to make an appointment for me.

I went. He listened, examined, and took endless tests. Then he talked. "What's bothering you?"

"Well as I told you, Doctor . . ."

"I mean what's troubling you here?" and he tapped on my forehead. He went on to explain how some people refused to admit to or face up to stress situations, choosing instead to bury or deny them. They'd seek relief by working or playing too hard and congratulate themselves on their "control." The body's defense mechanism, however, often chose a breakdown of bodily functions to indicate distress.

He diagnosed a severe gastroenteritis, verging on incipient

ulcers. I was put on a severe diet with pills for before and after meals, and told, "You must reconcile whatever your problem is, you can't hide it under a bushel, because you're ruining your health. Keep it up, I guarantee in a year I'll be operating on you for an ulcer."

That was my catalyst. Jim was only one and Cindy eleven, and I knew I had to be around a while longer. So now I had a reason besides my personal feelings, for activating myself.

There was one major problem: He wouldn't give me a divorce, nor a separation. He wouldn't even leave the house. They never covered that in any of the Hollywood movies. My reasons and motivations were so long and varied, suffice it to say that it started the week after we married.

I had been to marriage counselors and the whole bit, but they couldn't help, because he wouldn't come . . . so I gave up. I took Cin and baby Jim and Mary and we stayed in one room at my sister Vera's house. Vera tried so hard, but four people in a room is a pretty intolerable situation.

Meanwhile it was work as usual. All through the years, no one knew anything of my personal problems. We were brought up on my mother's "Never let anyone hear a breath you take," and I could never bring myself to talk about it. I remember once when I limped into one of the hotels to join the two teams assigned that I tried to stay out of the lights so no one could see the makeup job covering an assortment of bruises. I heard Toby whisper to Ed, "What happened to Marie, she looks like . . ."

Ed quickly interrupted with, "Sshh, don't let her hear you, it would kill her if she thought you noticed. That son of a bitch must be giving her problems again."

"Jesus Christ."

"Yeah, she thinks nobody knows."

I pretended I didn't hear. I couldn't talk about it. I put on my sunglasses and sipped my coffee. When they approached I said brightly, "Hey, you lazy lumps, what do you say we do some work for a change!"

While at Vera's, life was more than difficult. Everyone I knew was either receiving threatening phone calls or being solicited for help by my husband. Mary was promised a trip to England if she could give him information about another man. Jimmy was offered a trip to Puerto Rico for news of any indiscretions I might have committed. I guess he figured since Ed was a first-grader, he came higher because he offered him a new car. These were my friends, though, and I knew of these approaches almost as soon as they were received.

A much more interesting one we stumbled on by chance. While on patrol one evening about eleven o'clock, Jimmy, Ed, and I were circling around the Plaza Square at Central Park South when I spotted his Falcon parked by the fountain, with Lieutenant Mackin's squad car behind it. We pulled back and watched them talk for almost a half hour before they split. When the lieutenant got into his car he had radio transmission issue a forthwith to meet him at his location. Needless to say he was somewhat surprised to see us in about thirty seconds and almost swallowed his toothpick. He had nothing to tell us, nor any orders to give us, he was just giving us a "see," which in this job's parlance meant he was checking up on us. We were as a result of that car consultation to receive many more. What I didn't know then, and wasn't to find out for almost a year, was that the lieutenant was allegedly offered two custom-made suits if he could catch me off base and get me transferred, dumped, or thrown off the job.

Perhaps if I'd known it, I could have understood what happened several weeks later. The captain's long-standing efforts had finally been rewarded, and all the girls were being transferred out. The story had been around for two days, but we weren't very concerned, not after the interview I'd had with the captain.

Surprise, surprise, my name was included with all the others, and I found myself transferred to the Pickpocket and Confidence Squad with the rest of the mob scene. I wasn't surprised, I was stunned like a felled ox. I found the captain suddenly unavailable, the inspector was in conference, and the lieutenant had the day off again, of course. What I found out from J.J. the clerical man was that the dear lieutenant had spoken to both the captain and the inspector, told them I was having marital problems, expressed his concern over the possible effects it might have on the squad, and suggested that this would be an ideal time to handle the situation since all the other women were being transferred. I hope that old toothpicking lieutenant got to enjoy those custom-made suits, because he certainly earned them.

Things worsened at home, and I thrashed about in the death throes agony of a terminal marriage seeking some relief. Along with the agencies from which I had sought help, I also saw the police chaplain.

Chaplain William Kalaidjian was and is a very human person. He is married, has three sons and the loveliest little country-type church on Bainbridge Avenue and 201st Street in the Bronx. This is a man of God who responds to man's call to God. The cops know, you can't fool them because they're there—at the emergencies, at the hospitals when the cops are hurt, shot, killed. They know who responds. When the cops get in trouble and they're loused up, they ask to speak to Chaplain K, or Chaplain Bill, or just, "You know, the Protestant chaplain." I call him Padre.

The chaplain looks like Raymond Burr playing Ironside, has a deep resounding voice and a way of speaking and looking at you that makes the tensions ebb and the conversation flow. He heard me out, and just silently shook his head. Then he quietly admitted to knowing a bit of what had been going on from Mary, who'd joined his church and spoken to him a few times.

"You're going to have a problem with the job, you know that, don't you? You've got to take some action. You should report this to the Medical Bureau or else when something happens you'll be on the defensive. Your problem is you can't bring yourself to do it. Sometimes there isn't a peaceful solution, you may not be doing this man a favor by choosing to ignore him. Think about it. You owe something to yourself and the children. You must have peace of mind and some tranquillity to run a house. You're doing them an injustice, and he's not getting any help. Sometimes to hurt is to help."

I left the Padre with an awful lot to think about. When my husband heard I'd seen him, he ran to present his case as well. After listening, the Padre suggested we separate, and that he should seek psychiatric help. He left, but not before making wild threats to have me walking the streets, see me dead, and so on.

The Padre called me and I laughed. "I've heard that and so much more, it's like a litany."

"Be careful, if you won't do anything else I suggest, be careful."

My husband called and said he was going to Florida for three weeks with friends, and I breathed a sigh of relief. I took my entourage home to spread out, and had the locks changed. When he returned he seemed to accept it calmly, saying he'd stay with his brother for thirty days and give me a chance to think it over. I was grateful for small favors.

Four or five days later about eleven o'clock at night, I got a frantic call from someone who worked with him. "Listen, I feel it only right to warn you. He just left here and he's having a fit. He said he knows what you need, he's going up there to rape you and break your legs. I know he works with me, but I wouldn't feel right if, God forbid, something happened, I don't want it on my conscience."

"Sure, sure, thanks a lot, you say he left about a half hour ago? That means he'll be here in about five minutes. Great. 'Bye."

What could I do? Upstairs asleep were a child, a baby, and a housekeeper. I couldn't possibly wake them all and attempt to get us out. I hoped that the lock would act as a deterrent. If I had called the local police they'd report it to our department and again I feared he'd be brought up on charges or dismissed and this would give him more reason to rampage. So I shut off all the lights except a small lamp in the living room and waited.

It wasn't long, perhaps a minute or two, and I heard the key inserted in the door. When it didn't work, he forced it open. His momentum carried him inside and he saw me quietly sitting there, and became livid.

I was trying to carry the thing off as a sort of noncombatant conscientious objector, since all the normal and routine methods of resistance were considered taboo to the quasi-military standards set by the department for the personal life of its inmates.

The whole image was blown away when my daughter awakened with the noise, came downstairs, and became mildly hysterical. Mary rushed down, took in the scene, ran to my bedroom, and called the Padre reporting that I was being assaulted. That was it. No more pretending. The shit hit the fan and we ended up all covered with it.

Mary ran down shouting, "The police are coming," and he took off screaming obscenities and threats. I found out then that the chaplain had told Mary that he was notifying the local police and the Medical Bureau. What happened then remains as ridiculous and incomprehensible to me as putting a person in the public stock as a deterrent to others.

I went on sick report because I had to have emergency dental work. Meanwhile they caught up with him somewhere along the line and had him report to the medical office, which in turn sent him to an honorary psychiatrist. The psychiatrist had his weapons removed and scheduled him for a course of treatment.

He was furious and laid all the responsibility for his position on the fact that I reported him. He repeated his threats to take my life to the doctors, the chaplain, and the psychiatrist. As a result of some type of really weird thinking, I got a notification that someone was coming to pick up my guns for safekeeping. I ran down to the chief surgeon to see what that was all about and was told that since he was my husband and had access to my home legally and that threats had been made, they had to cover themselves by taking my guns away as well, since he might come in and use them on me.

"Doctor, if you take my guns that means you take my detective shield as well. I worked seven and a half years for that, I've had it less than two months. I need it to support my family. Do you realize you are doubly penalizing me. Isn't it enough of a sorrow to have a broken marriage, you're giving me an additional hurt just for no reason. It's only because I've seen this type of thing happen so often before in this job that I accepted what I shouldn't have accepted for so many years. You're making all my worst fears reality."

"Well, I don't believe in taking sides. I find that in these marriage problems, both sides should share the blame, so both sides should be hurt equally, that way the department doesn't look like it's taking sides. As a matter of fact, I'm going to send you down to the psychiatrist for an interview, and if he gives you a clean bill of health, then we'll restore your weapons and you can go back to work."

"Doctor," I said wryly, "I volunteered to go down the first day to see if there was anything I could help with. I will take your earliest interview, but I want you to know that you have just about killed my police career, the onus of this will hang over me for a long time. You've done me and my family a grave injustice. It's like breaking a guy's arm because he dared to have a broken leg. Your help in my so-called hour of need will be long remembered. Good day, Doctor."

I saw the good shrink, and he marked his report, which he was nice enough to show me before I left, "Recommend return of weapons and immediate restoration to duty." So I waited.

When I got tired and disgusted and in the spirit of ecumenicalism, I went down to see the Catholic chaplain to see if he could intercede for me.

"Oh, hello there," said he, "are you you, or are you your sister?" Well, I figured, that's pretty bright for a beginning.

"Well, since I'm not my sister, I guess I must be me," I said with brilliance.

"I mean are you the one who wears the hats, or the other one?"

"Father, I'm Marie Cirile and I'm here with a problem."

"Oh yes, well, you know that's a Medical Bureau case, and I don't like to interfere with their rulings, you know."

I described the situation, that both my local police surgeon and the police psychiatrist had stated that I could return to work, but that the department stated they feared giving me my weapons because he'd threatened my life. I explained that the department had ordered him to move out, that he had, and that I'd applied to the family court for an order of protection. I went on, "Father, be realistic. If this man is going to kill me, he doesn't need my gun to do it. He can do it with a knife or a club or run me down when I leave the house. It's sheer nonsense to expect me to accept a story with that many exceptions. I must go back to work. It's hurting me and it's hurting the children. What kind of rational explanation can I offer that a child would find understandable?"

"Marie, you must have faith and trust. Your sacrifices will not go unnoticed. Have you spoken to your local pastor?"

"Yes, as a matter of fact, I did speak to the monsignor and he unequivocally recommended that I seek a divorce to settle any legal problems that might arise. His attitude was that the church did not condemn divorce, it condemned remarriage."

He seemed slightly taken aback and then stated that there wasn't anything he could do, that he had to agree with the medical unit in that if I had a gun in the house he might be tempted to come and use it. "The Police Department has to protect itself, you see. After all, how would it look if he killed you, with your own gun, and after he threatened to do it. It would be embarrassing to the department, and they can't take the chance."

"Oh, now I understand. If he throws a bomb at my house, it won't reflect on the department, but if he shoots me with my gun, they'd be embarrassed, is that it?"

"Yes, yes, oh, I'm glad you understand our position."

Oh, I understood, all right. I understood that he couldn't care less for what I was going through, what I felt, what I or my children needed, or what happened unless it happened to embarrass the "job."

So I waited some more, and then went down and saw the chief surgeon again. By this time I'd heard that he went out of his way to zing the women on the job. I suggested that perhaps he was a little on the gay side, but they assured me that he was known to ask, "Who's the broad with the big ass?" as he tossed down a drink at one of the affairs.

The sum total of that second conversation was for him to send me to the psychiatrist a second time, despite the fact that he had the previous report. The psychiatrist, somewhat incensed, bellowed, "What the hell are they doing up there? How many times do I have to say the same thing?" In large oversized letters he wrote: I REITERATE . . . RECOMMEND RETURN OF WEAPONS AND IMMEDIATE RESTORATION TO DUTY. "Now go on, get out of here and go back to work."

A lot easier said than done, despite the intervention of the psychiatrist, the chaplain, the then Inspector Melchionne, and others. Finally I got angry, hired an attorney, and prepared to file a show-cause order against the city. The attorney filed a notice of intent and within two days I was restored to work. One man, and one man alone, the chief surgeon, had run roughshod over me.

Eighty-two days later, or just under three months, I got back my old policewoman's shield and was assigned to the Policewomen's Bureau. I was one pretty miserable person and a damn disgusted cop. It was hard to believe it was actually happening to me in our so-called enlightened society; and I decided that there had to be some recourse. I wrote a letter asking for an interview with the Police Commissioner. I was granted an appointment, and my hopes rose as we got closer to the fateful day.

In the interim, Peg Disco, who was then director of the Women's Bureau, was as nice as she could be. Peg and I had worked together as detectives on a couple of special assignments, so our new roles were somewhat strange for us.

"Marie, what do you want to do? Do you want to sit back and catch your breath, let the traffic pass you by for a bit? What can I do for you?"

"Thanks, Peg, I appreciate your thoughtfulness; people have been more than kind except for some characters who only know me through the newspapers. You wouldn't believe some of the nutty things strangers have come up to me saying. Things like, 'Are you the one who had a shooting war with her husband?' It's unbelievable!"

"Well, you may as well know that that story is making the rounds. This job is full of washerwomen, and I don't mean the policewomen. They'll repeat anything they hear and add their own flourishes. I didn't have to see the reports to know how unfair it is. Of all people you'd think that cops would know that if you ever pulled a gun in your private life, you'd be suspended and dismissed so fast your head would spin . . . but then there wouldn't be anything to talk about."

"That's true . . . last week's hero and this week's goat. Those papers play you up pretty grand but all they're really good for in the long run is to wrap up fish. So much for that. Peg, listen, I think I'd rather work. I want to keep my mind and body occupied. I might even get you a couple of collars, and do us both some good."

Patrolling in the area of Fortieth Street to Fifty-second Street, from Fifth to Sixth avenues, with a young policewoman of Peg's choice as my partner, would be my new assignment. She was supposed to be able to pass for about eighteen years of age and Peg said that she was very ambitious, so I thought I'd give it a try.

Patricia Pucker was small, about 5'3" and petite. She had dark hair and blue eyes and she played the baby bit for all it was worth. She had a way of looking at a guy with a big blank stare that reminded me of a Kewpie doll, so that I swore she was putting her finger in her mouth as she'd lisp, "Oh, I didn't know, I didn't think goo goo gaa gaa ooooh." I saw her try it on Peg, who swallowed the bait and ended up offering her reassurances on something. I shook my head, this doll was unreal. This had to be the best example of "Miss Goody Two-Shoes" I had ever come across. I couldn't wait to see her in operation on the street.

She tried the softsoap with me when we first met and went out into the big city. "Ohhh, I'm so happppy that you picked meee to work with. I know you could have had anyone in the whole office, but you gave meee a chance. I want to be just like you . . . I want to learn everything you'll teach meee. Ohhh, things are going to be soooo goood. Thank you. Thank you." And she grabbed my hand as if she were going to start skipping down the street.

I looked at her. Very quietly I said, "Patti, do you really want to work with me?"

"Oh my God . . . yes. Goodness gracious, I've . . ."

"Patti, then do me a favor, will you?"

"Ohhh, anything . . . you'll see . . . anything."

"Would you can the bullshit . . . I'm just not in the mood, okay?"

"Oh," said she as the air left her mattress leaving her inner spring showing bare, "you don't have to get so fuckin' bitchy."

"Ah, that's a little better, that's the mamma doll I thought was buried under there. Now maybe we can get along and work, as long as we respect each other. Right?"

"Sure, Marie, if that's what you want, I'll do my best, you'll see. Are we going to work on something exciting?"

"Peg, Peg," I thought, "what have you done to me?"

We spent a few days answering out minor complaints and making court appearances on some of my old cases. During our long gab sessions I tried to give her some of the basics that had stood me in stead and had given our burglary squad team its most valued nickname, "The Wide-awake Detective Agency." We used to laugh and say our motto was "We Never Sleep."

"Patti, everybody has eyes, but they can't all see; everyone has ears, but they can't hear. This is where you can go them one better, by training your eyes to observe, to take in, to transmit to your brain; and teaching your ears to listen and to comprehend.

127

Not just the superficial things ordinary people see and hear, but what's beyond."

We discussed cases and types of arrests and she told me that she'd made arrests in the Broadway Squad.

"Perhaps she's good under pressure," I thought. "I'm as bad as some of the male detectives, I'm putting her down without finding out for myself. What the hell, give her a try."

That was it, I made my big decision. "Patti, how would you like to work on something that could be big, but might be dangerous?" She seemed to stop bubbling and said very seriously, "Just try me. I've been waiting for so long to do some real police work. Just tell me what I have to do, and you can count on me . . . honest."

"Okay, Patti, but we're not playing tiddlywinks, remember. I don't play games when I'm out on the streets. Now, I'll tell you what I have in mind, and what I would love to do. This just might be the perfect opportunity." (I gave her a complete rundown on how junkie burglars dispose of their swag through a receiver and explained the importance as well as the difficulty in arresting one.) "The biggest operator here in midtown is a guy called Three-finger Jack. We've never been able to get him right, although I know of over ten junkies a day that sell to him. I arrested him once at a table with five junkies that had done business with him, but we never cracked his system. He has the junkies put the stuff in lockers before he buys anything. Then he has different runners that go and examine the stuff and report to him before he'll pay off. All we were able to get on them was a loitering charge, which is garbage.

"But he knew the guys and now he knows me too, but he'd never figure on two women. Patti, if we get him right we take out at least three or four burglars as well. Do you want to give it a shot, or shall we let it pass? Tell me straight because it doesn't bother me either way, but if you commit yourself I want you to know what you're in for."

Patti let out a deep breath and said, "I have no intention of spending the rest of my life locking up exposers in the balcony; I intend to get into the Detective Division."

"Fair enough. This guy operates out of Horn and Hardart on Forty-fifth Street and Sixth Avenue, and that's where we'll be tomorrow. I'll tell you what, you try to look as young as you can, and I'm going to look as old as I can, because I'm not going to have him recognizing me. That way we can hang out all day if we have to. In the morning we'll meet right in the cafeteria, okay? Now, would you please give the office our last ring and see if they have anything cooking." She toddled off as I sat there wondering if I was doing the right thing. "Can it be you're too used to working with men?" I thought back to the old Women's Bureau and girls like Gloria O'Meara, Johanna McFarland, Claire Faulhaber, Olga Ford—all good, smart-thinking, fast-moving cops. No, that's not it . . . but something sticks in my craw.

Goody Two-Shoes flitted back and gushed, "Oh, they said to remind you of your appointment to see Commissioner Murphy the day after tomorrow at ten o'clock. You're going to see the Commissioner?" she said in awe.

"Nothing special, kid, see you in the morning, take it slow." I left thinking, "the day after tomorrow," as if I hadn't been counting the days and the hours.

The next morning I took a trip back in time. I resurrected my "little old lady" that had served me so faithfully during the abortion investigations. As I applied the putty creating those deep grained furrows and age wrinkles, I could see myself aging at least thirty-five years. I turned my eyebrows silver and smeared purple eyeshadow on my lips instead of lipstick which gave me a look of imminent heart failure.

Then I shook out the gray wig and brushed it carefully into an untidy bun; dug out the old suit, now three years older and approaching my antique category; and rescued my elastic Ace bandages, which my daughter had wrapped around her ventriloquist's dummy to create a real "mummy."

It took me an hour's effort to hear Mary say, "Blimey, they're going to arrest you for vagrancy. If they saw you in England, I swear they'd put you on the dole! Oh, I can't get over how terrible you look. You're old! Perhaps I had best take James inside. I don't want him to get frightened when you leave."

That was music to my ears! It made me feel great. I'd carried the character in a different direction than before. I used to be an old lady, but now I was an old crone. There was a big difference. The old lady was genteel. The crone was a derelict. I used the suit skirt but topped it with an old shirt covered with a very large decaying sweater of prehistoric origin. The gray wig was slightly askew and loose tendrils flew about in disorder. My final touch was a big cloppy-looking shopping bag in which I had old newspapers, magazines, and assorted nothings; a sight I'd observed so many times in the homeless vagrant women who drifted about the train stations, bus terminals, and all-night cafeterias.

What couldn't be seen was the shield pinned inside the sweater collar, and the gun on a belt around my waist with a pair of handcuffs slung over it. I didn't carry a purse—I consider them a drag and a handicap. Through the years I'd always tried to get rid of the darn thing if there was a chance of any kind of action. In the theaters I'd check it in the manager's office; on patrol I kept it locked in my car trunk. My equipment was always on me, not in my bag where some idiot could grab it and run. I knew how important it was to have the use of two hands. There was always another thought as well: If anyone suspected you of being a policewoman they expected you to carry a big oversized valise for a purse. I think they have that listed on page one of the "cop spotter's handbook," right next to all flatfoots wear black socks and black shoes regardless of what clothes they're wearing.

I dragged this poor old creature downtown where she wearily drifted into the automat and sat down near a young pretty little thing in black slacks and ponytail, having a cup of coffee.

I dropped into a seat and heaved my shopping bag onto the empty one. My table mate glanced hastily and moved her seat a few inches farther away, in physical withdrawal, her nose unconsciously wrinkled in distaste.

"Don't be so disgusted, miss, someday you'll be old," I whispered huskily. She got very upset, and gathered her things to leave. "Sit down, Patti . . . I can see you still haven't learned how to use your eyes and your ears."

She used her eyes then. They opened incredulously; so did her mouth, which gaped ridiculously. I had to laugh. "God, Patti, I know I look bad, but you look as if you can count the lice in my hair. Let me assure you that under this grotesque mess is a body that did have a shower this morning. Whatyasay you be a nice girl and treat a poor old thing to a cuppa coffee?"

"Oh my God, I don't believe it. What did you do to yourself?" She laughed. "How could you let yourself look that bad? I wouldn't even let anyone see me without my makeup on."

"Patti, before I age anymore will you get me a cup of coffee, so I don't have to hobble all across the room? Meanwhile I'll look the place over and see if anything's alive."

I glanced around and then watched Miss Goody as she returned. She was conscious of male eyes on her and promenaded as if she were coming down a runway, seeming to seek visual approval. I really didn't give a damn, but my coffee was sloshing all around in the saucer.

"Nothing's happening," I said as I tried to rescue at least a half cup of coffee. "It's just a pretty motley assortment of bums and hanger-outs. It'll pick up around lunchtime, and be good for cover, so maybe we'll see something around then. Meanwhile you may as well settle down. You can call the office, or get a drink of water or anything else you may want if you get tired of sitting, but it looks like we'll be around for most of the day.

"Oh, by the way, let me get one thing straight with you, just in case something happens. I don't want you taking any chances or pulling any fool heroics. I don't know you well enough and I've never seen you work in a pinch, so we'll go slow and easy. Okay? I can't tell you what to do, when I don't have any idea of what could happen. All I can tell you is one very important thing . . . let's call it a rule that we all have in the Detective Division. We live by it and die by its being broken. You stand behind your partner and you back him up. So, my love, that's it . . . whatever I do, you just be behind me, watching and protecting my back."

"I wish I could do more, but I guess you're right until we get to know each other. But you can count on me."

It was about a quarter after one and I'd managed to slop my way through a couple of coffees and even appear to doze off for a while, while Patti had chewed her way through about three packs of gum, made three or four trips to the ladies' room, innumerable trips to the telephone, and flirted with the cafeteria manager.

While I had my head down, apparently asleep, two white males met at the very next table. I glanced at them and saw that one of them was in bad shape: he really needed a fix. His hands trembled so they were virtually uncontrollable. The other one was a little older than the young hang-out users. He was about twenty-eight and in good shape, about six feet tall, 195 pounds, with good muscular meat on his body. If he was on junk, it couldn't have been for very long, his skin was still good and his co-ordination was evident. So was the mean searching look in his eyes as he said to the shaky one, "How much money ya got?" "Mr. Shakes" fumbled in his pocket and extracted a jumbled collection of folded dollars which he handed to his friend saying, "Here, you count it . . . I can't do it."

The big guy riffled through it. "You've got nineteen dollars, and I've got a dollar. Now, that's not bad; we've got twenty dollars altogether. Now we've got to find someplace to cop." He pocketed the money and they left.

"Hey, Patti, let's walk these two characters for a bit. There's nothing happening in here, and we can always pick it up later. Once that receiver gets here he's good for a couple of hours. We just might happen to stumble on who's peddling the junk here on Broadway."

"Great, that's wonderful. How close to them should I walk? What should I look for and things?"

We're already out of the automat and watching them walk up toward Broadway. "Patti, I want you to follow me. Don't worry about their ducking out on you, just keep me in sight, 'cause I'm not looking to ditch you. Just hang loose and stick with me, and if I step into anything, remember—back me up."

I cut the distance between me and the future "coppers" of America and saw that Patti had fallen about twenty or twenty-five feet behind me. They walked over to Duffy Square on Forty-seventh Street and Broadway and sat down on a park bench. My shopping bag and I dragged ourselves over to the park bench whose back joined the one they were seated on. Overhearing their conversation was a breeze then because the back of my head was practically hitting the backs of theirs. Patti sat on the base of the Father Duffy statue and kept a sort of panoramic sight in view.

We just sat there with male and female junkies drifting up and asking if they'd scored, or seen anyone around. Everyone seemed to be uptight and hanging in there.

At about ten to two a tall young white guy with curly brown hair came up. "Another six-footer," I thought. "This one's about

190 pounds too." He put one foot on their bench, leaned over, and whispered into the big guy's ear. Mr. Big pulled out the folding money and handed it to Curley saying, "I told you I got it . . . here's twenty." Curley nodded, "C'mon . . . just you," and he and the big guy walked to Forty-seventh Street and Broadway and talked. I tried to get close but the heads were swiveling and I felt words at that point weren't of such great consequence, so I stood a few feet away waiting for the traffic light. I signaled to Patti to cross the street ahead of us, and she did, waiting in front of Liggett's Drugstore.

The two men talked for several minutes on the corner and then started to cross; but instead of crossing completely they walked through the streets diagonally covering the ground, but sure of detecting anyone that followed in like manner.

I noticed what they were doing and glanced across to Patti to make sure she was aware. I saw her engaged in conversation with some guy. I did a double take and flew across that intersection, coming right up to her as she was smiling her sweet little-girl smile up into some strange face. I swung my shopping bag, hitting her a glancing shot as I dove back into the street trying to make up for some of the lost time. "That stupid bitch," I thought, "if she wants to pick somebody up, let her do it on her own time, not on mine."

The guys were cutting across the street now at Forty-fifth and Seventh Avenue and I'd had to work to cut down the space between us. I was still angrily thinking of Patti. "Well," I thought, "that stupid ass thinks she's going to jeopardize me for some fathead in pants, she's got another guess coming. She's going to bitch about getting whacked with that bag, but that's just too damn bad, there's too much at stake here."

As they cut across the street, they were still about 250 feet in front of me; they came to a halt when they reached the corner of Seventh and Forty-fifth. The curly one looked up. A black in a second-floor window of a cheap hotel there leaned out and waved his arm at them shouting, "It's okay," as he looked up and down the block from his vantage point. Curley waved back, "Okay," and they continued walking east toward Sixth Avenue and I started to close the gap between us.

They stopped at the rear entrance of Horn and Hardart on Forty-fifth Street off Sixth Avenue. Curley went in and left the

133

big guy doing a slow jig of impatience. I sat on a building sprinkler about fifteen or twenty feet west of the door.

Curley came out, put his left arm around the big guy's shoulder, and they walked toward me. Curley was talking as they pulled abreast of me. "Here, stupid." His fingers were pressing and tapping on the big guy's shoulder to arouse his attention.

"It's here, you stupid bastard!" The big guy then reacted and reached up with his left hand to catch a batch of glassine envelopes which fluttered into it from Curley's palm.

As they walked past me I got off my sprinkler and fell in about four feet behind them. I flipped open my sweater collar that showed my shield and took out my gun.

"Police! Hold it! You're under arrest!!!" The two immediately broke into a run. I fired a warning shot straight up into the air, warning them again to stop, that I was a police officer, and summoning assistance.

The big guy stopped abruptly and whirled about with a ten-inch knife clenched in his right fist shouting, "Go on, go on, I'll get this fuckin' old whore." Curley veered to the right and ran into a jewelry exchange at 111 West Forty-fifth Street.

I backed off to get some space between us when I saw him pull that gravity knife, but it was too fast. He lunged and I side-stepped; the impetus of his thrust carried him past me. I fired a fast shot and he went down like a felled ox. He tried to get up, but I could see that his right leg was useless. The bullet had struck him in the thigh and apparently hit a nerve. The surprise on his face turned to raging fury. "You fuckin' old whore . . . you son of a bitchin' fuckin' whore . . . you . . ."

"Shut up, you creep bastard . . . next time I tell you to stop, you'll know I mean stop," I said as I kicked the knife away from just outside the reach of his outstretched hand and retrieved it as well as the fallen bags of heroin. He just lay there with his useless leg, spewing obscenities as a drunk would vomit.

As I threw cuffs on him I thought, "Christ, where the hell is Pucker?" The whole world seemed to be collecting, the streets were becoming a mob scene . . . but my backup was non-existent. I shouted at some civilians, "Call the police, tell them policewoman holding prisoner, send an ambulance," as I left my fallen prisoner to go into the building I'd seen the pusher go into.

As I ran in, I saw that the floor layout was like a maze. The space divided into individual cubicles each belonging to a different jeweler. The outside noise and excitement had seeped in and worry and excitement vibrated in the corridors. They looked in amazement and some without comprehension at what appeared to be a crazy old lady flying in, gun in hand, demanding, "Okay, where is he? Which way did he go? Police, goddammit. Where did that guy run to?" A voice shouted out, "He ran all through the place, looking for a back door, but there isn't any, so he ran into the men's room," pointing to a small corner door, all wood, which was closed. "Is there a window that he could get out of in there?" "There's a window, but it's too small for even Houdini, he'll never make it."

The door was locked. The old brain versus brawn routine, I figured. Well, I've no time for this nonsense; I left a prisoner unattended outside, a partner I don't know where, and who knows what-all else.

I banged on the door with the gun butt. I shouted at everyone to step back, and then hollered in my best truck driver voice, "Okay, you son of a bitch, how do you want it? Your partner's on the sidewalk outside with a bullet in him, and if you want to be next that's fine with me. Now, I'm going to count to five, mister, and you better walk out with your hands way up in the air, 'cause if you don't I'm going to start shooting right through this door and when those bullets start ricocheting off those fixtures you're going to look like a tin can full of holes. Now, come out or join your partner! One . . . two . . . three . . ."

The door opened and he faced my gun with his hands on his head. "Okay, smart guy, nice and easy now. I want you to move toward the door, and remember, I'm watching you like a hawk." Just in case, I asked employees in the exchange to call the police and the ambulance, and to tell them that a policewoman was holding two and would need transportation. As we approached the door, Curley could see that it looked like Times Square on New Year's Eve, there must have been five hundred people mobbed out there. "Unbelievable," I thought, "everybody and his uncle except Pucker. I don't even have a pair of cuffs for this crumb."

Curley figured it was time to make his move. I felt his body tense up and he pulled to get into gear. I gave him a taste of the gun butt on his skull, "Curley, your minutes are numbered . . . you better play it real cool." He became jelly again as we walked outside, to the tune of sirens ringing, blowing, caterwauling, making lovely raucous music.

I had Curley spreadeagled against the building in front of where the big guy was stretched out on the pavement as a police car pulled up to the curb. My mind was going a mile a minute thinking in the newly defensive way that has become the watchword for survival for cops in New York City. "Let's see what they can find wrong. I've got the knife, I've got the junk, I've got the buyer, and I've got the seller . . . and thank God they're both white!! But where is that stupid little b—"

"What the hell is going on here?" A couple of guys rush from the radio car and Detective Bill Duffin from the squad car. I grabbed Bill, with whom I'd shared a couple of tours in the Hotel Squad. "Bill, it's me, Marie Cirile, I need cuffs for this guy and an ambulance for this other one."

Bill put cuffs on Curley but he was shaking his head laughing. "The phones and the police radio are going crazy with calls. Everybody and his uncle's calling in. Hey, who you working with?"

"Bill, if I told you, you'd never believe it."

The ambulance took Mr. Big Guy, still spitting venom, and carted him away. "Bill, can you have Curley Locks brought to the squad for detention? I'll get there as soon as I can, I have a few things to check out."

The newspaper photographers were already on the scene, about a dozen squad cars and I don't know what else, because all I wanted to do was hide.

Bill said, "Don't worry, I'll try to stall them for you but don't take all day. I can see this is going to be a big one and the brass is going to start beefing."

Brass . . . beefing? Good God, I just remembered the appointment coming up with the Police Commissioner. If this collar ruined anything, I'd go bananas. Where was that dopey broad? Everything went off like clockwork, except she took a Brody. Now I had to worry about her and I had a prisoner in the squad room, one in the hospital, and a million reporters waiting for the story. I knew I had to find her.

I put in a call for my Wide-awake Detective Agency partners and got Ed on the phone. Tersely I told him the circumstances. "Stay where you are, we'll be there in fifteen minutes. I'm working with Jackie Coyne today, but he'll make the shape. Don't worry, stay put."

Twelve minutes later they were at my public phone booth on Broadway. "Ed, you can't lose your partner in the middle of a collar. I've got to find her."

"I know it's hard, but you've got to stay here. Jackie and I will ride these blocks. If she's anywhere, we'll deliver her to you. Now, keep the faith, tiger."

They left and the hardest part began—standing there like an idiot. Unmarked cars passed me on the way to the precinct, news and photo cars were all going the same way. It was mildly hysterical after a while.

About an hour and a half later, and more than two hours after the arrest, the guys drove up delivering guess who—Miss Goody Two-Shoes. She started to expostulate, "Oh, Marie . . ."

"I don't want to hear it . . . I don't want to know it . . . this is what happened this afternoon."

"Oh, Marie, how can I say that? I'll never be able to remember the story."

"Listen, you . . . do you know they'll hand you the biggest fattest complaint you ever heard of on this job?"

"Oh, I don't know what to do."

"Let me tell you that the precinct is full of TV cameras and newspaper photographers and bosses anxiously awaiting your story. Maybe I will ask . . . what *is* your story, Miss Prim?" I saw the fellas standing back, with their eyes rolled up toward heaven —a good sign.

"Oh, oh, well, I just lost you. I didn't see you after you were standing waiting for the light on Forty-seventh Street."

"What do you mean you didn't see me? I saw you, you were talking to some clown in front of Liggett's. Who was he anyway?"

"Well, he's just a very nice fella from out of town. He said I looked lonely and asked me if I wanted a drink."

"A crummy pickup . . . you . . . wait a minute. After I crossed the street I hit you with my shopping bag to make sure you saw me. What about that?"

"Well, you see, I only talked to him for a minute, honest, but I forgot for a second you were dressed like that and when you hit me, I just thought you were an old lady. All of a sudden I realized and looked around and you were gone. I didn't know what to do, I felt so terrible. But I felt worse later when I heard all the sirens and the noise. I knew it, I said, that's Marie, I'll betcha. I was afraid to call the office, and I've just been walking around ever since, hoping I'd bump into you."

"Why didn't you call the precinct and find out where the run was? Or ask one of the uniformed men to find out on the walkie-talkie—make some attempt?" shot out Ed, "instead of standing on a corner with your finger in your mouth! If you were my partner, I'd flatten you. She's alive, no thanks to you."

"All right, Patti, how do you want to handle it? Do you want to take your medicine, or do you want me to cover for you and give you a rundown on what happened this afternoon?" Naturally she chose the latter and then went through a briefing session. She'd say that the reason she wasn't at the scene was because she couldn't get across the street due to the traffic, but that she'd observed from across the street.

She managed to smile sweetly and demurely all through the interviews and photographing sessions, gracefully accepting congratulations on a job well done. "This," I thought, "is what keeps women where they are in this job. Who the hell would ever trust any other woman after hearing a story like that? You'd have to whack a guy on the head to work with a female if this story gets out." I was truly angry, she had muffed a shot that doesn't always come your way: a chance for a female team to do a competitive job in a male-dominated world.

The big guy was Thomas P. Hornett, alias Thomas Patrick King, alias Thomas Hart, alias Thomas C. O'Neill, whose history of thirteen arrests ranged from assorted drug charges to grand larceny, burglary, criminally receiving, burglary and tools, and felonious assault with a knife. "Ho so," I thought, "he's tried this little game before." I charged him with possession of drugs, possession with intent to sell, and felonious assault with a knife.

Curley was Harvey P. Tuyman, whose yellow sheet ran the

gamut from possession of pornography, possession of drugs, and grand larceny–auto, to assault and robbery with a knife. Curley was charged with possession of drugs and possession with intent to sell drugs.

I went to see O'Neill in the Bellevue Hospital prison ward to which he'd been transferred, and found him a little more tractable. "Geez, next time aim for someplace else, will ya? This'll keep me from dancin' for at least a coupla months . . . and I got this girl that's all she lives for is dancin'."

"Well, Thomas, you tell your girl she's lucky she's not dancing at your wake . . . be thankful for small favors!"

Meanwhile the papers, television, and radio carried the story like crazy. Everybody and his uncle were looking for interviews. Despite the approval of the department's Community Relations Board, I tried to avoid as many as possible. It bugged the hell out of me to have to include Patti in as a facet of the operation, but how else could I explain her total absence without setting her up for a complaint?

Besides, right in the middle of this mess I had much more important things on my mind that had me tied up in gastric knots. My appointment with the PC was for the following morning, and I was hoping that all this publicity wouldn't upset or unnerve him or alter my chances for an impartial hearing.

Ten A.M. on May 26 I saw Commissioner Michael Murphy in his office. He had my personnel file spread across his desk and was reading as I walked in. He continued reading it for at least ten minutes without ever raising his head, acknowledging my presence, or in any way giving evidence of knowing I was there, alive and breathing.

What a feeling that is. My stomach had already sunk down to about my ankles and hope was a thing they named ships after; nobody could have felt any more morbidly pessimistic.

Finally, he raised his head. His face seemed to be all eyes that bored right through me. "Tell me what happened." No greeting, no niceties, just a fast knife stroke. I swallowed and accepted at that point that my mission was hopeless.

Quietly, in almost a spiritless monotone, I gave a factual diary-like account of what had happened. It took about ten or fifteen

139

minutes. He jotted down several things, and as I finished, threw his questions at me.

They were the first intelligent questions asked by anyone from the department, excluding the chaplain and the psychiatrist, and therefore the easiest to answer. You could see his razor-sharp mind evaluating, discarding, concluding as he weighed every aspect. He was shaking his head when he was through.

Then he pinned me with those eyes again and said in his clipped direct way, "We will disregard what has occurred. I will personally see that your shield is restored. It will take a day or two for the paper work, so don't get impatient. I've given you my word, and I regret what has occurred." He got up concluding the interview, and as I was about to thank him he said, "This does not require thanks, I expect you to justify my faith in you. By the way, I want you to know that I'm aware of what's happening in my department and that your recent exploits have in no way colored my thinking. Good day and good luck."

My twenty-four-hour deodorant spray never got me past 11 A.M. that day. I came out of that room reduced to ribbons. My exhilaration as I went back up to the Women's Bureau turned into the "weeps." I was finally able to let down and give up the "good fight" just as I was beginning to think the world was getting a bit queer. What a relief . . . now all I had to do was wait some more.

It was a cinch now, because suddenly I was a celebrity. I got fan mail from all over the world. It was unbelievable, people sent me copies of newspaper stories to autograph. Letters of thanks and "well done" came from strangers. I found this remarkable, that people took the time and trouble to dash off a letter to someone they'd only read about.

One of my favorites was a postcard that came from Virginia Beach, Virginia. This gal had pasted a copy of a small story, "Old Bag Unmasked," and it had two small photos of me—one in the wig and one without. Under this she'd written:

Dear Mrs. Old Bag,
You look better in the white hair, put it on and wear it with pride, Old Bagging becomes you!

Teenie Morris
Another Old Bag

It really cracked me up. I wish she'd put her address on it, I would have thanked her for her humor.

A letter from London came from Louise Ernst, one of our New York policewomen.

Dear Marie:

Picture this if you can. Yours truly is just having tea in a lovely old English Inn located in the countryside about twenty-five miles from London. I picked up a newspaper and there you are. What an unexpected pleasure. I've enclosed the article. As they would say over here, Marie: "Good Show . . . Job well done!"

You certainly had a time of it there for a while, but you do us proud, Marie.

Will you take care of yourself?

Love,
Louise

Between the mail, requests for television appearances, the mundane routine follow-up police procedures like checking my gun out with ballistics, checking the confiscated drugs at the police lab, and making court appearances more than filled the three days it took for a notification to come through from the PC's office. On May 29, 1965, seventy-seven days after the Medical Bureau had taken it away, the commissioner returned the very same detective's shield and reassigned me to the Pickpocket and Confidence Squad.

I'd worked only ten tours with the Women's Bureau, but was more than ready to leave. I couldn't bear to watch Patti's simpering face as she goo-gooed and gaa-gaaed all over the place. I thanked Peg for her hospitality, but she thanked me instead and said I'd done wonders for her unit's morale and that she intended to write us up for departmental recognition.

"Peg, you can if you want to, but I'm never going to push for any again. You know I've got more than my share already, but boy, when the chips were down, they sure didn't count for very much within the department. So if they come, they come, but I won't go looking for them anymore."

Pickpocket & Confidence Squad

So here I am, where I never wanted to be, another bastion of male versus female. The unit covers the five boroughs and actually is the most active mixed squad next to narcotics. The big difference is in the utilization; they're subdivided by sex within their own framework. The males work with male partners; the females with females. There aren't any mixes by either choice or design. The caliber and type of work expected is different also.

PP&C work falls into three main categories. The first naturally is the apprehension of pickpockets. The second is the investigation of confidence swindles such as the pocketbook drop, the Murphy game, the phony jewelry con, and so on. The third is the investigation of gypsy confidence swindles.

The men got all the complaints with any substance and that involved the confidence games for investigation. The women seemed to revert back to what Commissioner Melchionne called her Shoplifting Squad; that is, they hung aroung the bargain counters in Macy's or Alexander's on sale days watching to see if anyone tried to filch a wallet while the women went bananas at the counters.

I was welcomed by the sergeant, who seemed impressed with their operation. "I know it will take awhile for you to understand our procedures," he explained. "That's why we put everyone transferred here on a probationary period. We don't want you to carry responsibilities while you're learning, so for three months we'll carry you on probation. You won't get credit for any arrests for that time. Your partner, who is your training officer, will take any arrests and will give us a weekly report on how you're doing."

"Sarge, I was making pick collars seven years ago, and I've made just about any other kind you can think of; I don't mind being broken into your procedures, but this probie period seems a bit way out."

"Well, we'll see. Maybe we can cut the time down in your case, it depends on the reports your partner submits. You'll be working with a first-grader, Marilyn Boeing, as your partner."

"Oh no . . . Sarge, I hate to start out this way, but can you change my partner. I defeated Marilyn in an election in the Policewomen's Endowment Association and she's never forgiven me. I think it would be a bit unfair to put her in a position to pass judgment and issue me grades."

"That's strange . . . she requested you. Perhaps you're exaggerating. I'm sure she's forgotten all about it. If it doesn't work out, we'll see what we can do."

I was given the rest of that tour off to transfer my things and told to meet Marilyn and a third female detective, Mary, out at the World's Fair in Queens the following day.

The surroundings were different at least. I hadn't gotten a chance to take in the fair, so I was enjoying that part of it. Marilyn, my erstwhile teacher, was 5'11" and weighed about 190 pounds, but was a contradiction within herself. She looked like a linebacker for the New York Giants but thought and acted like little Miss Buttercup.

We made the rounds at the fair and stood on all the crowded lines to see what we could see. On the line in front of the General Motors Pavilion we saw a little more than was normal. Three men seemed to be bucking the line, edging and pushing their way in. Then two of them maneuvered and pushed a well-dressed man from behind right into a third man who was standing in front. The third man in the hustle and confusion reached into the "mark's" back pocket for his wallet.

We all saw it and I jumped up ready to take action. "Marie, you go see if you can get one of those special guards to help us," said Marilyn.

"What for, for God's sake, let's take them. There's three of us. By the time you reach out for someone, who knows where these guys are going to be? You expect them to sit and wait for you?"

"You tell her, Mary," Marilyn smirked. I darted a glance at

Mary, who had a somewhat abashed look as she said almost apologetically, "Marie, that's the way we work it here in this squad. The lieutenant has strict orders that any woman who wants to make an arrest has to get help first."

"You mean to say that's the way it'll always be? What the hell do they give you a gun and a shield for, then? Any civilian who sees something can run for help, you don't have to be a detective to do that."

"The lieutenant says he'd rather lose a collar than have one of us hurt. That's the way he feels."

"What about the men? Do they have to find a cop to help them make an apprehension?" I asked.

"Oh, don't be silly, of course not, they're men."

"Shades of Mother Macree," I murmured. I looked at Marilyn, close to six feet tall, and Mary, who, though she was only 5'4", weighed in at about 185 pounds, and thought, "We need help?"

Marilyn ran and secured somebody or other and we arrested three Ecuadorians very quietly. One was 5'5", the second was 5'3", and the third behemoth was 5' even. What I found most interesting was that they were all in this country illegally, spoke not a word of English, and were incredibly simplistic and affable when I spoke to them in Spanish.

In Ecuador they'd gone to a pickpocket's school for professional training, and were as proud of their prowess as any skilled artisan. The scheme thought of in Ecuador and executed here was to come in on visitors' visas, and overstay their return dates. Meanwhile they'd "work" at their trade like crazy, keep sending the money to Ecuador, and continue until something like this arrest, which would cause them to be deported. They'd get a free trip home on Uncle Sam and be big heroes when they arrived. They smiled with pride when one of the men shyly told me that his mother had almost finished paying for her little farm. I guess Sonny had made good.

So much for my first day in the Pickpocket and Confidence Squad. The next few days were uniformly drab as I got to meet the security personnel of Klein's, May's, Macy's, and A&S in Brooklyn. As I trotted alongside my partner I felt like a puppy on a lead, but I was being very good; I never even peed on her foot once.

On the afternoon of the third day the skies burst open with sunshine . . . roses . . . rainbows.

I'd made the two o'clock ring and was told there was a notification for me. "Shoot," I said, scrambling for a pen.

"It's from the office of the chief of detectives, and it directs you to be in the board room of Police Headquarters, 11 A.M. tomorrow morning, to receive the New York *Daily News* Hero of the Month Award as well as the *Journal-American* Policeman of the Month Award. You are directed to bring a member or members of your family to accept the cash award. . . . Hey, Marie, congratulations, that's really great. The whole office is buzzing, I don't think I ever remember a woman getting the Hero award before."

I was talking to one of the fellas that I hadn't even met yet but he was feeling that camaraderie that made some of the squads so great. "You're right, no woman was ever honored by the *Daily News* before. I was always aware of it, but last week one of the reporters told me that he was going to suggest it to his editor, because they've been giving that award out for forty-two years— that's 509 News Hero Awards—and he said he was finally going to throw a winner into the hopper. But you know, sometimes there's excitement and eagerness and tension during an arrest scene and I've learned not to put too much emphasis on what's said. You get promised an awful lot of things that never materialize, and if you dwell on them you could get pretty disillusioned.

"So I just smiled my thanks and kept working, and now son of a gun . . . it just quietly came through. Oh my God, it's just starting to get through to me!"

So I went home and cleaned up the act. I told Cindy she could come and she was nervously excited. She was eleven then and they wouldn't give the cash award to a minor, but they couldn't stop her from being my cheering committee.

I called Mom and Pop and invited them. I think that for once in his life my father was proud even if I wasn't a boy. Our group greeted First Deputy Commissioner John Walsh in the starkly impressive board room. The photographers from the *Daily News,* the *Journal-American,* and *Spring 3100* (the police magazine) were there snapping like crazy and the reporters were talking and chatting. Poor Mom and Pop were almost petrified with a mixture of fear and pride as Mom was pressed into action holding the $350 cash award that went with the honor certificates.

Finally it was over and I was able to sigh with relief. Nobody goofed. Nothing would have embarrassed them more than if something, who knows what they were worried about, had gone wrong. Now they could relax, and maybe enjoy the surprise I'd cooked up for them.

"How about a little lunch . . . anybody feeling hungry yet?"

"My stomach shesa cry, only a cup coffee today," said Ma. "In da howsa, I gotta nice-a peppa witha da meat. We go home and eat."

"That's all you think about—your stomach, your stomach," said roly-poly Pop, who weighed about 220 pounds and sure wasn't tall.

I just drove to the Plaza Hotel, where I'd made reservations in the Oak Room. "Okay, we're here, let's go, you've got to help me spend some of that money I got today. This is a special celebration." With Cindy's help we ushered them inside where the maître d' took over. He turned on his Italian and had them seated with suave smoothness.

"Listen now, I want you to order anything at all that you ever wanted. I'll translate it for you Momma, and don't give me any of your usual baloney about just having a ham sandwich."

When Pop ordered oysters Rockefeller and Mom had melon and prosciutto as appetizers, I knew they were on their way. The musicians danced attendance and we got front-office celebrity attention. Pop was in his glory when they lit his cigar, which they'd presented, and placed a brandy snifter in front of him. It was posh all the way and we all loved it; Pop was to talk about it for quite a while.

I was thrilled. Inwardly I felt that I'd come to terms with the job; I hoped that I had given my parents something to be proud of, and Cindy something positive after a pretty crummy year. The only thing that stuck in my craw was the knowledge that if it hadn't been for the foul-up with the shield, this last arrest would have meant my getting second-grade money. I refused to dwell on it, though; the job had to some extent made me a fatalist and if it was meant to be, it would be.

Getting back into routine wasn't bad, getting used to working

146

with Boeing was another matter. After a few days there was no doubt in my mind that she felt that I was "given" to her to expiate my sin in beating her in a public election. Never were two such dissimilar people made to work together. Marilyn liked a highball or two or three with lunch; I was an abstainer. I couldn't even afford to eat lunch in the places she liked to hang out in. I liked to work and head home, while she liked to hang out and socialize. My so-called claim to fame was work; hers was fraternizing with the bosses. I think my favorite story on that score was the one in which at a line organization cocktail party, being I hope somewhat crocked, she gaily went up to the former Police Commissioner, greeted him by his first name, and goosed him. Everybody said it was "Beeauuutifullll!" Now, that girl really had the job by the connections.

As we walked the streets, I'd point out junkies and car workers. She'd shake her head, "That's not our work," and head for the next department store. Leaving Klein's, we were right in front of a Horn and Hardart automat and I explained to Boeing how these places were notorious for sellers and receivers.

Son of a gun . . . this little short fat guy came trailing out of the place with two junkies in his wake. I held Marilyn's arm to stop her and watched them. The little guy gave a cursory glance around and then, like he owned the street, whipped out a jeweler's loupe and held his hand out to one of the junkies. Junkie fumbled in his pocket and gave something over. Fatso held up a lovely gold floral spray pin, about three inches in diameter and covered with precious stones, and peered intently at it with his magnifying loupe.

"That bastard is louping the swag—right out here on the street. Marilyn, look, we've got to take them. That's a stolen piece of jewelry and he's going to buy it from those junkies who've probably burglarized some house this morning."

"That's not pickpocket work. We don't get credit for that and I'm not going to take a chance. You can't either. The lieutenant said I'm in charge and I say we don't touch them. As far as I'm concerned, I didn't see anything, and that's what I'm going to say." The three men re-entered H&H, and I stood there wondering if I disliked her or myself more at this point.

I put in my tenth request for a change of partner and but-

147

tressed my remarks by telling them that I'd request a squad transfer if it wasn't possible. I'd worked with her for months, feeding her collars so that she could retain her first-grade shield. On the job we call this "carrying," and I was tired of saying, "She ain't heavy, she's my partner."

They switched two teams around and I got myself another first-grader, Laurette Valente. Considering that there are only four female first-graders, and one shield is held in reserve for the director of the Women's Bureau, it was pretty unusual.

Laurette looked like what the average person expected a policewoman to look like. She was about 5'10" and built pretty sturdily. I could probably use her skirt as a dress. I was beginning to get a complex, I was always trotting two steps behind like a Chinese wife as I attempted to keep up with the large strides. She was a nice person, quiet, withdrawn, and completely wrapped up in her family. Despite her seeming quiet, I think the feature I liked most was that she called a spade a shovel. She was honest to the point of being outspoken when she felt a situation warranted it. We got our quota of arrests, and retained our status on the evaluation sheets until we got involved in a fiasco that seemed to come out of a Hollywood script.

Laurette and I were working the buses during the crowded rush hours when the pickpockets attacked in all their glory. It was 5:15 P.M. when we got on the Fifth Avenue bus at about Forty-fifth Street. We stood near the driver and looked over the passengers to see if there was any undue activity. A flicker of interest was aroused by three well-dressed dudes, who although they were seated separately were busy watching every movement that anyone made.

One of these cats was an absolute vision in emerald green. He was about thirty-three, a well-built 5'10" and sported a green suit, green knit shirt, a soft furry green, five-inch-wide-brimmed fedora with feathers, green lizard shoes, and was carrying a green leather coat. Even in jaded Manhattan he was worth a second look.

My interest mounted when the chap in the rear got up and peered out the back window. I sauntered midway in and noticed a sharp late-model gold car following directly behind the bus. When the bus stopped to discharge passengers, a number of times, all the other cars behind the bus managed to pull ahead, but the gold one made no effort to leave.

I pushed up to the front and leaned over Laurette. "We've got something here, baby. I think they've got a whole operation going for themselves. They've got a car following right behind this bus. I'll bet the wallets are going right out the window; and in an emergency they've got a standby getaway car. Ming, what a setup! There's three in here and one out there and they don't look like the kind that play games over Macy's sales counters. Listen, we better concentrate on the three in here and worry about the other guy when we come to it."

"You know, that big good-looking one in the green looks familiar to me. Either his picture's in the file, or one of the guys locked him up and I saw him in the office," said Laurette. Meanwhile the bus got a little more crowded and conditions were, therefore, more favorable for the picks.

"I'm going to tell the bus driver to keep the doors closed if we step in and take any action. We've got to contain them, and I don't think it'll be easy. We can't pull a gun, there's too many people and they'd panic on us."

I sidled up front and told the driver, "If we take any action, stop the bus, keep the doors closed, shut off the ignition, and pocket the key." He knew who we were, we had identified ourselves when we got on. "And remember, no matter what happens, *don't move the bus,* and *don't open the doors!*"

He was young, eager, and willing to co-operate—what a pleasure! "My name is Patrick Carr, you holler if you want me and I'll do whatever I can."

Laurette and I each had a pair of cuffs and I had a billyjack, thank goodness. The yellow car was still behind us, where it had been for ten blocks.

"Mr. Green," apparently the spotter, had gotten up a number of times when people clustered about the rear exit, but didn't seem to find what he was looking for. The second one was fortyish, wore conservative clothes, and looked more like an economics professor. Number three was a little guy, about 5'6", but real slim. He was carrying his trenchcoat too, although it was March and darn cold. He was Mr. Nervous compared to the professionals he was with.

149

On Thirty-third Street between Fifth and Sixth avenues the bus slowed for one of its scheduled stops. At least thirty people were already up and crowded about the front and rear doors. This stop was the hub of one of the world's largest shopping areas, and almost all of the passengers seemed to be destined here, including our three suspects and, of course, us.

We spotted the mark. They'd apparently singled him out when he was seated and waited for him to get off. He was an affluent-looking businessman dressed in a great-looking gray pinstripe, carrying a hand-stitched leather portfolio, a copy of *The Wall Street Journal*, and a stink of money.

Our three surrounded the intended victim. He was flanked by the Professor on his left and Mr. Nervous on his right. Mr. Green was to be the big gun in the rear. They maneuvered him into position, then together they thrust and shoved and propelled the crowd toward the door. The Professor and Mr. Nervous pushed against the mark at the same time that Mr. Green leaned into him and put his left hand into the guy's left-hand trouser pocket. The crowd meanwhile was muttering discontent. "Hey, stop pushing." "We're all getting off, what's your hurry." Our three were among the noisiest.

When we saw him "dip" or go into the guy's trousers that was all we needed to make a jostling arrest under the penal law statute which reads: "Any person who, with intent to provoke a breach of the peace, interferes with any person in any place, by jostling against such person, or unnecessarily crowding him, or placing a hand in the proximity of such person's pocket, pocketbook, or handbag, shall be deemed to have committed the offense of disorderly conduct."

If we'd let them get the guy's wallet then we'd have had a larceny pinch, but since we're purported to be pickpocket specialists we're supposed to stop them right in the act.

Laurette and I hollered together and loud enough for the driver to hear, "Police, you're under arrest!!!" We both had our cuffs out, but all of a sudden there was nothing to put them on. The three of them started bellowing so they could drown out our voices, "Hey, driver, open this door . . . what the hell is going on here?" "Hey, lady, you crazy or something? Anybody here see me do anything? You're afraid to answer me 'cause I'm colored. Right?"

Meanwhile they ran up to the front of the bus and tried that door, without results. They turned to the driver's seat but he wasn't there. Patrick Carr had smartly sat down and taken off his hat.

There was a crowd of people gathering outside banging on the bus trying to get in. Pat shouted out the window, "Go call the police, tell them we have an emergency on the bus." Meanwhile what we did have was pandemonium. Laurette and I were chasing these idiots up and down that bus and they were skittering and shouting and kicking up a storm. I had taken out my jack but couldn't get a good shot with it. Every time you approached one of them, they'd toss a passenger at you like a bowling ball, shouting, "Help us, help us, somebody. This is persecution."

Mr. Green turned to a college-age girl clutching an armload of books and wearing a five-inch button on her shoulder proclaiming, "Make Love Not War." "Now, miss, you're my soul sister, right? You gonna let these pigs tell these lies? Help me, sister. Love . . . peace . . . that's all we want."

I tried to slip the cuff on while he was making his big speech, but he was doing a dance and there were forty people eyeing every move. I tried to hide the jack and give him a hidden jab in the back with it, as I hissed, "Will you stick up your hands? You're going to get Inciting to Riot along with all the other charges."

"Brutality . . . oooh, she's killing me."

Miss College jumped up. "Leave them alone . . . they didn't do anything. What're you picking on 'em for. No wonder they hate us." She grabbed my hands and Green ran to the back of the bus.

"Sit down and shut up, you don't know what you're talking about," I spit out.

"Don't you talk to me like that. You're a servant, we pay your salary, you pig, picking on those poor men because they're black."

"Sweetheart, they tried to steal somebody's wallet, so be a good girl and—"

"*Marie* . . ." I wheeled to see the Professor trying to wrest the cuffs away from Laurette. I went dashing back so they tried another tack. Mr. Nervous ran to a colored passenger. "Momma, help me, you gonna let them get your brother?" The woman seemed terrified. He whirled to face the others and clutched his privates, "Lord, what they've done, I'm so nervous, I'm gonna pee." He ran madly about with his hand on his zipper and they were really getting out of his way now, afraid they were in for a shower of urine.

Miss College was back exhorting the passengers. "The poor man is a wreck. Have the police no mercy?"

"Hey, Sarah Bernhardt, you keep that up you're going with your friends when this little fiasco is over."

"She threatened me. You heard her. It's fascism, I tell you."

"My heart . . . I've got to get off this bus," a little middle-aged woman screamed. "I'm a sick woman. . . ."

"I've got to pee . . . I'm going to pee right here in the bus. . . ."

"Help me, brother, we're being victimized. . . ."

"Let them go, let them go, we'll all be killed," a skinny, bespectacled woman moaned.

"So vat did dey do? Vy is everybody crazy?" asked an old man.

The driver, back in his seat, was blowing the horn to attract attention and assistance. The Professor ran up front. "Open that fuckin' door." Pat just leaned harder. The Professor reached under the metal barrier to get at the driver and started to kick and punch him.

The screams and anguished shouts rose to ear-shattering heights. Cars, trucks, and buses stalled behind us blended their horns in a raucous cacophony of discord, a perfect musical background for our turbulent tableau.

I saw Pat struggling and ran up and gave the Professor a shot over the head with the jack. He bellowed like a wounded bull, "They're killing us! The fucking pigs are killing us."

Then a voice shouted from outside. "Open the window . . . quick, I'll help you out . . . the Man's coming." The driver of the gold car had put in an appearance.

The horn blew . . . people screamed . . . a woman fainted . . . Laurette took a good kick in the groin . . . the driver had had his lumps, and our three-man team was still performing. They attacked the windows with a vengeance, each one operating in a different section of the bus. Pat, Laurette, and I flew about shutting them as fast as they were opened. Sometimes the men were partway out and we'd heave to retrieve them while the outside character hauled from the other side.

As the Professor opened a window, I finally managed to cuff him to the hanging rail, so he appeared suspended like a half side of beef. "One down," I muttered and turned to see Mr. Nervous actually step on a woman's lap and start to clamber out the window behind her head. The woman remained frigidly immobile, almost catatonic, as this character used her for a stepladder.

I saw him being tugged from the outside and managed to grab the last leg as it was disappearing out of the window, and got his shoe for my trouble. The bus dispatcher outside tried to stop him but was attacked by the driver of the gold car, and they were fighting it out.

"Hey, Laurette, let's get this last one!" We cornered him as people flew out of our way. "Mister, I'm going to put a nasty bullet hole in that pretty green suit; you'd better think cool," I threatened. I had my sweater pulled back so he could see my hand on my gun butt . . . and he looked. The passengers were huddled into groups trying to avoid the dangling Professor and now us.

Mr. Green knew he was cornered. Nothing moved but his eyes. "Laurette, throw the cuffs on him. *You! Turn around!* Put your hands behind your back. *Now, bastard!!*" He was cuffed at last when I heard Pat shout, "The cops are here!"

The bus was surrounded by the heavenly blue of uniforms and nightsticks pounded. "Hey, what's going on in there? Are you stuck or is there something wrong?"

"Detectives," I bawled back. "We're holding two; one escaped. We need transportation."

"You've got it. There's a couple of squad cars here already."

"Beautiful . . . Patrick, open the door and let the passengers out first." I apologized to the passengers for the somewhat unusual ride and asked five of them to leave their names and addresses in case we needed them as witnesses. In two or three minutes we got the Professor down and recuffed him behind the back and took him out with Mr. Green. As Laurette and I limped down we heard an old lament, "Don't let them take our brothers.

Help me, help them." Son of a gun . . . the driver of the follow-up car had stayed behind to spring them.

This character must have studied at the same acting school as the others. As he was shouting he was grabbing at Green and the Professor and trying to wrest them away. "Look what they do . . . they rape our women and kill our children. Stop the pigs and help the brothers."

Laurette said, "Okay, mister, you're going with your friends," and she turned to grab him. He kicked her in the leg before we got cuffs on him and dragged him punching and kicking all the way.

When we finally got down to booking them we threw it at them, charging them with (a) jostling, (b) attempted grand larceny, (c) resisting arrest, (d) disorderly conduct, (e) felonious assault on an officer, (f) felonious assault, and (g) interfering with a police officer. If they wanted to scream, holler, shout, and bellow, they might as well have something to bitch about.

Two pretty sad looking females dragged themselves into the PP&C office after court the next afternoon. We were a vision in technicolor, with multicolor bruises. Mentally we were pretty elated though. When we'd picked up the prisoners' yellow sheets we had found they all had at least two pages of arrests—and our Mr. Green had almost forty in all. I wished I could have waved those records in front of that busload of people who sat and listened to them mouth off about their innocence.

I checked Green's old arrest record for known associates and saw that he was last arrested with a man named Alvin Boone. We got the photo unit to run off Boone's picture and we had Mr. Nervous, our escapee who'd gotten out the window.

Laurette and I limped a jig around the office and transmitted a wanted alarm for our escaped prisoner. The one who gets away always clogs your craw, but once identified and with an alarm out on him, we'd be notified if he was picked up for anything, including spitting on the sidewalk. Then I went home to soak in the tub.

A few days later I stopped in at the Women's Bureau to say hi to the girls and to exchange a little gossip with Peg Disco. I was chatting with Marge, and we were going through the usual routine, when she interrupted and said, "Marie, you know I'm not the type to say something behind your back. If I have something on my mind I tell the person, that's the way I feel."

"What gives, Marge?" I asked curiously.

"Marie, I don't think it's fair what you did to Patti Pucker."

I almost swallowed my vocal chords. "You don't think what's fair?" I found myself speaking through clenched teeth.

"Well, Patti and I were talking and I told her what a great piece of work you two had done, and that it was good to see a woman get the award for a change. And then she told me, 'Well, I guess it was good for Marie, but she didn't even have the decency to share the award money with me.' I'll tell you, Marie, I said, 'Patti, Marie wouldn't do something like that.' And she said, 'Well, she did. I didn't even see one penny of that money.'"

"Marge . . . Marge, shut up. I've never been so damn mad in my time on this fool job. Margie, I'm going to tell you something that only Patti, I, and two guys I used to work with know about. It would have stayed that way too, if it wasn't for this. Listen and then let me know if you'd have shared that award money with Miss Sweet and Simple."

I gave her a fast rundown and Margie's eyes opened wider and wider. Marge is good out in the field, she's a worker who's not afraid of tackling a job, so she knows what a partner means. As she listened, she was sucking in her breath and finally let it all out in a big noisy "Jesus Christ!"

"So you tell that broad she's lucky to have been included in the application for a departmental award. I got a Commendation and Patti got an Excellent Policy Duty, her first and unless they start handing them out for pickups, probably her last. I'm sorry if I sound like a pig, Margie, but she's got everybody buffaloed."

The weeks and months went with monotonous regularity and I was stagnating in position when I heard of an opening in the Property Recovery Squad.

For years I'd wanted to get into that unit, but it was very small, possibly ten members, and each one virtually handpicked. There were a number of reasons for its looking good, the first being that Peg Disco had been in that squad and had gone from third grade to second to first, and now was director of the Women's Bureau. I felt that with this precedent combined with opportunity and plain work, lightning might strike twice. The second most important factor was that you worked by yourself . . . it was the type of squad where you sought and developed your own information.

So I did a lot of thinking and a lot of calling and got someone to ask the then chief of detectives. After a week that seemed like a year, I got word back. "He says okay!"

"You're kidding, tell me what he said."

"Well, I told him that I had someone who'd like a transfer to another squad, and he sorta grunted and said, 'Who? From where to where?' When I told him, he looked a little surprised, but then he said, 'At least you came up with a winner. Yeah, I can't see any reason why not. It'll take a few days.'"

"Wonderful . . . that's something . . . he said that about me, it makes me feel good."

As we were finishing up a tour several days later, I got a message from the chief's office. "Hey, Marie, you've been transferred. It says, 'Notify Detective Marie Cirile that effective 8 A.M. on February 2, she is transferred from the Pickpocket and Confidence Squad into the Missing Persons Unit.'"

"Wait a minute, wait a minute, uh, would you read that again." It sounded just as bad the second time I heard it, and all I could think of was, what could have gone wrong?

I found out that evening after a few back-and-forth phone calls. The chief of detectives and the lieutenant in charge of the Property Recovery Squad were old drinking buddies. Over lunch the chief mentioned that he was transferring a woman into PRS. The lieutenant had a fit and a half. "It took me three and a half years to get rid of that other broad, I don't want any others."

The chief said, "Take it easy, you don't even know who it is."

"I don't care either . . . I don't want *any* woman."

"I promised I'd transfer her, so I'll put her in the Missing Persons Unit."

That was the whole story; the positioning of females was tantamount to distributing token liabilities on a more or less even basis. I didn't know this lieutenant, he didn't know me—and he was going to keep it that way.

Missing Persons Unit – 1967

Here's a squad I never thought I'd find myself in. It's a big outfit, forty or fifty assigned, about fifteen of them women. The men looked upon the women as a threat, as rumors flew about that they were to be replaced by a totally female squad.

Most of the men assigned had a particular reason for being here; most of them couldn't function in a normal squad routine. In this unit, the hours are stable, the chart is known a year in advance, there are no arrests to be made, no competitive quota system, and no overtime.

The reasons for being here ranged from working another job; having an invalid wife at home or a chronic illness; going to school or studying for promotion; to being afraid of working the streets. Three or four really belonged here; they were licensed morticians and were an absolute godsend and necessity in a time of disaster.

Most of the women, however, got here in more or less the same manner as I. Someone couldn't figure out what to do with them. The same week I got transferred in, another woman whose boyfriend was president of one of the line organizations came in as well. She acted as if she was the king's consort as she bragged about how she'd asked him to arrange the transfer so she could manage her social commitments and appearances, not to mention her three children.

A week later, much to her chagrin, two women got transferred in from the Pickpocket Squad because of inactivity. So to some people it was to be a contract, and to others a punishment detail. When the captain called the four of us in for an interview, he asked confusedly, "Uh, which of you got transferred in for inactivity?" "Captain, Marie and I came here on a contract," the princess hastily threw in. I felt sorry for the captain, it was a pretty strange setup.

The MPU was responsible for three sets of circumstances:

They were assigned all cases of missing individuals under the age of eighteen and over the age of sixty-two, and any age if there was reason to believe the person was not a voluntary absentee, or that there'd been foul play of some sort committed.

Any DOA (dead on arrival) in a public place; or who passed away without being under a doctor's care; or was unidentified or had no relatives or friends to claim the body, became one of our cases.

An aided case—that's anyone sick or injured who's removed to a hospital or other institution by the Police Department—also comes within our purview.

Under one or both of these last two categories we'd cover plane crashes, train derailments, and other major disasters.

All in all one of the main reasons I shied away from the unit was that it was so overwhelmingly, constantly depressing. I used to say that on the average the cheeriest notification I made was to tell some woman that I'd located her missing sixteen-year-old son. On a slab in the morgue. Dead from an overdose.

I railed and ranted for a few weeks trying to get out, but then I looked around and got a taste of the creeping insidious pervasion. "What are you beating your brains out for? You're getting the same salary as everyone else. That's a jungle out there in the street. A person is crazy to jeopardize his life . . . the bosses don't appreciate it. You just do what you have to do, no more, no less, and pretty soon you'll be eligible for your pension, and you'll be alive to enjoy it. Don't make waves. . . ."

So I took a few notches in my skull and substituted other goals. I enrolled in John Jay College of Criminal Justice so that I too could become brilliant . . . although it took more courage to enroll as a freshman at this stage of the game than it did for me to make an arrest. I marked time.

It was 1968 and Jim was now going to school full-time. We were having to make do with a procession of varied household

help since the Padre had introduced Mary to
and the nasty creatures had gone off and gotte

I looked at other working mothers in this squa
they were able to dispense with help and were mai
selves. That's almost as good as a promotion. I grabb
who was now fifteen, and talked. "Kiddo, if we manage th
without help for a year, we could put that money away and
a trip to Europe." Her eyes opened wide. "Do you want to gi
it a try? Remember, though, you're going to have to really help
me." She was more than willing.

That year I was into psychology, sociology, Italian, creative
writing, drama, a police science course, art history, and (ugh)
math. I was also back to scrubbing floors, doing the wash, ironing,
as well as all the gardening and maintenance work. In addition,
I handled a load of four hundred to six hundred cases a year.
When you average anywhere from ten to fifteen cases a day, it
is virtually impossible to go out into the field and investigate
them. The powers that be know this, but it's sort of a shut-your-
eyes type of thing. If each day you receive, say, fifteen missing
persons cases, how can you go out and look for one teen-ager?
You learn to pick and choose and hope and the office watchword
is "Leave them alone, and they'll come home."

The single most important thing to do is to check the morgues
every day for unidentified dead and see if you can match them
up with any of your missing. Not too much fun, when they've
got a new floater, or a jumper, or someone removed from a fire
and you have to pick out details that might identify them, like
bridgework or scars. Most of our morgue men are first-grade detectives; it's hard to feature anyone begrudging them their money.
They fingerprint the corpses and sometimes do unbelievable restoration work. Most of these men are really nice guys, but one of
them and some of the regular morgue attendants are pretty weird.
All the fellas would hint at strange and bizarre happenings at
this one morgue, and warn the girls never to go down alone. Although one detective said they'd probably be safe, because their
bodies were still warm.

"If I drop dead in this office, you'd better make sure that degenerate doesn't get his paws on me, or I'll come back and haunt
you all," I warned them.

you might get a case that had a dif-
at looked just like a hundred others.
sing. Twenty-eight years old, she'd
aving a fight, the mother-in-law told
band to tell him I intended to close
voluntary absentee, having left him
t a case for Missing Persons.
l told me she'd never leave without
ecially since the female was preg-
or so. The dogs had been featured
News magazine section, because the
st litter known for a poodle. She'd
hand-fed and cared for those pups like children, and now until
her disappearance had been deeply concerned about the dog's
pregnancy. Well, okay, I bought the story and gave it a little
whirl. I got a list of her closest friends and decided to talk to them
and get the story a lot faster than I would from him.

The closest address was a block away from the office on
Broome Street. So I started there. It was a broken-down old tenement walk-up. My knock was answered by a pretty, curly-haired
gay boy wearing trousers and that's it. "Yes, sweetie?"

"Hi, where's Sheila?"

"Oh, come on in, she's just having a cup of tea," and he walked
into the tiny kitchen with me right behind him. "Sheila dear,
there's someone for you," and he led me in.

I looked and my eyeballs crossed. Boing. She was sitting there
in a lacy open-knit shell sweater with a neckline slashed to the
belly button. It was sleeveless and just met at the waist under
the arms. The real eye-opener was that she wasn't wearing anything underneath, and that she had the most prominent pair of
door knockers I had ever seen, and a helluva tan.

She waved a cigarette idly in my direction. "Do I know you?"

"Well, it all depends . . . are you Sheila Mack?"

"Yes, but how did you know I'd be here? I just got back in from
Puerto Rico less than an hour ago, and no one knew when I'd be
getting back."

I told her who I was and why I was there and she was impressed at my locating her within an hour. I wasn't going to tell
her differently. We talked and she admitted she'd left him volun-

tarily, and had been in P.R. with some guy who wanted to set her up in "business," get her an apartment, and so on. "Well, that's your business. Mine is just making sure nothing happened to you that you didn't want to happen."

She laughed, "That bum thinks I'm going back and waste myself living on his truck-driver pay. I must have been crazy to marry him. I thought I was in love. When I think of the time and money I've spent . . ." I was putting my case folder away and the last phrase caught my interest. "What do you mean, money?"

"Are you kidding? It cost me over three thousand dollars just for these!" and she cupped her breasts up and forward and seemed to caress them lovingly.

"Whaaat . . . are you talking about?" I dropped my attaché case and sat down again. She was laughing and gay Danny was simpering.

It seems she was a he and had undergone two years of different operations to arrive at what she had. They'd implanted bags of silicone on her chest bones to make those interesting-looking mountains; they'd injected silicone into her hips and backside so they would lose their lean lanky male look and become rounded; she'd had a series of operations in India whereby they removed the penis, and then in subsequent surgery here in the States they'd created an artificial vagina. She had undergone massive hormone therapy to discourage facial hair growth, and extensive electrolysis to remove existing body hair. It had cost over ten thousand dollars, and she was sitting there saying, "I wonder if I did the right thing?"

I admitted to being completely fascinated and she went on freely discussing her personal life. She had been legally judged a female, and had in fact received a marriage license after a court battle and she and her husband had walked down the aisle and been married in a Catholic church. The bride wore white.

Sheila admitted being a prostitute after a series of operations, and bragged she'd made a fortune. "I couldn't keep up with them. The guys were anxious to pay a hundred dollars a pop because they were so damn curious just to see what I looked like and how it would be. I had a beautiful apartment and clothes and everything and then I had to meet this truck driver and I thought it was love, and then he asked me to marry him. I flipped out at the idea of doing the whole bit, wedding gown, bridesmaids, priest . . . I fell for it."

"Did he know about you, about the operations and all?"

"Sure, I told him and he said he didn't care, but not to tell his friends or his mother, that lazy bitch. It was all so romantic at first, we got a little apartment, three flights up. I stayed home and cooked and dusted while he worked . . . and now after a year I'm through watching him flop into a chair and guzzle beer in front of the television set. So I'm waking up. I tried it and it's not for me. This guy said he'll pay my rent in one of those apartment houses on the West Side and I can do what I like, he doesn't care if I hustle, as long as he can share the wealth."

Miss America got up to put the kettle on for more tea in a swing-and-sway strut that made me look like a block of cement. "That's it, lovey . . ." and she posed against the cabinet smiling. "All in all, they didn't do such a bad job, did they?" and she did a pirouette seeking approval and reassurance again.

"If you're happy with it, baby . . . 'cause you got it."

I marked time for a few years and tried to channel my interest and attention into school, home, travel, flag waving, apple pie, and mother. My negative feelings about promotion opportunities for women had been further re-enforced after being in Missing Persons for a while.

It was the first opening for a second-grade female in about two years, and every third-grade woman wanted it. I was no exception. God knows I was far from complacent, but when I started to review the applicants mentally, I figured that they couldn't overlook my arrest record, citations, and all that nonsense . . . especially since so many of them had said at different times, "If there was only an opening, I'd give you grade . . ."

The interview in the chief of detectives' office brought me to earth with a thud. The lieutenant seemed virtually indifferent as he ran down the list of questions, barely raising his eyes from the scrap paper he was doodling on.

When he got through taking the pedigree (name, shield, rank, assignment, date appointed, date promoted to grade, number of complaints, number of citations) he zoomed in on what was to be his big question, "How many arrests do you have for this year?"

"This year? You have me in the Missing Persons Unit, it's a non-arresting agency, how can I make any? I've tried . . ."

"Oh well, that's our criteria, the shield must be awarded for activity. We can't give someone a second-grade shield when they're in a unit like Missing Persons . . . we have to reward people for their zeal," and he got up.

I shook my head in disbelief. "Loo, I've been trying to get out of that squad from the day you transferred me in. You can put me in an arresting squad anytime you want. I relish the chance to get back to fieldwork.

"If you look at my record for any other year that I've been on this job, you're not going to find anyone else to beat me. How do you think I've gotten nine citations? And if you put me somewhere else, you'll get the same caliber work, I promise you."

He stood there with closed face and cold eyes and I knew before he said anything that a decision and a promise had already been made. "We'll keep you in mind, but as I said, the shield must go to whoever is putting forth the most activity. You'll hear from us."

I didn't . . . but I heard from everyone else in the office, about ten days later when I waltzed in. "Well, what do you think of Marcia beating you out?" . . . "Marcia said Kevin had promised her grade money, and he delivered!" . . . "My God, she acted like she was a princess before, now she'll think she's queen." They said a lot more nasties and felt like they were entitled. Some termed it sour grapes, but others felt it was deserved when promotions were given to those who were blatantly unentitled to them.

Marcia had come into Missing Persons with me, had no arrests nor any citations to my knowledge, but she was the "Comare" of the president of the Detectives' Endowment Association. She didn't try to be subtle about it, flaunting it like a white fox scarf. When a couple of the guys tried to congratulate her—"Hey, Marcia, Kevin came through for you, that's great!"—she lifted her head regally. "Kevin wanted to make me first-grade, but I said second was enough for now, I didn't want people to think I was a pig."

I didn't disappoint them when I reacted. "Marcia? *Marcia?* From here? From Missing Persons? Oh that quiff lieutenant . . . I should've known better. I don't even know why I bother anymore. Why the hell couldn't he be honest? . . . makes me go through the motions like a goddamn fool . . . and they got a goddamn contract in already. 'What have you done lately?' the bum says to me. 'I'm very sorry, but we have to give it to whoever is putting forth the most activity.' He meant to whoever is putting out, the creep son of a bitch. If I knew it would do any good, I'd go over and ask him to justify this promotion, but you know you'd never get to see anyone. Where did she get transferred to?"

"She's not going anywhere, she's staying right here in Missing Persons so she can be available for all those fancy organization affairs and host the brass and go on those vacations and tours and take the P.C. to dinner and all that there jazz. The Queen's not going anywhere she doesn't want to go."

By this time I figured I had given the guys their two cents' worth of excitement for the day and bottled up my feelings and zippered my mouth but not my mind. If I could only be commissioner for a week, I dreamed, I'd make some of these guys line up nude and tell them I was inspecting their equipment for advancement in grade. If sexuality was to be their yardstick for promotion, I'd tell them I'd have to see how they measured up. Let them cringe in disgust or mortification at my premise for promotion. I broke up laughing at my conjecturing.

In December we were blessed by having a lieutenant transferred in to fill a long-standing vacancy. When you got a new boss, everyone minded their p's and q's until they found out what kind of a person he was. What we heard that first week set everyone on edge. I had desk duty one evening and took a call from someone obviously under the affluence of incohol.

"Hey . . . you got our boy Quincy Churchman, ha? He's your boss, but he usta be our boss, right? He's there . . . permanent . . . right?"

"Do you mean Lieutenant Churchman? If you do, yes, he's been transferred into our squad. Who is this, anyway?"

"Ha-ha-ha . . . We're detectives from his old squad. I just wanted to tell you something about him. You know how some guys are on this job, they should have been priests, not cops.

Right? But not Churchman. No, sir! He should have been a *nun!* But lemme tell you, I want to tell you that we're having a party for him."

"Oh, well, let me take a message for him, I'm sure he'll be . . ."

"Lady . . . don't you dare. We're having the party because he's been transferred, and he sure as hell isn't invited. We just want to make sure there's no way he can get back. He's a bad-news guy, you watch him . . . tell your people. I felt I had to warn you. He had two cops locked up . . . I knew them . . . they hadn't done anything. He personally pressed charges against them. One guy committed suicide and the other one's in the booby hatch. Yeah, he's a real nice guy, and we're drinking to his rotten memory. Don't forget what I told you. Watch yourself. Good night, sweetheart."

This story made the rounds and was augmented with bits and pieces from other sources so that everyone was exhaling with disgust and apprehension waiting for the ogre to arrive.

Lieutenant Quincy Churchman slipped in quietly one morning disguised as a human being. He was about fifty-eight years old, with parchment-white skin and apple cheeks, and eyes so gray they were virtually colorless. He held his lips tightly pursed, and his white hair (no trace of previous color) was very short and just as tightly combed back. I glanced at him and saw a study in repression, everything was taut and restrained—his lips, his hair . . . his hands tightly clenched in front of him . . . even his walk, which was slightly pigeon-toed.

When he was safely ensconced, the office buzzed. All the gossip and stories made their rounds again.

"He studied to be a priest, but chickened out just before he was ordained." "I heard he did it to keep out of the service." "Yeah, then how come he never got married?" "I don't know but the guys say he's really creepy, they don't know what he is." "I heard that the last two or three places he worked, the guys signed petitions to get rid of him."

At that point the man of the hour emerged with a "grin" on his face. His lips were still pursed but somehow they were showing teeth, large white teeth in his white face, under his white hair. With his red cheeks and split red lips I thought he was going to make like Bugs Bunny and go hippy-hopping out of the office.

The captain walked out with him to the desk and introduced him to everyone who was there. He gave them all his tight tooth smile and repeated all the names, sometimes asking that they be spelled. Even the captain seemed uncomfortable.

The next time I saw him I was hung up in traction in the Hospital for Joint Diseases. The day before Christmas I was on my way into the office to turn in reports on some eighteen cases before going off on vacation. The East River Drive traffic was heavier than usual for ten in the morning, and I attributed it to the impending holidays. There was no way to make time, but this nudnick behind me didn't want to know that. I kept watching him in my rearview, and thinking that he spelled trouble. He was pushing a red Caddy and dressed real sharp, plaid overcoat and big shades, and kept racing his engine and then braking as he looked for any little hole to slip into and make time. "This bum looks like he's trying to get the work in, I'll bet he's a number runner or a book. The way he's pushing, he's going to ram somebody for sure."

He did. Me. He smashed into my rear; I went into the car in front of me. Then he got zonked again from the rear. The guy in the radio car who responded told me afterward that he was still there when they arrived, only because he couldn't get his car extracted from the fender sandwich. Otherwise he would have taken off.

My Christmas presents were a broken bone in the back of my neck, cervical sprain, concussion, and the inheriting of Lieutenant Churchman.

Maybe there's something about a helpless female strung up in traction, with weights suspended from here and there, or maybe he was doing his Christian duty; whatever it was he drove me nuts. I was pretty heavily sedated for pain, and would often doze off to awaken and find Churchman looking down at me. Now, if you start with surprise in traction, you'll end up with one leg six inches longer than the other.

I was a mess, hair couldn't be combed . . . no makeup and feeling miserable . . . I didn't want to see anyone. Yet every morning he'd be there with his smile and the New York *Times* and the *Daily News,* which I couldn't even pick up to read. We had nothing to talk about, even if I had felt like talking.

The longest conversation we had was when he came in one day with satisfaction smirking on his face. "Well, young lady, I decided to check out the criminal record of the driver who struck you and I must say that your instincts proved completely correct. He has a previous history of arrests for bookmaking and policy."

"Thanks, Loo, it was kind of you to take the trouble," while I chortled to myself, "Son of a gun, you haven't lost the old touch, kid."

He must have decided that this poor helpless female needed him. He started calling home to check on the children, offered to help them with marketing and to drive Cindy to the hospital if she needed transportation. They always declined (but politely). When Cin came to the hospital she asked how come he was calling the house every couple of days. Then I found out he was subtly interrogating her about our life-style. Do we go out to dinner often? Do we travel? Alone? Together? Do I have anyone to help me around the house? Do I like anyone in particular? What does she think of me? He had kept her on the phone for extended periods of time, and between politeness and awe at his being my "boss" she was constrained to answer.

"Can't you get him to stop calling, Mom? He makes me awfully nervous."

"Me too, baby, I keep telling him every day that my family has everything under control, that there's nothing I need or want, but it seems to slide off his back like water. I'll be home in a few days and then he won't have any excuse to call; just try to put up with it for a little while longer, okay?"

Maybe he didn't show up carrying the papers after I got home, but he managed to make his presence felt nonetheless. You never knew when he'd call, and it got to the point where everybody reacted whenever the phone rang, and none of us wanted to answer it. On the fifth or sixth ring someone would chicken out and pick it up in case it was the medical unit doing a house check.

I could tell by the frozen face when it was Churchman, and I would close my eyes wherever I sat, so they could say, "Mom dozed off," or I'd stumble into the bathroom—"Mom's in the bathroom now."

We solved it to a small degree when I hired a Spanish-speaking housekeeper who didn't know one blooming word of English. On

167

a piece of paper I had written phonetically, "Missi sliipin," and that's all you could get out of her. The trick was to pick up the extension phone at the same time and see if you wanted to speak to whoever had called.

So I started getting little notes:

Greetings and salutation,
Your beloved daughter had some wonderful things to say about her outstanding mother. It seems to me that with the halo you are wearing there will be no need for artificial illumination when you return to the office.

> Best of everything,
> Sincerely,
> Quincy Churchman

Det. Cirile . . .
Please!!! continue to refuse the Hollywood and Broadway contracts. Our department would never recover from your loss.

> Sincerely,

What made it absolutely wild was that they came in Police Department envelopes, with his two-inch-high flowing script:

Commissioner Marie T. Cirile
World's Most Beautiful and Photogenic Officer
oo Pennsylvania Avenue
Yonkers, New York 10707

Another beauty came addressed to:

Mrs. Universe of 1969

———

I returned to my work, filled with apprehension and forebodings which didn't last long, as they were very quickly replaced with the actual problems.

Of course, everybody else thought it was hysterical, and it became the major source of conversation. The office was split into three factions. Those who thought he was a religious fanatic who had gone overboard in doing his Christian duty; those who were convinced he was half a fag and couldn't quite assimilate what they saw; and then the group that thought him an old degenerate.

Everyone felt free to go into each other's boxes, where the new cases, telephone messages, and anything that came in for you since you were last there would wait for you. Never had a message box been checked with more regularity—by anybody and everybody. No wonder, with little gems like:

Princess Marie Terese,
It is with great appreciation and a deep sense of humility we are privileged to apprize you that in recognition of your outstanding performance of duty in the Dunckley case, you will be excused from all duty on Friday, August 29, and again on Saturday, August 30.

Gratefully,

Dear Marie,
All your office associates express their appreciation to you for your action in initiating repairs to the time machine. Many, many, many thanks.

He'd smother me with attention in the office, run over and remove my coat, shove a chair under my behind if I happened to be standing up and talking on the phone, mouthing, "Rest, you must rest!"

In addition to the notes, my box would be jammed with jokes he had cut out, articles he felt would interest me, clothing advertisements he felt I would like, and coupons like "Buy one hamburger, get a second free," "25¢ off on purchase of Nescafé," and comic strips for Jim.

I had innumerable cans of soda, containers of coffee, pieces of cakes and cookies pressed upon me, because he could tell I wasn't taking care of myself. I knew I was in for trouble when he walked across our three-hundred-foot expanse of office with that pigeon-toed walk and the way he had of having both hands sunken into his trouser pockets. The guys used to sit and wonder if he had any pockets, and just what he did inside those pants all day.

As he got closer the voices would zing me, "Oh, here comes Marie's boyfriend." "Woo woo, Churchman's a real lover boy." I never had this problem in my whole life. I could always turn a guy off . . . do it easy . . . do it hard, depending on the person; but this weirdo was a case unto himself.

There were two guys that brown-nosed him and were his favorites. One at a time when they displeased him he zonked 'em good. He had a cruel vicious streak running through him, barely covered by a veneer of pious Catholicism. And I know this medieval job . . . no one'll listen to you because he's a boss, he's a man, he studied to be a priest and that's the whole shmear. You're a loser. If I tell him it displeases me, I lose; if I let him go on, something's bound to happen, and I'll lose.

He was standing in front of me, with his hands in his pants, and with that smile. "How are you? How's Cindy? How's Jim? You're so blessed to have such fine children, but you must take care of yourself. You don't look like you've had enough sleep, are you all right? I called your home last night, but Jimmy told me you were out. I just happened to be in the neighborhood, and, uh, thought I'd drop in for coffee. Did you have a nice time? Oh, never mind . . . here, I have this for you." He pulled out a big green lollipop. I looked at it and at him. "Green, Jim's favorite color, he'll be so pleased. I'll save it for him and give it to him after dinner."

He snatched it up and snapped, "I didn't give it to you for Jim, I'll get you another if you want to take it home. This one is for you!" He smiled again and started to peel off the paper. "It's really very good for you, dextrose you know, you'll get energy. Now eat it, right now."

Never mind the ribbing and comments after that one. I survived by volunteering for any and all special assignments, garbage details, night duty, and anything that got me out of his clutches.

This pious man meanwhile attended mass every day, persuaded some of the men to go on retreats, and on Sundays would question to see if everyone had attended church.

One afternoon he asked me if I had ever considered working part-time. "You mean in addition to the PD job? I've got enough on my plate, Loo, I couldn't handle any more and do it justice. Between the house, the kids, the job, and school starting again in two weeks, that's enough for me to handle."

170

"That's why this job's perfect. It's temporary, you work by the hour whenever you can; the whole thing will only last a few weeks, so you'll only get a few days in anyway. With school starting soon, you probably could use the extra money to buy the children school clothes." That argument always made sense.

"Just what's it all about? What kind of work and where?"

He told about getting a call from a personal friend, a retired lieutenant and former squad commander, who'd opened up a private detective agency in the Wall Street area. The state had just passed a law compelling the fingerprinting of all employees in the stock market industry and given them about a month in which to comply. These large firms had given out the fingerprinting contracts to private agencies and they in turn were stuck with getting experienced people to do it for them. They turned to a ready source, police personnel.

"But, Loo, that's against department regulations. Our rules specifically state you can't be involved with detective agencies."

"Yes, you are absolutely right. In fact I questioned him myself on that point, and he assures me that he spoke to Deputy Commissioner Walsh and that they obtained special permission because of this new law that's been enacted. They're classifying it as clerical work and not investigative work, because all they want is to get the prints—you don't check them out, they'll go to the FBI for that. The pay is good, and as I mentioned, it's only for a few days. I wouldn't want to see you doing anything for much longer than that and risk your getting run-down. You're too important to Cindy and Jim, and of course the office, to get sick. We all want to see you happy and smiling."

Churchman called up his friend, made the connection, and I ended up working a total of four and a half days, in a period of about ten days. You earned your money—they just came at you, the lines never seemed to end. You stood there and rolled those prints and averaged about 100 to 125 a day, and that's a lot of printing.

Besides the monetary reward I garnered another accolade drawn up by the good lieutenant, which provided the office with their mirth for the week.

171

ACADEMY OF POLICE SCIENCE

1969 A.D.

TO OUR BELOVED PUBLIC:

BE IT KNOWN THAT THE HONORABLE MARIE TERESA CIRILE IS AWARDED THIS CERTIFICATE IN RECOGNITION OF HER HIGHLY PROFESSIONAL ACHIEVEMENTS IN THE FIELD OF FINGERPRINTING. IT IS AN HONOR FOR US TO COMMEND THIS YOUNG LADY TO YOU FOR OUTSTANDING PUBLIC SERVICE.

So much for fingerprinting, I thought, as I registered for the new fall program in John Jay and tried to figure a way to handle the "Churchman problem." It was really getting to me. He'd invite the children and me out to dinner, and I'd produce some excuse; then he'd go ahead and call home and invite the children directly to see if he could get confirmation or denial of the wedding or family affair that I'd probably manufactured. He'd ask Jim if he'd like to go to a movie and when he'd eagerly accept, would tell him to ask me if it was all right. Of course Jim couldn't understand why he couldn't go, and I'd have that problem to contend with.

I didn't want to go directly to the captain, so I figured I'd use the chain-of-command system. I went to the sergeant (who knew all the stories) and told him how I felt.

I found out afterward that he was the father of seven and that his wife was expecting again. The office swarmed with devout Catholics.

I asked him to either transfer me out or somehow get word to Churchman that he was making a jackass of himself.

The male confraternity closed ranks. The sergeant looked blank, forgetting how often he'd joined the laughter in the lunchroom. "The lieutenant? He's a very religious man; he's studied in the seminary, you know. He's a clean-living man, doesn't smoke or drink, has never been married; I've never known him to go out with a woman!"

"Then maybe he thinks I'm a guy, what can I tell you? I don't smoke or drink, but I'm not deaf, dumb, or blind either and I know when a guy's making a pass at me; the problem is, does he know what he's doing? I don't think I should have to take this from him just because he's my boss."

"Well, gee, Marie, I don't know what to do. After all, the lieutenant hasn't done anything, right? I think you'll be better off if you don't make any waves. Why look for trouble, you know what I mean. He'll get tired and it'll just blow away and nobody will get hurt."

"I wonder if you'd take that attitude if it was your wife he was hounding? Shoving lollipops and Tootsie Rolls into her mouth and calling your home at all hours to check up on what she was doing." He had the decency to blush, confessing, "Listen, I'm on the lieutenant's list and expect to be made in a few weeks. I can't take the chance of lousing it up!"

"Why didn't you say so, I could have saved my breath. You're the guy who doesn't want any waves."

So I had a heart-to-heart with Churchman, and told him I couldn't take the ridicule and jokes from the rest of the office. He was ready to fight them all, he wanted names, he would take care of them.

"No, that's not what I had in mind. I think perhaps if you treated me like everyone else, and didn't give me any 'preferential treatment,' the stories and laughter would die down. I'm sure you understand that a woman alone has to guard her reputation, Lieutenant."

"I didn't realize I was being an embarrassment to you, or rather that you felt that way about it. That's unfortunate . . . yes, very unfortunate." His face was tightly screwed up; even his cheeks were white.

The pendulum swung full tilt. The office wasn't laughing anymore, they were shaking their heads in collective sympathy at just what I knew was going to happen. I'd told everyone right along that he was irrational, and that if I'd told him "No thanks, I'm not really interested," to any of his offers he'd flip over and become an enemy.

Now he was busy giving me the shaft. Every extra detail was mine, and all of my cases were now rejected for various reasons ranging from punctuation to just "leave it open a while longer." I was still getting notes in my box but they were somewhat different in tone:

Det. Cirile—
Please leave a written report on my desk listing by date and giving in detail your efforts to locate the parents, relatives,

guardians, etc., of the four-year-old who is at the Children's Center. The time and date of the teletype message that was transmitted will be entered on this report.

In addition I am interested in knowing what investigative leads you are pursuing and your plans for a solution to this case.

Thank you
Lt. Churchman

In his desperate urge to crush me for rebuffing him, he unwittingly provided my escape. The Auto Squad was mired in stolen and confiscated cars. The newspapers had brought a lot of attention to the fact that the pounds contained thousands of cars that had been sitting there for months. Now they were attempting to do something about it and the Auto Squad was screaming for additional help. Missing Persons was told to donate three detectives on a temporary basis; Churchman picked two men and me.

Auto Squad

The Auto Squad sure did need help. The desks were piled high with cartons of paper work. The two fellas with me smiled happily, "Boy, this should be good for a couple of months before we have to go back to Missing People."

My happiest discovery was finding that Paul Reilly, one of the detectives I'd worked with in Safety Lock Company, was now one of the sergeants in Auto. Once you've worked together, there is always a common meeting ground. I respected Paul and always called him Sergeant Reilly, in the office or in front of any of the other detectives unless they happened to be personal friends. It wasn't a put-on, but an indication that I wasn't seeking to take advantage. This was considered police policy etiquette and therefore *de rigueur*.

Paul said they were drowning in paper work and cars and had to push the stuff out. I asked him if they could use a woman in the squad but he doubted if their lieutenant would buy it. I explained my eagerness to stay as long as possible and Paul, who was one of the most sympathetic of people, shook his head in disbelief. "You poor kid, whatayougotta put up with that for?"

"Paul, tell the lieutenant I'll make a deal with him. He told the guys this morning that this backlog will take about two months to clear up. Tell him I'll have it caught up inside of three weeks, if he'll give me a chance to work out in the field. He's got nothing to lose—if I don't convince him, or prove myself, 'cause we're only here on a telephone message anyway."

A couple of hours later I was inside talking to the "Dutchman," a tall, powerfully built man, good regular features, cold blue eyes, and a Nazi crew cut hairdo. He talked in a rapid-fire staccato

175

voice, and when he got excited he sounded like a burp gun. "Okay, then, what's this about you're interested in working in the field?" He was now brisk, efficient, and very U-boatish. "Y'have any idea what we do here? Y'know that it can be filthy as well as dangerous? Talk it over with the sergeant, and if y'still interested, and if they can think of some way of utilizing you, I'll give it a try; but don't forget you owe me production on the clerical end."

"It's a deal . . . and thank you."

The Auto Squad maintained automobile storage yards in each borough where all cars, trucks, and motorcycles that had been abandoned, were derelict, found after being stolen, confiscated in an arrest, held as evidence, or towed away, were taken. These pounds were glutted because we couldn't dispose of the vehicles —that would leave the city open to lawsuits. Each had to be examined individually in an attempt to identify the owner.

If the car had plates it could be fairly simple, but often the plates were taken from one car and put on another stolen car. The most accurate way to check was by the Vehicle Identification Number, which is stamped in a number of spots by the car manufacturer.

Professional car thieves replace the plastic plate in the front windshield and sand off the one on the engine block, but usually they don't bother to remove the hidden VIN number. We had books listing the various locations of these hidden digits, which differed with the make, model, and year; what they had in common was inaccessibility.

The car had to be raised and we had to lie or crawl underneath with a flashlight and clean off spots with sandpaper, hoping to come up with something. The whole thing was time-consuming and the stockpiles grew.

There were also valueless cars—burnouts, husks left after a fire, wrecks deserted by people too lazy to junk them, and stolen cars that'd been abandoned after being picked clean. We zeroed in on the fastest way of eliminating these gutted wrecks. With the lieutenant's blessing we went out to the pound and took Polaroid pictures of the "derelicts," as the best argument we could provide in favor of destroying them. We wore waterproof boots because there was always mush and puddles, and valueless baggy pants or overalls. I had a hat that covered all my hair, and good heavy gloves.

We also carried a blackjack, because the place crawled with rats—big ugly water rats over a foot long. As we approached the line of cars we clunked on the fenders and set off enough noise (we hoped) to send them flying. The guys permanently detailed to the pound said that every once in a while when the rats got too bold, approaching the trailer or refusing to be chased off, it would call for a practice session with their shooting irons. This would control them for a couple of weeks but never came close to solving the problem.

It was freezing, dirty, and I caught a miserable cold, but it was a lot of fun. I felt so great to be alive and doing something. I clambered over and between these derelicts to get good shots before we put the big X on their windshields okaying them for the crusher.

Herr Lieutenant was expansive, saying that he was considering requesting me as a permanent member. "I'm flattered, Loo, and of course that's what I was pushing for. I know it's not protocol to give stipulations but . . . I'll be glad to work here if you give me a partner and let me work like any of the other detectives. If you're figuring that you'll use me mostly for clerical and maybe once in a while on an investigation, then very frankly I wouldn't be interested."

"You're certainly honest and to the point. You think you could work on stolen car rings, and make arrests and handle investigations?"

"I don't claim to be a car maven, but I've seen a lot of guys who know less than me. And as far as the case load and arrests, that doesn't make me lose any sleep. Whenever you're new in a squad there's a certain breaking-in period and this one shouldn't be too different."

"Okay, Cirile, I'll go see the inspector."

I was really not too surprised when he told me, a few days later, that the inspector hadn't approved the transfer. It seems Lieutenant Churchman had asked for my return, claiming I was desperately needed and that they were shorthanded.

"But I went out on a limb telling the inspector how sharp y'are and what a waste to keep you downstairs. I said that y'had good info and were working on cases already and expected to make some collars. He was very interested; he wouldn't transfer you in, but he didn't order you back. You'll stay on a temporary assignment which lets Missing Persons think you're going back, but actually keeps you here. I'll give you a partner and y'see what y'can do, and then we'll hafta take it from there."

Which wasn't good, but wasn't all bad either . . . at least it was something to work for. I had managed to make a liaison with the Department of Motor Vehicles, which when combined with other information proved invaluable in coming up with people who had purchased stolen cars. This made it pretty easy to have a ready supply of partners willing to work with you. I didn't get to work with a steady partner because they were all assigned specific areas, and my information could be anywhere in the city. I'd just pick my team and ask them to work with me for a week or so.

It was working out beautifully and we were recovering stolen cars like mad. My recovery rate not only equaled any of the male detectives, but in most cases was much higher and my position became pretty well entrenched.

One of the messages I took while making a ring on August 24, 1970, asked me to see a Lieutenant Dumpson at the Department of Investigations, 111 John Street. Today, warning bells would start to bang and clang in the brain department but on that overly hot day, it was just one more humid stop to make.

"Lieutenant Dumpson, I'm Detective Cirile."

"Oh yes, officer, sit down."

"Can you tell me what this is all about, Lieutenant?"

"You mean you don't know?" he said incredulously. A stenographer carrying a speedwriting machine and a youngish wild-haired chap scurried in. The lieutenant cleared his throat nervously and the stenographer started recording. "Ah, I'm Lieutenant Dumpson of the Department of Investigations, would the rest of you please identify yourselves."

"I'm Frank Watson, stenographer." "Irving Kern, special prosecutor for the Department of Investigations." "Marie Cirile, detective, New York City Police Department."

I felt hackles growing up my spine, and every pore was oozing an eerie feeling of impending disaster. "Lieutenant, I want to know what I'm doing here."

"Detective Cirile, I, uh, hereby advise you that you have the right to remain silent, that you . . ." He put on his glasses and was reading from a prepared text.

"I don't understand. You sound like you're reading me my rights . . . what has that got to do with me? What's this all about?"

The prosecutor and the lieutenant exchanged glances and young Kern said, "I'm sure you know, officer, we've had forty others in your position here for questioning and you're probably aware of the scope of this investigation and should realize that you'd better co-operate with us."

(What in Christ's name is this all about? This has got to be a hallucination.)

"Mr. Kern, I don't know what the hell you're talking about. What I do know is that I'm entitled to this information."

"Officer," the lieutenant stepped into the breech, "your name has come up in a criminal investigation we're working on. We understand and have evidence that you did fingerprinting for the Double Crostic Detective Agency in violation of Police Department and possibly criminal laws."

I was dumbstruck as he went on. "We have over ninety members of the department involved so far and have interrogated forty of them. They've all agreed to sign admissions and co-operate, which is what we're asking of you."

"Fingerprinting? . . . big hotshot scandal . . . corruption . . . graft . . . you people are sick. You got some cops willing to break their behinds working a second job to *earn* money to bring home to their families and you're going to prosecute them? You should give them a goddamn medal for not taking a bribe or looking for an easy buck. You should try printing all day and see how easy it was to *earn* that money!"

"Strike that out," Mr. Kern snapped to the steno.

"You leave that in! I'm saying it and I want it to be part of the record. You keep a total record, not just what you cull, Mr. Kern. I want you to be able to read it back as I say it, not as you choose to hack it up. Working, the glorified capitalistic American birthright. It's become a crime now.

"For this, you're reading me my rights? You're looking to hang something on somebody, but it's not going to be me. I've seen too many of you 'special' prosecutors trying to make a name for yourselves on the gravestones of fallen cops, and I'm not going to lie down for you to crawl over me, Mr. Hotshot."

"Officer, you have the wrong attitude, we're here to help you. Just give us a statement, it will go no further. In fact I can assure you of a whitewash here. We started it, and have to go through it so we can mark it closed. I'm sure you understand, after all, aren't we really in the same field of work? Why should I look to hurt you?"

"I'd sure like to know. I've handled enough investigations to know that if I have a stenographer taking down every word and I read someone their rights, I intend to arrest them. So, Mr. Kern, can the bullshit. I'm not in the mood for it.

"If I recall, Lieutenant, I interrupted you while you were reading me my rights. Well, Mr. Prosecutor, and Lieutenant, under Part One of the Supreme Court decision we're all aware that I have the right to remain silent. I chose to exercise that right as well as the right to obtain counsel."

"Officer, that means making another trip down, when we can dispose of it now and you'll probably never hear of it again."

After being greeted with a lengthening silence, Mr. Kern said, "Well, what's your attorney's name and telephone number, I'll have to call him and arrange for a date this week."

"May I be excused?" I stumbled out, blinded by tears, looking for the elevator and found myself in a dead-end corridor. It seemed like too much, and I stood and bawled.

What had I done? What heinous crime had I committed? I worked for four and a half days, on my own off-duty time, with my commanding officer's permission and at his solicitation, and with the permission of the first deputy commissioner. I stood for hours with my legs crying to sit down, printing until the people blurred and I saw only fingers, to earn five dollars an hour.

Now, someone had decided that this was wrong. Coldly and callously fourteen years of good police work were dismissed and I was treated like a criminal. My rights! I was shaking with humiliation and anger. My dead end had me backed up to the entrance of the men's room and I looked at it dully, thinking, how appropriate.

"Officer . . . Detective . . . oh my, I don't want you to take it like this. There's nothing personal here you know. . . ."

I turned to the aspiring prosecutor. "Mr. Kern, go take a flying pee for yourself and leave me the hell alone." I took what was left of my dignity and drew it close like a tattered shawl but it didn't keep the wind from whistling through.

During the next few days I reached out for other people that had printed, and found that they'd all been assured that the work had been approved. Now they were told that the deputy commissioner had denied permission having been requested or issued. Most of them had worked for longer periods; my four and a half days was about the shortest they'd heard of.

The majority pleaded guilty and gave voluntary statements after conferring with lawyers from the line organizations (DEA, PBA) because of the department's proofs of guilt—canceled paychecks and no applications on file for moonlighting. Their reasoning was based on the verbal assurances they'd received that the commissioner was not looking to be punitive, and that the most anyone would get would be a reprimand.

I thought about copping out to save embarrassment. If I pleaded not guilty the case would go to departmental trial, which is nothing more than a kangaroo court. To me there was no alternative. I felt mentally and morally justified and couldn't give in without a fight.

While the case was waiting for a trial date I found out that over eighty men had pleaded guilty. Their cases were hanging fire awaiting the outcome of mine, and they were impatient with me for delaying what they thought would be a clerical reprimand.

I got my lawyer off the deck of his fifty-five-foot boat long enough to represent me at the trial. He might as well have stayed and basked in the sunshine for all the good it did me. When you find yourself talking to a group with downcast eyes, sneaking furtive glances at their watches while their impatient fingers nervously drum a tattoo, you know that you're not going to get very far. Courtroom rules don't apply . . . and when they state, "there is nothing that you can say that will refute this canceled check," they're telling you to close your attaché case and go away.

The upshot of it is that they threw me a bone. I was found not guilty on one specification (doing it maliciously) and guilty on two others, namely working, and working without official permission. It was now entered as an official complaint on my record and I was ironically fined four and a half days' loss of pay.

Unofficially my lawyer was told that they had to find me guilty because otherwise the other eighty men would all appeal their cases and they'd be swamped. Unbelievable. Most of the others involved who pleaded received five-day fines; I guess they gave me a half day's pay as a token of my defiance. My lawyer, so used to the criminal law system, couldn't get over their bureaucratic high-handedness. "It's like a mother killing her own offspring, it makes you sick."

We walked over to Ferraro's and drowned our sorrows in black espresso.

I was now back among the rats and the pigeons at the Fountain Avenue Pound. Of all the auto cemeteries, this one had to be rated as the choicest-smelling because it was kissing cousins with the Fountain Avenue garbage dump. You really took your chances out here when over a hundred pigeons took wing in lazy circles looking for a choice morsel and casually dropping the remains of their last one.

To add to the flora and fauna, the place also swarmed with packs of wild dogs. These were not your domesticated animal, they were closer to the coyote or wolf. They lived and bred among the acres of garbage; generation after generation without gentling or any touch of humanity. When they fought, they fought to the death with the others yapping discordantly about them.

They usually kept their distance, but if you had to pick up a car from a rear spot, you might have it ringed with eight or ten of these creatures, wild-eyed, filthy-looking, flinging themselves against the car with bared teeth and creating an unholy din. That would sober you up in a hurry. Discretion being what it is, I found it nobler to retreat. I understand, though, that the fellas occasionally conducted "birth control clinics" when they felt that the overpopulation was becoming a threat.

When the inspector was transferred everything hung in

midair until he was replaced by Captain Kissane. My last contact with him had been when he was a lieutenant and we were involved in the Union Square shooting. Now he was the commanding officer of Burglary Larceny Division, whose subunits were the Safe and Loft Unit, Property Recovery Unit, Auto Squad, Forgery Squad, and the Missing Persons Unit. That's a lot of units.

With Churchman gone from Missing Persons and a new boss upstairs, the lieutenant tried to get me permanently assigned to Auto. Kissane heard out his reasons. "I'll think about it for a few days. Is she down there now? Good, send her up, will you . . . let me talk to her."

"Marie, come in . . . sit down. . . . It's been awhile, hasn't it?"

"It sure has, Cap."

"I have a request here to assign you to Auto and I want to know why you want it, and if you want it, before I act on it."

"Cap, your question is a novelty in itself. I was going stir crazy in Missing Persons, and Auto was my only available out at the time." I gave him a capsule version of wanting Property Recovery, getting Missing People, and how I'd grabbed Auto to get away from it.

He sat there deep in thought. "Would you work on a special case now and then if it came up in Safe and Loft?"

"I'd jump at the chance."

"You know I've had the germ of an idea that is so alien to American police work, and yet so necessary, that it may form the nucleus of a whole new squad."

Interested? I panted waiting for his next words. Then I heard what I'd never expected to hear in a police office. "Marie, do you have any particular interest in art or in any of its ramifications?"

"Art? You did say art, Cap?" He just nodded. "Well, that's a new hairpin. I could be facetious and say, 'Of course, after all I'm Italian,' but you asked it straight. So let's see. I had a couple of college courses, the usual Art and Art History, and I think an afternoon in a museum is a treat and not a chore. I'm an antiques freak and collect silver, so I haunt auction sales, garage sales, and estate sales. I'm no genius but at least I know the difference between a Picasso and a Gainsborough."

"I know you're wondering about my question, Marie. Here's what I have in mind. I'm trying to get approval to start an Art

Squad. Scotland Yard has one, the French and Italian, in fact most of the European police departments, all have special units to handle crime in this area. Safe and Loft has uncovered seven art thefts over the past sixteen months and that was by practically stumbling over them. The guys didn't know what they had when they had it. This is what I'm trying to change."

"This is still the New York City Police Department? And I'm listening to a captain going out on a limb to initiate a squad because he foresees a need? This shows more perception than I've been exposed to for a mighty long time. Captain, I think at this point you could assign me to latrine duty and I'd smile and do it willingly."

He turned a little pink and started to stroke his new red moustache, then leaned forward conspiratorially. "Off the record, I've arranged for four people to attend special instruction in all phases of 'art' at Sotheby Parke-Bernet, one of the leading art auction houses in the world. They've agreed to train them and will have lectures, demonstrations, and visiting experts. It'll be full-time and last about a month and a half. What we're waiting for now is approval from Chief of Detectives Seedman, and I think the chief is inclined our way."

"Suppose I told you that I'd happily pay to attend this special course—would that answer your unasked question about whether I'd be interested? To me this is almost as good as first-grade money. Imagine being able to do police work surrounded by the world's art treasures. Cap, I'd love it."

"We'll have to sit tight and see what happens across the street . . . if all goes right we're in business."

I laughed quietly hugging a new secret as I went back to work.

A week or two later a notification signed by the chief of detectives came through that temporarily assigned me directly to Burglary Larceny Division to attend special training classes in art identification.

The Auto Squad boss had a fit. "BLD—what kind of shit is that? I'm the one who asked for you! I'm going up and see the captain right now."

"Uh . . . Loo . . . sit down a minute, will you, and let me try to explain this thing. You see . . ."

Assembled, we were a rather motley-looking crew as we prepared to storm the hallowed sanctuary of Sotheby Parke-Bernet in our quest for knowledge and culture. For six weeks we were to be classmates, and from there who knows?

Jack Armstrong, the All-American Boy, was there disguised as Sergeant Thomas Connolly of the Safe and Loft Squad. Tom is what every mother hopes her daughter will bring home—blond, blue-eyed, well built, clean-cut, teetering between conservatism and adventurousness, intelligent but quiet-spoken, loyal, and just disgustingly nice. I'd worked with him as a detective, and he hadn't changed much except to get a bit quieter, which I hadn't thought possible.

Peck's Bad Boy, also known as Jimmy Roberts, was a detective assigned to Safe and Loft. Jim ate and slept the job and often looked it. He was a great "more butter, more beer" man with a fluctuating weight problem that had him busting out of his clothes. Street sharp and with a hell of a lot of moxie, he wasn't afraid to speak his mind or take a stand if he felt justified. Dark hair and a babyish face probably led him to smoke the big pipe that he was always either cleaning, packing, or puffing.

An unknown quantity came into our midst as a last-minute replacement for a detective who was detailed out on sudden notice. Lieutenant Erasmo Germano was fiftyish, portly, and had never worked in the Detective Division before he made lieutenant. This made us dubious. The Detective Division is a very close coterie, and word-of-mouth recommendations are the quickest form of acceptance. In a unit where your partner is often responsible for your life, you just don't accept people all that readily. If nothing is known about your background or past performance, your co-workers usually adopt a wait-and-see, time-will-tell attitude.

Here we were the Police Department's answer to the art world's needs, knocking at the door of PB for them to ladle out knowledgeable largesse. We were given a grand-slam introduction to the staff and building by the impeccable Mr. Marion before being turned over to John Block, who would be our chief mentor and guide.

Here I expected some old fruity type with glasses hanging on a ribbon; who was riveted into his still starched white shirt with at least a hearing aid if not an ear trumpet, and instead darling John could well be one of Cindy's college friends. He had a large unruly shock of darkish blond hair, light blue eyes that peered earnestly at you through heavy shell glasses, and a complexion pink from skiing in Vermont. He was twenty-two but looked eighteen, when he allowed himself to be indiscreet enough to laugh out loud.

John had the responsibility for our entire training and planned an itinerary of visits and lectures to augment his own teaching. I was awed by the amount and variety of material stored in John's head. He knew a great deal about almost every facet of art from furniture to porcelains and was able to pick his way about skillfully in most areas.

We covered porcelains from Tang to Chin Lung, from Meissen to Limoges. In furniture we ranged from early American through the French cabinetmakers and all the English periods. We learned how to interpret the markings inscribed on silver and the phrases so dear to those who spieled the descriptions. After all, if a collector reported that a silver vase with repoussé chasing was missing, it behooved you to know that the silver motif was beaten from the inside out.

We explored Art Deco and what was to become one of my favorites—Art Nouveau, with its whiplash curves and emphasis on quality. I loved the curvilinear flow of growing things, the fluidity of water and hair.

We covered glass from Cameo to Lalique and Tiffany before we delved into Objets de Vertu, and in sculpture we flitted from Hellenistic Greek art to Alberto Giacometti and Henry Moore.

The Renaissance, Baroque, Impressionist, and Post-Impressionist painters gave way to the Nonrepresentational, Nonobjective, Cubists, and Modernists. In prints we learned of the varieties: lithographs, engravings, etchings, silk screens, woodcuts, linocuts, combinations, and drypoint.

What made it all fantastically interesting, besides the material itself, was that we were clued in as to how they approximated the value of each art work. How they determined its authenticity was another eye-opener. We also learned how furniture of a certain period was put together, and how to inspect a canvas for age and silver for fraudulent markings.

186

Under the guise of training our police team, John wangled special permission from the Metropolitan Museum of Art for us to go down to their special workrooms. No private citizen is allowed here. In fact it's off limits to most of the museum personnel. There's another special world down there under that big museum.

We saw one of the Empress Josephine's desks being taken apart for wood refinishing treatment. Each piece of ormolu had been removed, every wooden section laid aside like a giant jigsaw puzzle by loving hands.

In the fabric room they had swatches, centuries old, woven with fine metal and gems, worth hundreds and hundreds of dollars a yard and kept just to replace what might wear out on the museum pieces on display.

As a special treat one day we were allowed to go into the restoration room. They showed us how they were able to see if there was more than one painting on a particular canvas, and if there was, how they removed the top one without destroying the bottom. Then we were allowed into a really closed-off area.

One lonely soul was working, completely absorbed, sitting over a large wooden crate packed with a special excelsior in which sat a handful of pieces of pottery. He jumped up quickly when he heard us, almost shielding the contents from our physical presence.

He explained that he was restoring a Greek vase, a "Krater," from the eighth century B.C. The vase was about three to four feet tall with two handles and geometric designs. He had assembled it replacing the missing pieces with composition in order to better view where the remaining pieces belonged.

Jim meanwhile hauled out his trusty pipe, found it filled with old tobacco, and looked for a place to dump it. Well, where else but in this convenient vase . . . force of habit. Jim casually clunked his old oatburner on the edge of that twenty-eight-centuries-old vase. The curator almost had a heart attack as the vase did a crazy dance and four sets of hands reached out to grab and steady it. Jim whispered "Oh, Jesus Christ!" We led him, mummylike, out of the restoration room as we became personae non gratae and condemned his peace pipe to lower Siberia, for the duration.

We attended auctions at Sotheby Parke-Bernet and many exhibitions in other museums and galleries and suddenly we were ready for graduation. The Police Department's art identification experts . . . ta ta ta ta.

Well, we got our training, but the department hadn't as yet gone along with the idea of an Art Squad, so Captain Kissane assigned me temporarily to the Property Recovery Squad. Roberts and Sergeant Connolly went back to Safe and Loft. Lieutenant Germano returned to the Burglary Larceny main office where he had been before . . . and it was almost as if the training hadn't taken place.

I had vacation coming—two weeks—so I put in for them hoping the Art Team thing would be okayed in the meantime.

I filed my 49's and became a woman of leisure (ha!) as I did my Christmas shopping; put up the outdoor lights, the Christmas tree; assembled a three-story garage, with elevator, for Jim as well as an outdoor jungle gym; crammed for my finals; and wrote two end papers.

In mid-January I returned and was temporarily assigned to BLD again. This began a seesaw play that was to continue for some time. By the end of February 1972, I was back in the Property Recovery Squad, and starting to feel like a Yo-Yo. Though I was in PRS I was being forwarded all sorts of art complaints that were begging for attention, and I was trying to serve two masters.

On March 15 I proudly made my first art arrest. It sure wasn't any big hullabaloo, but it was a start. I recovered a five-inch-high glossy red Tiffany vase that had been stolen from the New York Coliseum Antiques Show, and was valued at about $3,500. The owner, who had circulated photos from his home in Cleveland, Ohio, was unbelievably happy, I was happy, the prisoner was not happy.

I had promised to take the children away during Easter vacation, so Jimmy, Cin, and I were in Eastern's wings of man on our way down to sunny Puerto Rico.

I came back with a whale of a suntan and it was business at the same old stand, but with a new twist. I tried to do a sort of public relations job for both the department and—particularly—

the Art Squad. I told everyone that touched the field in any way about the people the department had trained, that we were open to any complaints or information, and that we'd be glad to help them in any way we could.

The shopkeepers and gallery owners were astounded. They said that they'd often felt that they were without any representation whatsoever. Everywhere I garnered stories of con jobs, deceits, outright thefts, forgeries, and substitutions. The field opened up like a hothouse plant upon exposure. I left the PRS and BLD phone numbers, figuring, let the cases come in and prove the need for the squad. I was trying to create "friends" who would tell me what was happening in the field.

Two weeks were spent planting seeds while still having to do routine Property Recovery Squad inspections. I had my assigned area as well as that of the adjoining sector to cover because that detective was on vacation. It was a pretty big nut to chew. I was working alone and the PRS area ran from East Fifty-ninth Street up through Harlem to the Triboro Bridge.

I made a Harlem stop and was scrambling back to art country when I got zonked driving on the East River Drive. This character in front of me jammed on his brakes as he came abreast of an exit; he'd overshot his turn and braked before he realized he couldn't make it.

I leaned on my brakes and came to a screeching halt, almost kissing his bumper. Just as I took in a deep breath, sighing with relief thinking, Boy, what a close call, I got clobbered from behind by another car.

Sayonara Charlie . . . I was taken to the Hospital for Joint Diseases and admitted through their emergency room with a severe brain concussion and sprain of the neck and back. I was there for a week, feeling as miserable as one could feel, but just grateful that Lieutenant Churchman hadn't heard about it this time.

I was kept pretty much sedated, as it seemed to hurt to do almost everything that needed doing. I pressed to get home early, thinking that if I was to feel that gross, at least I wouldn't have someone waking me at five in the morning to ask if I was feeling that way.

The fellas started calling to say that the Art Squad idea was catching hold. Complaints and information were coming in and the media were calling with inquiries and requests for interviews. They knew that I would start chafing at the bit and hoped to give me a goal to aim for.

The end of May I learned that we had acquired a new detective, transferred directly to Burglary Larceny just to work with Art. He was Robert Volpe, with a background in the Narcotics Squad and the PC's office. He was also an artist who had had one-man shows and received critical acclaim.

Captain Kissane told me that Volpe and I would comprise the Art Identification Team working through BLD and we could reach out for Jimmy Roberts and Tom Connolly in Safe and Loft when necessary. It was enough to drive you nuts. Six months I waited for this and now it came through when I still found it hard to clear the fog from my brain and manage my equilibrium.

The next week I spoke to the captain again and he asked when I could get back to work, that the Art Team was really percolating and needed setting up. In addition he wanted me to go out to New Jersey with them to check out a new system of registration for the identification of works of art that was supposed to be akin to fingerprinting.

My doctor said it was too soon to jump into a full-time schedule, but I figured this art bit had such potential I couldn't let it get away from me. So I told the Cap, "Okay, you win, strap me back in harness. I'll call Jimmy and make arrangements for this Jersey trip."

On the trip to Jersey, Jimmy told me that he and our new team member Bobby had started to set up a file system. They'd established contacts with the FBI and Interpol and things were rolling.

"Jimmy, why in blazes don't you and Tom work this thing with us? You both were in on the ground floor and the way things are snowballing we have a tiger by the tail. We could have a hell of a thing here. Can you imagine if they make us an actual squad and put Tom in charge, we could turn this town upside down."

"Listen, Marie, I like this stuff, but Safe and Loft was my first love. I'll help out any chance I get, but I don't want to transfer over. Besides, I'm on the sergeant's list and if I get made they'll automatically transfer me anyway, so what's the use of two moves?"

"I guess you're right. Say, listen, what's this kid like, this Volpe? What do you know about him?"

"Bobby? Well, he's different, I'll tell you that much. He seems like a nice guy. You know he paints? But you'll see him soon enough."

Bob Volpe looked like a little kid dressed up for graduation, with his chocolate brown slacks and shirt and brown-and-white sport jacket. His light blue eyes missed nothing as they darted around, and his light brown wavy hair was cut long, styled around his face and down to the collar. The most outstanding feature, which had to be of fairly recent vintage since it was fingered so often and lingeringly, was a bold, prospering handlebar moustache, its turned-up ends lovingly touched with a bit of moustache wax. I smiled inwardly thinking of about eight thousand bosses who would rise in collective foment and force him to conform to their plastic image. I could see that there was a lot more here than met the eye, as I said, "So you're the guy who's been bugging me to get back, eh?"

"And you're my missing partner, boy am I glad to see you. Hey, I'm so sick of hearing, 'Well, maybe when Marie gets back,' maybe now we can actually see where we're at, and where we'd like to go."

Then the three of us went on to the International Art Registry, Ltd., where we got a demonstration of their patented process of coding two- and three-dimensional works of art for positive identification.

The amount of mail and interdepartmental communiqués that had accumulated in the six weeks I was out amazed me. Other police departments were asking for information about the Art Squad, and wanted to know if they could send personnel into New York to be similarly trained.

Circulars and wanted posters for lost and stolen works of art came in from Interpol and other agencies. Private citizens also wrote in, sometimes complaining of things that had been missing for many years.

It was evident that we had a massive amount of paper work on our hands, as well as a get-acquainted program that I had worked out with Bob. We spent two days running to Sotheby

Parke-Bernet and some of the other leading galleries that had promised us co-operation, and attended an auction. Bobby and I were building a tremendous rapport with the art community and establishing our lines of communication, but most importantly we were letting people know we were there. We even surprised ourselves as we garnered information and expertise, set up our files, and put in a request for an itemized art reference library. We got requests to address press groups, associations of insurance adjusters and dealers' leagues, but put them off for a while as we scrambled about, getting acquainted with our people.

I began to realize that the art field is especially receptive to crime for various reasons. In the first place, a collector of, say, Russian enamels, can be so into his collection that the monetary value is completely secondary. Acquisitions are his prime concern. He must have the pieces he wants—so that he and only he has them! This type of person would buy a stolen Rubens or Rembrandt knowing that he could never display it or ever hope to resell it. He'd be content to keep it in a hidden spot for his own enjoyment.

When someone like this is the victim of a burglary the pattern is different from that of an ordinary theft. The collector wants *his* things. Period. If he thinks he stands a chance of getting them back without the police, he won't file a report, or he will deliberately distort the facts. A collector may traffic with anyone in an attempt to ransom back a lifetime's accumulation, sometimes willing to pay as much as the market value to get *his* things back.

In some of the galleries I visited I found prints kept in open bins on a second-floor balcony with no one in attendance. One could riffle through Mirós or Picassos valued at from four to twelve thousand dollars each and roll one up and secrete it unobserved.

Some private collectors certainly had larger and more extensive collections than many of the commercial shops and their security might consist of a large overfed German shepherd.

What had really surprised me was that thefts in the art world had reached such epidemic proportions that worldwide associations had taken note and made attempts to curb and regulate the field.

1. November 14, 1970—UNESCO passed a treaty prohibiting and preventing the illicit import, export, and transfer of ownership of cultural property. It called for establishing a list of important public and private cultural property and giving appropriate publicity to the disappearance of any of these items.

2. June 5, 1972—*U.S. News & World Report* published an article entitled "Why Art Treasures Are a Growing Target of Thieves," subtitled, "Worldwide market in stolen paintings and sculpture is booming. One effect: Organized crime is now moving in."

3. August 11, 1972—the United States Senate gave its advice and consent to the U.S. accession of the UNESCO treaty for the purpose of curbing the international trade of stolen art objects.

4. The 40th General Assembly meeting of INTERPOL called for increased activity on their part to combat thefts of cultural property by publishing special issues dealing with the most wanted stolen works of art.

It was easy to see why when we researched the crimes and saw the amounts involved:

May 1972—$3,000,000 worth of art—just two paintings—stolen from a church in Italy.

May 19, 1972—a $200,000 painting was taken from the Paris Opéra Museum.

June 1972—The Woolworth mansion in Maine was relieved of fifty-one works of art valued in the hundreds of thousands of dollars.

September 1972—$400,000 worth of paintings stolen from Gallery Tamenza in Paris.

September 1972—Museum of Fine Arts in Montreal was burglarized to the tune of at least $2,000,000.

These facts and figures were just smidges but enough for us to know that our little Art Identification Team was created out of a *need*. A need to protect those art collectors and dealers that were being victimized by a new breed of "thief."

Art thieves have achieved status within the crime community and are envied by the common "goon." They've almost managed to straddle the fence between the bad guys and the good guys;

after all, how can you be all bad when you appreciate and value a Raphael—even if you had to steal it.

Yes, it was clear that organized crime had discovered art. It was a heck of an investment, a wonderful hedge against inflation, and the return was infinitely better than fencing hot jewelry.

A call from our counterpart at the FBI art unit brought us to his office, where we heard about a complaint he'd received from the Museum of Modern Art about losing prints from their print room.

The FBI determined that it wasn't in their jurisdiction, suggested our team, and volunteered to pass on their findings to us.

We checked the print room at the museum and realized how vulnerable the prints were to theft. It's much easier to steal a print than a painting, because paintings are usually in heavy, elaborate frames in guarded galleries, whereas the prints are most often stored in rooms that are more library-like. The print room is open by appointment, and the visitor can request to see any particular artist's work or works. They're usually brought to him at a large table and he's given all the time he wishes to study them at his leisure.

Interviews at the museum confirmed the losses, and an inventory was in progress. Just on a hunch we visited the print room at the New York Public Library and asked if they'd suffered any losses. They were startled but promised to check and give us a fast rundown. Within three days we got our answer. . . . Yes, they had losses.

Following up on what seemed like an emerging pattern, we went to the print room at the Metropolitan Museum of Art and asked our same question. The horrified curator seemed to take it as a personal affront as she drew herself up, "No, we have had no losses."

We checked out the admitting system while we were there and found it substantially the same as at the other print rooms. An appointment had to be made in advance, although it could be done by telephone. The subject signed in and out of the room and had to obtain a special pass if he was carrying a package.

Back to Modern we went, checking the appointment book and compiling frequency statistics. Narrowing it down to three names, we started researching them. The first thing we did was ask the employees in the print room if they remembered anything in particular about these people.

Almost to a woman they remembered one of them because he was "brassy," "pushy," "arrogant," and "demanding." One young lady said he was "overfriendly," called them by their first names (which he knew from their desk signs), and "always tried to take advantage."

Now we gave them a job to do. Check out the boxes of prints that he had looked at and see if there were any losses, and if so, compile them. Our job was checking him out. To our surprise we found that Theodore Donson, our male white thirty-four-year-old, was a practicing attorney working for a New York City law firm.

At the New York Public Library Mr. Donson was also well known. The girls in the print room remembered him because he was always asking them out to lunch and soliciting special attention and favors. We assigned them the same job as we did Modern—trying to compile loss sheets.

The Metropolitan Museum was somewhat thrown when we asked them if Donson had been a frequent visitor there. Offhandedly the curator stated that the name was unfamiliar to her. Very casually we mentioned the losses suffered by Modern and the library and the coincidence of Donson visits and suggested that they look into their records.

Late that afternoon as we were sitting in the office typing out reports, we got a frantic call from the Met print room. "Oh my God, we do have losses . . . and Donson has been in and out of the place at will . . . and the print girls all know him. . . ."

"Try to draw up a list of things that are missing, but more importantly, at this point we must stress the need for internal security. I know the most important thing to you and the other museums is the recovery of your art work, and that's what we're working on. This story is not to be given out, not even an inkling. You're to handle the checking and listing discreetly so that we can attempt to catch Mr. Donson in the act if he is our thief, as we suspect.

"Now, when Donson seeks an appointment we want you to give it to him. Then call us immediately so we can set up coverage."

There was a long-drawn-out sigh. I could almost see her face reflecting the emotions in her voice . . . her sacrosanct chamber of the arts invaded by the alien police hordes.

"You realize of course that our print room as well as the other museum and library print rooms are closed for August and will reopen after Labor Day?"

Everybody was placed on standby alert as the New York art world slumbered away the hot month of August. We figured this was an ideal time for us to go on vacation for two weeks also. After Labor Day the galleries would blossom with their fall showings and the auction world would reopen, museums would put on special exhibitions, and art would be born again, one more year.

However, as things happen in this crazy job, our mentor, chief advocate, and troubleshooter, Captain Kissane, was arbitrarily transferred to Brooklyn instead of being promoted to inspector, and Chief Seedman, who'd approved our existence, resigned from the department. We were suddenly surrounded by new bosses that looked at us as if we'd crawled out from under a rock. Art Squad? What the hell is an Art Squad, I never heard of that in a police department!

In less than a week under the new regime the Art Team was transferred into the Property Recovery Squad and told to continue to work our art cases along with the regularly assigned work.

To make for more irony, *Newsday* applied to our public relations office and received permission to do an in-depth study article on the team for their weekend magazine section.

Amei Wallach, their cultural affairs specialist, was shocked to find that we didn't even own a desk or a telephone to call our own. "Amei, we're fighting for survival," I told her, and Bob chimes in, "They don't call what we do police work. They say, 'What the hell do you do all day? Walk around in the museums looking at pictures?'"

Amei deliberately sought out the bosses for their reactions, asking Sergeant O'Hooligan why he'd gotten the new unit. "I guess they're under me because we supervise secondhand dealers and pawnbrokers. Most art people are secondhand dealers. Paintings are a secondhand commodity."

"Do you think the Art Team's work is important, Sergeant?"

"Apparently the Police Department thinks it's important," he said, then added quickly, "so I guess I do too."

The atmosphere was far from conducive to growth. In fact we were actually harassed and hampered. Every time we got located anywhere to work on an investigation and would make our compulsory call into the office we'd get a forthwith, which meant we'd have to abandon everything and see what was wanted. There was usually nothing to see. We'd get into the office to find the sergeant gone and a message to wait. So we'd sit and vegetate. Chances are he wouldn't get back and if he did, would say, "Oh, never mind."

Every day we'd hear, "Hey, Volpe, I want you to get a haircut, and that moustache has to come off. You can't come here dressed like that. You look like a goddamned hippie." No matter how we tried to explain that when we wore our jeans and sneaks we were "blending" and being accepted and getting work done, it was like talking to a blank wall. That part wasn't too bad for me, because I had a reputation as a clothes horse in the job. If I had a chance, I loved to dress up, but by like token if I had a chance to dress down I relished that also.

But poor Bobby was strictly a nonconformist artist. I think he started putting Vigaro on his moustache to encourage the growth after they threatened him with transfer if he didn't get it taken off.

We were persona non grata in the squad. The word was put out by the sergeant that we weren't to be trusted because Bobby was a spy planted by the PC's office. He even went so far as to call a special office meeting (we were the only ones excluded) in which everyone was warned not to talk to us.

We begged him to get us transferred out or to let us seek an umbrella elsewhere, but he said it wouldn't "look good."

This was the fomenting atmosphere surrounding us when we decided to try to take our vacations. We were turned down, even though we told him about Donson and the galleries closing. "You can't go together. I don't care who goes, but it's only one of you."

We thought it ended when I took the third week in August and Bobby took the last week and the first in September. We found out afterward that Sergeant O'Hooligan had told the deputy, with a wink and a knowing leer, how he'd spiked our efforts to go on vacation "together"! Sicko . . . I know this job if nothing else. No one outside it can realize how much can be done to slaughter another person without saying one word: a certain look, a nodding smirk, or a rolling of the eyeballs can bury someone's career.

On the Friday of my week's vacation at about a quarter to five in the afternoon, I got a call from an "informant" that I hadn't heard from in several years. He'd seen a recent news article about the Art Team and realized that I was still around. Was I interested in some hot information? "Sure, why not, what's it involve?"

"Have you read today's *News?* Well, turn to page ten and you'll see an advertisement for information about a hijacked load of hosiery. The company is offering a five-hundred-dollar reward and the FBI is carrying the case. I know who's got it . . . are you interested and can you handle it?"

"Wow, sounds like old times. Listen, just stand by, I'm gonna have to get some clearance on this. I'm home on vacation and this boss I'm working with is a real pip. Let me try to get him, maybe I can talk him to death. You hang loose."

I called Property Recovery but got no answer since it was after five and they're a nine-to-five squad. I contacted Burglary Larceny, which supervised the PRU and spoke to the deputy outlining what'd occurred. He asked how good the information was and, from past experience, I was able to say, "The best."

The deputy said he was going to speak to the chief and would call me back. "Christ, this thing is building up like a pyramid," I thought, remembering the good old days when a call like that would send us flying to get our hands on the stuff before it disappeared completely.

On the return call I was told that I'd be recalled from vacation and temporarily assigned to work with the Safe and Loft Squad on this case, but that the chief's questions had stressed, "Isn't she on vacation now? How come she's getting involved in this? And why didn't she go through regular channels and get her sergeant's approval first?"

I was beginning to wonder why I was bothering myself, when he told me to expect a call from a lieutenant in Safe and Loft, and to work it out with him.

When the call came through and after the information was re-hashed, I was told to report to their office on Monday morning because "nothing much was probably going to happen over the weekend." I was going to tell him that I never found a crook with nine-to-five hours, but I was beginning to get the feeling that I was being treated with bemused tolerance, especially when he volunteered to take the information and work it since he was sure that I didn't want to come in off my vacation.

His attitude reflected his feelings that I must be weird when I said, "No good, I want to follow this through myself. It's my information and my responsibility."

By Monday I knew that the shipment consisted of 308 cartons, 7,445 dozen or 89,340 pairs of hose valued at $3.50 apiece, with a total value of about $80,000. I knew where it came from and where it had been headed.

The lieutenant in Safe and Loft finally assigned a team to work with me mid-Monday. Some of the guys I knew took me aside and told me to watch my step; that the fellas they'd assigned me were both under an investigative cloud. "Hey, Marie, these guys know their days are numbered and they're not going to be out there looking to play cops and robbers."

"Oh, for heaven's sakes, you pulling my leg? What the hell did he give them to me for?"

They gave strained polite laughter. "Marie, he doesn't like you . . ."

"Doesn't like me! I don't even know the man. I never saw him before a few hours ago. What is there to like? Let him turn it over to somebody else who'll be glad to get their hands on this information."

"Off the record, Marie, he got a call from Sergeant O'Hooligan, who gave him a song and dance about your going over his head. In fact he insinuated that you made up the information to get off vacation, because you couldn't go with Volpe. You should have seen the lieutenant's face. It got brick red . . . I thought he was having an apoplectic fit. Then he said that he'd take care of you. Y'see what you're up against."

"That son of a bitching sergeant! Does this whole crappy department suddenly revolve around him? He's got everybody bull-shitted with his silver mines and his important friends and how he's worth three million, give or take a nickel. I don't think the bum's got a pot to put it in. If he did, what the hell's he staying on this job for after twenty-five years, free office and secretarial services for his business? Why the hell doesn't he go scootch one of his girl friends and get off my back, because I've like had it with him!"

They were right. Monday became a holding operation. Tuesday morning I spoke to the informant and found that the stuff had gone over the weekend for fifty cents a pair. He was upset and asked why the hell we sat on the information, after all he'd hoped to garner the five-hundred-dollar reward money when we recovered the property.

I apologized. What else could I do?

"Well, I'll try you one more time. I've been offered four million pills. They want thirty-five thousand dollars for the load."

"What are they?"

"I don't know what they are, but he said it was called something like 'nurnel.'"

"Let me see what I can find out. I'm on my way to the office now and I'll get busy on the horn."

I called a pharmaceutical laboratory and found that there was a birth control pill called Norinyl manufactured in Palo Alto, California, and that the firm had suffered a loss of seven drums containing 4,200,000 tablets. The FBI and the Treasury had all the details on the case. I conferred and both were extremely interested, so I promised to keep them informed and reach out for them if I needed them.

I tried to keep the informant appeased by telling him that I was trying to convince the deputy to let one of the Safety Lock guys pose as buyer.

"I've got an even better one for you. I have somebody else who wants to buy the pills. I'm going to try to set it up between these guys, that way you can step in clear and get them both buying and selling."

"Hey, wow, that's fantastic. We'll have bad guys coming and going, and won't have to worry about the detective being made. That's too much . . . stay cool, baby, I'll be in touch."

Wednesday morning I met the informant and he had good news. The mark had agreed to the price quoted for the pills and told him to set it up. He would get back to me with the time, place, and details.

At approximately eleven-fifteen that same morning, after sitting around for more than an hour waiting for the lieutenant, he came over and very brusquely said, "This office is discontinuing this investigation due to its lack of activity."

"Lack of activity! We just lost a load of hijacked stockings because we weren't fast enough and now we have a load of stolen pills. I've got a buyer and a seller and it's being set up right now. Where's the inactivity? If every case was this inactive this department would be in good shape."

"As far as I'm concerned it shows lack of activity," he said snottily. "I suggest that you give the information to your own immediate supervisor for redirection. That's where you should have gone with it in the first place, miss."

I looked at him with venom, thinking, "You crummy bastard, you let yourself be used and can't see what's under your goddamn nose."

He could probably feel my ire as he hastily threw out, "You are returned to your command."

"Sir," I said, dripping sarcasm, "need I say it's been an experience working with you."

I returned to my command all right. I was in that office, which was about five blocks away, by eleven-forty because I was looking to punch this sergeant right in the face. He had stymied my entire police career, first with his little innuendos that Bobby and I were "too friendly," chopping down my efforts in the Art Team, and now actually stopping my case work in Safe and Loft. I had never been smirked at or had my work denigrated and I wasn't about to let it start now.

The squad member doing day duty said he'd gone out to lunch, so I started knocking out reports and getting all my information down on record. The day wore on and he didn't return. One of the fellas brought me in a sandwich because I wouldn't chance missing him by going out. I stayed there until six-thirty, but he never showed.

The next morning I was still trying to see the elusive boss of Property Recovery. A call came in with a forthwith for me to report to the inspector's office and they notified him that I was there. Since his office was one flight down, I got there in about thirty seconds. With a face as long as the door, he said, "I'm going to have to issue you a complaint. . . . I just got a call from the chief's office and he's furious."

"May I ask what I've done?" I said dispiritedly.

"Lieutenant Dim of Safe and Loft states that you were unaccounted for yesterday after he dismissed you and ordered you back to your command. You were supposed to come back to Property Recovery, Marie. The chief was livid; this lieutenant has him all charged up. Where were you? Can you give any reasonable excuse that they might consider?"

"Inspector, I don't have to invent an excuse. I tell you this is the straw that breaks me. I've had it, and it's got to stop right here." The inspector almost flinched with surprise at my intensity. "This is a deliberate cold-blooded attempt to set me up. Only they're so stupid they didn't double-check the facts before they went out on a limb. I'm going to tell you what happened yesterday, Inspector, and then you're going to have to listen to me tell you a long sad story of harassment and abuse that's finally ended in this attempted frame. I want a transfer, I can't work under this man any longer, and you'll see why.

"From just past eleven-thirty in the morning until six-thirty at night yesterday, I was one flight over your head, just where I was ordered. I sat in that office waiting for Sergeant O'Hooligan all day."

He was visibly startled. "Can you prove that? Was anyone in the office?"

"Inspector, I signed in . . . I'm in the day book. Look in his basket, I must have turned in over twenty reports including a report on the Safe and Loft case. And the office was jammed. First there's the guy on desk duty, and then there were about five or six of the men getting their reports up to date. I never left the place, in fact Monahan brought me up a sandwich and coffee."

He picked up the phone and dialed our extension. "This is the inspector. Is Monahan there? Tell him to come down to my office and to bring the day book." A few minutes later an apprehensive Monahan stood at the door looking from the inspector to me. "Monahan, I understand you were in the office yesterday. Did you see Detective Cirile, and if so, what time was it?" The poor guy was on the spot. He didn't know what the inspector was after, but he had no alternative but to answer.

"Yes, Inspector, I saw her. We were all catching up on reports. I'm not too sure of the time but it was early afternoon, I think."

"Thank you, Monahan, you can go now. Just leave the book here." He started thumbing through and located the entries. "Yes, you signed in at 1140 hours and out at 1830 hours, which certainly confirms what you said." There was a knock on the door and Monahan reappeared.

"Excuse me, Inspector, but I just remembered. . . . I bought Marie a ham and cheese hero yesterday and I didn't go out until about two o'clock and I know she was around for a couple of hours before that and . . ."

"That's okay, Monahan, thanks. I think we can straighten this out. It's just a misunderstanding."

When he left I asked the inspector if he could transfer the Art Squad to someone who could visualize us as an asset or, failing that, to transfer me to another squad. We talked for over two hours and he was more than receptive—he was normal and even nice. He told me to sit tight as he had to see the chief, explain the circumstances, and get him to agree that a complaint was unfounded.

Several days later I heard that the S&L lieutenant had been reamed by the chief for making him look like a fool. The inspector checked things out, but the lieutenant admitted that he'd never verified my return to command. He'd based his actions solely on a conversation with the sergeant in which he stated that he'd returned me. The sergeant, who was calling from God knows what restaurant, said that he hadn't seen me. So the lieutenant figured now he had me, and took it upon himself to become the sergeant's avenging angel. They should have gotten a complaint for impeding a police investigation, dereliction of duty, harassment, and false official declarations.

But that wouldn't happen because they'd never give justification to a subordinate at the expense of making the brass look bad. It wouldn't be good for "discipline."

In a follow-up conversation with the inspector, I was assured that he'd have a long talk with the sergeant and that in the future I could feel free to come to him directly with our problems. I figured this to be a temporary standoff, a holding maneuver. Let's face it though, a dying man, or woman even, will grab at straws.

On Tuesday September 5, the day after Labor Day, I got a message from the Metropolitan Museum of Art print room that Donson had made an appointment to view prints. He would be there at one o'clock that afternoon and every other day that week. I urged them to let Donson keep the appointments and assured them that I'd arrange coverage. The powers decided that since Bobby was on vacation and notice short, they'd utilize Jimmy Roberts and Sergeant Connolly from Safe and Loft.

The three of us hightailed it over to the museum print room and set up shop. There was a door with a small center glass panel that led to the print storage room. We covered the glass with cardboard leaving just a peephole for Jimmy, who would stay inside peering out into the viewing room. Tom Connolly and I were going to chance it at the tables examining prints.

I took a seat on the far side of a corner table, requesting and getting several boxes of Henri de Toulouse-Lautrec to busy myself with. Tom, in a blue worsted jacket and an aura of being ill-at-ease, established himself across the room. Most of the staff had been made aware of our presence and urged to conduct "business as usual," except for the receptionist, who'd been asked to notify us when he signed in.

Shortly after two I felt him coming into the print room. I got goose bumps on top of my goose bumps as I saw this really very ordinary-looking thirty-four-year-old bloke smiling up at the sign-in girl. He was about 5'9", 180 pounds, and a bit bulgy in the midriff area. Very curly dark hair grew onto his collar, and shaggy sideburns framed his face. He had brown eyes, a rather large nose, and a somewhat unkempt-looking moustache. A gray glen plaid suit hung somewhat baggily around his white shirt with wide red stripes and a blue tie. You'd think he was a friend of the family's as he stood chatting, causing people to look up from their viewing at the distraction.

The receptionist left the front desk and came by, hissing sotto voce, "That's him, that's him," and continued on by.

Donson left the desk carrying several parcel-like packages, approached the viewing area, and looked everyone over. Then, making a decision, he strode over and took a seat opposite me. I gave him a vaguely irritated look at the interruption and continued taking notes from the piles of research material and prints I had surrounded myself with.

He started to make himself at home, swinging a portfolio about the size of a desk blotter onto the table and placing what appeared to be a sealed brown-paper-covered parcel alongside the table. The size of this package was interesting. Bigger than the portfolio, but less than half an inch wide, it could easily pass for a packaged painting.

After telling a print girl what he'd like to view, he began shifting through notes and papers and what appeared to be several prints he'd brought in with him. When the girl gave him the cartons of prints, he sorted and shifted and piled and repiled. He used the files and cross-indexes and then requested a book to cross-reference. He'd return a batch of prints, request additional ones, and be up and down like a blooming Yo-Yo.

After about two hours he seemed to be settling down. I saw him slip an index card into his portfolio and make an erasure on one of the museum's prints. He kept holding the print up comparing it with the catalog's description; finally he removed it from its mat and placed it over the ones he had in his portfolio while I watched intensely.

"Oh, you're not supposed to do that. That's against the museum rules," one of the print girls said in hushed horrified tones, as she hastily placed the print back in its mat.

"Oh, sorry, I didn't realize. I was comparing it and took it out to get a closer look. I'm finished with these anyway, will you bring me Picasso prints size III and IV?"

I winced, knowing that the day was shot down and so were we. After a few cursory glances at the Picasso prints, Mr. Donson packed up and fled like a bird.

"What spooked him?" Tom had joined Jimmy after about an hour because he felt that he was getting too many of Donson's glances. "You wouldn't believe . . ." We walked over to the young lady who was sitting there with her head in her hands. As we approached she burst out, "I'm sorry. I'm truly sorry. It just came out automatically. I knew it was wrong as I said it, but I couldn't stop and I've ruined everything for you. When he took that print

out and picked it up in his hands . . . all sweaty and ooooh . . ."
She started nervously biting her nails.

"Hey, take it easy, there's no sense having a heart attack over it. Let's just hope that he has the nerve to keep his next appointment. Tomorrow, though, you'll play it our way. If he comes, everyone make themselves scarce. Keep a girl at the desk, but everyone else is to stay away from the print tables. I'm going to give him so much rope he can tie up his own birthday present. If he doesn't bite then, we'll know it's a big waste of time. Okay? Now you can start worrying about tomorrow instead of what happened today. By the way, is he allowed to bring in those things that he carried?"

"Well, he's allowed to bring in his portfolio and he had a pass from the main desk to carry in a sealed package."

"Hm, just curious. Listen, it's almost closing time. Go home, take a long soak, relax, give yourself a manicure, and tomorrow take a tranquilizer before you come to work. Things'll work out, you'll see."

In the A.M. I became "different." First of all I wore a pants suit because I had on a dress the day before. I figured he might be a leg freak. Sometimes a guy won't remember what your features are like, but he'll recall that portion of your anatomy that he's got a fixation on. Anyway, I covered the legs.

I'd worn my long hair down yesterday, so now I covered it with a short brown wig and put on a special pair of glasses that I'd had made with lenses of clear glass. I changed the color tone of all my makeup and altered the shape of my eyebrows and lips. I especially changed the color of my nail polish and put on an engagement and wedding ring. With all those hours of glancing over, God knows what details he might've observed.

When I walked into the Safety Lock Company the detective at the desk looked up, "Yes, can I help you?"

"Frank," I laughed, "you don't know it, but you already have!"

I sat and watched the clock, but nothing happened. My meet with Sergeant Connolly was set for eleven-thirty in order to cover Donson's one o'clock appointment. But a team in Queens had called in for the sergeant earlier that morning and he'd gone out there. At twelve-thirty I stopped pacing and got ready to leave. "When you hear from Sergeant Connolly, tell him that I've gone to the museum. He'll know what it's about."

"Why don't you hold on? We've got to hear from that Queens crew soon."

"Can't do it. This guy is overripe. Too many people around the museums and libraries know we're interested in him and it's only a question of how long before he knows also. Just can't take a chance on blowing it."

At the museum I had to reintroduce myself and then reinforce the previous day's request to keep busy or get lost. I chose the same table as yesterday, but today I took the front seat that Donson had occupied the day before. This way I had my back to the print room. Pop art, my very unfavorite, was my choice for today's viewing. I wanted to make sure I wasn't going to be intrigued by anything I was looking at.

Donson came, right on schedule, and signed in. I could hear his voice. I glanced and saw he had the same portfolio and package that he'd carried the previous day. As he came into the viewing area his footsteps died. I knew he was looking around. The footsteps started, the sound got closer, and then he sat down in the chair directly next to me.

"Unbelievable," I thought. "Yesterday our papers and eyeballs were mingling, today our elbows will be kissing."

He went into the same bit as on the previous day, but with time he got bolder. When he was on his fifth or sixth box of prints I hoped that Judy, who was servicing him, remembered I told her to count them before she brought them to him and immediately afterward, and to make note of any losses.

Donson had now erased the accession number on one of the prints and was continuing his shuffle or comparison with the book's description. He put it down, picked up another print, and examined that; picked up one of the prints he brought with him and examined that under his magnifying glass. Then he dropped that over the whole thing and went to the files. I saw him remove a file card and return to his seat, where he pitched it into his portfolio. "Son of a gun," I thought, "this guy's a beaut. No wonder they didn't know if they had losses. How can they, he not only steals their prints, he takes their files. How can they see if anything's missing when the listing's removed. To compound the felony he's erasing the accession numbers on the prints and any other identifying marks; once they're gone the museums will have a problem knowing and proving that it's their copy of that print."

As I was thinking this, he was busily erasing more of the penciled numbers on another print. "Time is running out," I thought, and called Judy over.

"Will you get this box for me?" I said, and handed her a note asking her to call Sergeant Connolly. She came back with a box of prints and a note saying that the office hadn't heard from him as yet.

"Okay, kid," I said to me, "you're on your own. It's four o'clock and they close at five, so things'll have to move." And they did. Another file card went from the cabinet into the portfolio.

A tiny razor blade, the kind used in injector razors, was suddenly in his hands and very casually he managed to reach over and cut along the top of the wrapped parcel he had leaning against the desk. A few deft shuffles and elaborate wavings with the magnifying glass, and the two prints that he'd erased the numbers from were slipped into this manila package. Then he took a pencil out of his pocket; but it was no ordinary pencil. It had Scotch tape wrapped around it like a roll. He removed the tape and sealed the package containing the two prints. He had a pass reading "sealed package" to come in, and by cracky, he'd be going out with a sealed package also.

When they announced that the print room would close in fifteen minutes, he picked up speed. He kept consulting little slips of paper and I swore he had taken prearranged orders. In the final box he seemed to find what he was looking for and got busy with his eraser removing the marks from the engraving.

"The print room is closing, please return everything in their proper boxes. The print room is closing," announced Judy.

Donson started to put things back and to pack up, only he managed to shuffle the last engraving under some papers in his portfolio. That made three. Boy, if he could knock off three a day, this guy could open up his own museum soon.

I got up to leave first so he wouldn't think he was being followed. Passing the files, I saw a funny face hiding behind them. It was Tom Connolly of the Royal Mounted . . . getting there in the nick of time.

I walked out, beckoning with my eyes. Outside the door and behind a statue, "Tom, he's got them. I saw him take three. They're in his things and he should be coming out right now."

A very nervous Donson, now that he was out of the insular lining of the print room, eyes darting wildly about, made his way down the long corridor before he reached the huge marble stairs leading to the main floor.

"Are you sure now? He's got the stuff on him?" asked Tom.

"Tom, I'm taking him. I was going to step into him before you got here and if we don't move we're going to lose him." With that impetus we both took off down the elongated hallway to the head of the stairs which gave a clear view.

Donson was already midway down the massive marble steps and making time; this was no casual exit. Tom and I looked at each other and made tracks. Suddenly it was a chase scene. It was so out of place people stopped to stare. The echo of those hurried scrambled steps made a deafening crescendo. The sound reached Donson, who quickened his pace. When he reached the base, he acted like a real pro. Instead of turning, he made an abrupt stop at the water fountain, bending to get a look at what was behind him. When he saw two bodies coming for him, he did a sudden about-face, abandoning his idea of going out the front door, and headed for the side.

"Tom, he wants to play games."

"You're right, let's take him now." We broke into an open trot, got him from both sides, and announced, "Police! Let's go to the security room, we'd like to ask you a few questions."

He was a little green around the gills but still cocky as he claimed he had permission to remove the prints. So the print curator was called down and said no one ever had permission to remove prints. Period. Then he agreed that he might have inadvertently mixed up some of the museum's property with his own and reached in and removed two sixteenth-century old master woodcuts by Hendrik Goltzius, "Landscape," and "Landscape with a Shepherd," and a sixteenth-century engraving by Israhel Van Meckenem, "Panel of Ornament with Dance of Lovers." He reclosed his folio, straightened his tie, and brazened, "I guess you've no further need for me, so I'll leave now."

"Mr. Donson, I don't think you're quite aware of the seriousness of your position."

"How do you know my name? You never asked me."

"Theodore Donson, you live in Irvington, and you're a member of the bar. Right?" The air escaped from Donson like from a punctured balloon and he reached out shakily to hold onto the desk.

"As a practicing attorney may I assume you are familiar with your rights under the *Miranda v. Arizona* decision, or do you want us to spell them out?"

"No, no, it's . . . I . . . oh God! . . . yes, of course I know my rights, but I've given you back the museum's prints."

"Donson, we're not museum security. We've been working on you for months, and I've been watching you for two days straight. So far we want you for losses here, the library, and Modern Art, and we're just scratching the surface. You know, it'll go a lot easier with you if you return some of the things that you've stolen. The museums are primarily interested in getting back their art work. Now you know we can hit your house and office with search warrants and God knows what we'll come up with. But that'd be doing it the hard way. All your neighbors and friends will be aware of it, and it won't do you much good at the office either. Or we can do it easy: Give us a list of what you have and what you've disposed of and we can take it from there."

Donson had been sitting there with his head in his hands listening and nodding. "I just don't know what's best. I don't know what to do. Let me talk it over with my lawyer first."

The Central Park Precinct, usually overrun with squirrels and nuts, was mobbed with newspaper reporters and photographers as we booked Ted Donson for grand larceny–art, burglar's tools, and altering business records.

Among the things entered as evidence was Donson's unique "booster box." These boxes, usually the tool of a good shoplifter, appear to be wrapped packages or boxes, but are contrived in some way to open so that stolen merchandise can be quickly shoved in. Donson's box consisted of two large flat pieces of corrugated cardboard cut larger than desk-blotter size and wrapped up in brown wrapping paper with all the edges fastened with Scotch tape.

In checking out his background I found he'd been convicted two years before of trying to sell the personal letters of Mrs. Aristotle Onassis. These letters had been written by Jacqueline Kennedy to former Deputy Defense Director Roswell Gilpatric. Gilpatric said that they'd been stolen from his locked office files.

Donson, who worked in Gilpatric's law firm at the time, claimed that he'd received the "Dear Ros" letters in the mail and offered them to an autograph dealer who placed them up for sale. With the ensuing publicity and Gilpatric's statement that they'd been stolen, the dealer removed them from the market.

Donson pleaded guilty to keeping property which "he did not have permission or authority to take, possess, or use." That seemed to be the story of his life.

Donson was flabbergasted at the amount of press coverage he received in both TV and the press. "Donson, you can forget about ever moving another piece of art. You're so hot you couldn't sell anyone a two-cent stamp with a bill of sale. You won't even be able to hang anything on your own walls, besides your children's drawings, without your friends or neighbors giving it the eye.

"Every museum, gallery, and private agency is going to go crazy now inventorying. We've notified Interpol, the FBI will be here this morning to interview you . . . forget it, you're shot down. You remember all those nice trips you made to Switzerland? You know those nice auctions and art sales in Zurich where you did your wheeling and dealing? Memories, my friend . . . just memories.

"That's why I tell you, whatever you got stashed away you ought to turn in. 'Cause if we get to it first, we'll zing you on each and every count, but if the museums get it they'll be ready to make peace. You keep thinking about it."

In court, much to our disgust he was released without bail, because he was a member of the bar and therefore (ha) a reliable member of the community. This spiked our effort to get an immediate search warrant. The assistant district attorney said, "He's on his way home. By the time we finish the paper work and get a judge to sign it, the stuff'll be gone."

We weren't about to let things end here, though, and sure enough by "strange coincidence" the museum got an anonymous phone call several days later telling them to watch for two keys in the mail that would open coin lockers in Grand Central Station. They came and we set up a "stakeout" in Grand Central in case someone wanted to add, subtract, or just check on. Jimmy Roberts, Tom Connolly, and Bobby (who was back from vacation and fuming mad because he hadn't been called in for the "big caper" that we had worked on for so long) and I sweated it out.

Finally we gave up and opened the lockers, and found one large package and three smaller ones. They were handled carefully to preserve any prints and brought to Safe and Loft. The peeling-painted office started to take on beauty as we spread out forty-five works of art valued at a minimum of $200,000.

There were four rare books and forty-one prints, engravings, woodcuts, and etchings. Among the artists represented in the haul were such European and American masters as Henri Matisse, Jean Dubuffet, Edgar Degas, Mary Cassatt, Odilon Redon, Joan Miró, Lionel Feininger, Toulouse-Lautrec, Francisco Goya, Emil Nolde, Edvard Munch, and Hans Holbein; there were also numerous Japanese prints by Utamaro, Choki, and Sharaku.

As the word got out the New York art world all hoped to get back whatever they were missing, and we clocked over fifty inquiries in three hours. We displayed the prints on the desk tops as well as we could and the cameras and TV men zoomed in on them. I began to feel like Old Mother Hubbard as I flitted around saying, "Don't touch that, please don't pick that up"; and answering questions from some of the regular men assigned to SLATS who asked, "Is that stuff really worth money? You mean some people would hang it in their living rooms? What the hell is this? Ugh," as they picked up Redon's "The Spider" or Munch's "Vampire."

"Honest, fellas, would you take my word for its being worth more than a load of hijacked cigarettes!"

Within twenty-four hours we knew that twenty-six of the prints and books belonged to the Museum of Modern Art, ten to the Metropolitan Museum of Art, and nine to the New York Public Library.

When Paul Richard, the knowledgeable columnist from the Washington *Post*, contacted Donson that day and asked him of his connection with the art return he was told, "on advice of counsel, I decline comment."

But things started rolling. Within days a plain brown-paper-covered parcel arrived at the Cooper-Hewitt Museum without a return address. Between stiff pieces of cardboard it contained a valuable Rembrandt etching that had been missing for five years.

The Library of Congress got one of the brown paper packages, containing a dozen prints by Dürer, Schongauer, Mary Cassatt, Rembrandt, and other famous masters that they hadn't even known were missing! Another package was mailed to the National Gallery of Art, with prints missing from Alverthorpe, a private museum in Philadelphia that now houses the Gallery's invaluable print collection.

One museum man described the mysterious returning of missing prints to the country's most important libraries, galleries, and museums as a "blizzard of goodies."

The Brooklyn Museum got back their nineteenth-century Degas lithograph, Yale University their Dürer print "Adam and Eve." Two Rembrandt etchings were returned to Associated American Artists, a commercial gallery that had listed Donson as a customer. Parke-Bernet recovered two Rembrandts as well.

They were coming in thick and fast. It was interesting that Donson was known at the museums and galleries that recovered prints, as a dealer as well as a private collector.

There had been a tremendous amount of interest generated by the museum arrest as people became aware of the Art Team. Bobby and I were asked to appear on "Midday Live," "Chris Kelly Presents," and the "John Bartholomew Tucker Show." He got a little miffed when I was singled out to do "What's My Line."

The Museum of Modern Art wrote a two-page letter of commendation and thanks to the Police Commissioner for our "diligent and imaginative work," and for "displaying extraordinary resourcefulness, discretion, and devotion to duty. . . . Thanks to their special training in the field of fine arts, as well as their specialized knowledge of the art world, all three detectives were quick to understand the problems involved in the case and to conceive almost intuitively the mode of their solution. . . . Their handling of the case has been a credit not only to themselves but to the Police Department, and I would like to take this opportunity to commend the department itself for its vision in establishing and specially training the Art Identification Unit. . . ."

Now, you don't often have someone go out of their way to say thank you, and a pat on the back sometimes is what keeps you going, so it would have been nice to have known about it. The Police Commissioner acknowledged the letter to the museum's director. "Thank you for your thoughtful letter of September 20, commending Detectives Marie Cirile, James Roberts, and Robert Volpe for their assistance and co-operation.

"I shall be pleased to convey your warm expressions to these officers and to their superiors, and I am sure they will be pleased to learn of your kindness."

By accident several months later, one of the museum's employees happened to mention how pleased the director had been that the commissioner had acknowledged his letter. We had several exchanges of, "Letter? What letter?" before he brought out copies, which we photostated, and that was how we got our news, despite the fact that the immediate supervisor is responsible for issuing copies of all commendatory letters.

Donson placed himself under private psychiatric care and on November 8, 1973, he pleaded to criminal possession of stolen property and was given five years on probation with the stipulation that he continue psychiatric treatment. As a result of the felony conviction, he was disbarred.

The museums and other places of public exhibit took a good long look at themselves and revamped their filing systems and methods of cataloging, improved their security systems, and in some cases even installed elaborate electronic equipment.

Bob and I didn't have to do much in the way of "hard sell" anymore. Most places greeted us with, "Oh, we've heard all about you and wondered when you'd get around to us." Places that cringed at the thought of police sought us out.

Including the mighty Met. The director wrote the commissioner about a special exhibition—Arts and Crafts from the Soviet Union. It was to be placed on view for about two and a half weeks as part of the Cultural Exchange Program arranged by the State Department.

This exhibition had toured other cities in the United States and efforts had already been made to destroy it. New York was the final viewing before the exhibit returned to the Soviet Union and it was felt that this might serve as added impetus to groups like the Jewish Defense League and other anti-Soviet organizations.

The museum held a high-powered conference with their officers and security people present, as well as representatives from the State Department, the FBI, and the Police Department, not to mention the Art Team, and arrived at the security methods and amount of coverage that would be needed—from outside uniformed men to bomb squad inspections—and it was put into the works.

Bob and I graduated from the Keystone Kop Kartoon Klub when we received heavy parchment envelopes that held a darned impressive-looking invitation. It was about ten inches wide with posh engraving and most cordially begged us to appear at an invitational preview of the Soviet Exhibit and reception, where the guests of honor would be the Russian delegates and the ambassadors to the United Nations. It was to be held in the museum at 9 P.M. and was to be a formal affair.

I must admit to having really looked forward to it. I couldn't imagine a social affair being held in the museum, but I did know one thing, they wouldn't be able to say they invited "à la Tradition" cops. I had a gown that I'd been saving for about three months, waiting for enough nerve and the right time and place to mobilize it for action. It came from Carnaby Street in London and I'd fallen in love with it. I bought it somewhat defiantly, telling myself, "Someday you'll *need* this." It was stark white and made of a silky-finish nylon knit.

Bobby and I'd agreed to meet for cocktails in the Carlyle so that he and his friend could meet my date and the ice would be broken before we did our thing at the Met. With the introductions I slipped off my coat, and Bob exploded, "Jesus Christ! Have I been working with that all these months?" We laughed and went on to the Met.

In the reception line I found myself being presented to the director, Thomas Hoving. "This is Detective Marie Cirile of the New York City Police Department." "Detective Cirile, this is indeed a pleasure. The museum is indebted to you and I'm pleased to be able to personally thank you for your work in our behalf. Now I'd like you to meet His Excellency Alexis Borodin and . . ."

Acknowledging this with a smile and a handshake, I was aware that my date was, with a helpless look, being introduced as Mr. Cirile while Bobby looked on laughingly.

That was the beginning, but by the end of the evening, I decided that someday I would have a monster party in this museum setting. It was a mixmaster blend for perfection. Paintings and statuary that defied time and stylish periods; masterful flower displays that pleased the eyes and the nose; music that soothed the ear and musicians that seemed unobtrusive, nearly hidden beneath the tapestries. It was a far cry from the jungle outside, and I truly loved this fantasy land.

By evening's end I had a lot of new friends, had shaken up a few old ones who'd never seen me socially, had acquired an orchid for my décolleté, and was rudely aware that we were due back at the museum at 9 A.M. to start our coverage of the Russian exhibit.

The museum's regular habitués were in for a change of pace. They had to thread their way through the large complement of uniformed police, as well as those mounted on horseback, to enter. Once in, they found themselves under the scrutiny of closed-circuit television.

The museum's uniformed security guards were conspicuously present as a deterrent and special cordoned areaways were established to control the ebb and flow of visitors. Detectives mingled freely to no one's awareness. I was the only female assigned and anytime anyone had someone who seemed the least bit "unusual, offbeat, odd, or suspicious," I'd get a call on my beeper and would tail them for their museum stay or until my suspicions were allayed. I walked so many miles on those marble floors some days, I felt like a piece of the statuary.

To get into the actual Soviet exhibit area, the men had to submit to a frisk and the women had their purses checked. I think if most of them had any idea of what the exhibit consisted of they wouldn't have bothered going through the trouble of going in. I found it sadly disappointing. Most of the contemporary items seemed comparable to what was available in our local five-and-dimes.

The exhibition was rigidly controlled. Except for demonstrations that were limited to the outside, and several people who had to be ejected, it was subdued, low-keyed, and regulated.

One afternoon, shortly after five, my beeper summoned me to a phone call from my FBI counterpart. "Listen, can you get away? We just heard that the Blank Gallery on Fifth has a bad Bierstadt. We're going up, so if you can meet us it'd be great. We don't know if it's our jurisdiction, or yours if there's no interstate angle."

"Sounds good. The museum's closing, so I'll meet you there in fifteen to twenty minutes. Bobby's at the Bronx DA's office this week, but I'll call him there."

"Meet you down there in twenty minutes" was all he said, and it released both of us to travel.

At the Gallery we found the painting in question and got a pretty flimsy story as to how it was obtained. It was the old "man off the street selling his inheritance" bit. We gave the owner the benefit of the doubt, however, when he said that he'd asked for identification and been shown a driver's license. This didn't mitigate the fact that seventy-five dollars had been paid for a painting that any gallery employee would know was worth about three thousand.

A fast check of the driver's license address with telephone information showed a listing in Queens, so Bobby and I decided to follow up on it. The painting, which had been reported stolen from an uptown gallery, was removed as evidence, and the nervous owner was told not to contact anyone since we'd find out about it anyway.

At the Queens address we interrupted two gay boys partying. Their simple explanation was that they'd been burglarized a year before and the license had been among the papers taken. A check with the precinct verified this and they were off the hook. Now we knew that whoever stole the painting was walking around with stolen ID as well. We left at about nine o'clock, and called in to the Crime Prevention office, which superseded us, to sign us out in their book so we'd be on record.

People are always wondering why you can't find a cop when you need one, and what had happened to incentive, motivation, honest pride in doing your job. I can answer for myself in my job: It was killed by merciless pounding administered in varying degrees until I could no longer judge the severity. Then a pause, and when I raised my head again, the whole learning process was reinforced with another bruise on the head.

We got ours the next day! Sergeant O'Hooligan gave us the works. "Why did you take it upon yourself to do anything without permission?"

"Sarge, I had no choice. The office was closed; whom could I ask? I wasn't going to go through that BLD bit again, and this wouldn't hold."

"You were assigned to the museum, not anything else."

"I'd finished my tour at the museum when this thing came up from the FBI."

"Yeah, that's another thing. Why did he call you?"

"Because we're the Art Team, remember? There isn't anybody else in the city. Who's he going to call, Narcotics?"

"I don't care. I don't like it. I don't want any working on your own. I want to know what's going on. You should've waited until some other time."

"Sarge, the guy's not going to sit on a hot oil. You've got to move on it as soon as the word's out. For heaven's sakes, you should know that. It's our case. It's Art Squad work and I wasn't going to let it go down the drain. Do you know how hard we worked to build up these contacts? We can't let them fall by the wayside through default."

"Yeah, another funny thing. How come you got Volpe up from the DA's office. I notice he came flying up for this one, but every time I reach out for him there they tell me they can't let him go."

"Listen, Sarge, Volpe was finished with his day's work. I should think you'd be thrilled . . . you know, dedicated staff working on their off hours to stem crime and all that jazz. Boy, I remember when I had bosses that hollered, 'Nobody punches a time clock around this office, when we have a case it's all signals "go."'"

"Listen, I put you up in the museum, that's where I want you. Volpe's in the Bronx, that's where I want him. That's it. I don't want any more of this monkey business going on behind my back. I don't trust anyone willing to work on their own time. It makes me wonder about their reasons. What's their interest? What's in it for them?"

"Well, Sarge, if you ask me, which I'm sure you won't, I'd say that's a damn unhealthy attitude. In fact, it's not even worth debating with you. After all, everybody knows I'm independently wealthy! What's important is, what's going to happen to the art cases? This museum bit is supposed to go on for about two and a half weeks, are we just supposed to let everything slough off or what?"

"Listen, I don't want this headache with you two. You want to be independent, you think you're your own bosses, well you just keep it up. I'm telling you that you're assigned to the museum."

"Yes, mein herr."

"What did you say?"

"I said I better get over there."

This could only happen in the Police Department, I thought. The P.C. himself sends letters commending us. I haven't even had time to acknowledge a request from the Voice of America for an interview; publications like *Art Gallery Magazine, Saturday Review of Art*, and the *Times* magazine section, with almost worldwide circulation, clamoring for interviews, recognizing our work, and a lowly sergeant, one step removed from a uniformed patrolman in the precious "chain of command" of this pyramid-type empire, can sit on your head like a chicken hiding an egg.

Grousing and bitching, I fumed my days away in my marble mausoleum. The office didn't like it too much either because they had to send up a replacement while Bob was assigned in the Bronx. Everyone got it in rotation, a day apiece. Some enjoyed it. Some looked around and asked, "Jesus Christ, what the hell am I supposed to do here? This place gives me the creeps."

I hadn't been feeling like myself for several months, in fact since the accident, but I didn't dare take the time out to do anything about it since Sergeant O'Hooligan had again declared open season on the Art Team. I figured we'd be either past tense or relegated to patrolling the Prospect Park reservoir if I didn't stand there, cudgel in hand, beating its antagonists off. I was disgusted. If he was looking for it, it was only a question of time before he caught me doing "something" and could give me a complaint. Just as in civilian life, you could hardly go through a day without breaking some minor infraction comparable to jaywalking, spitting on the sidewalk, smoking on the subway, littering, or not curbing your dog.

In the department, rules cover you from eating to defecating. You have to make an entry in your memo book before going off post, whether it's stopping for a soda or finding a place to pee. Can you see a good police officer taking time out to make so-called proper entries after someone has dashed up to him, "Officer, officer, there's a man with a gun in the check-cashing place on the corner!" That's why some good cops go dead—fear of a "shoofly" boss whose job it is to issue complaints, not to make arrests.

The sergeant was trying to take care of me in his own way. He monitored my every move. The fellas warned me to watch out, that he was poking and prying and looking to get me. "Let 'im look! It's probably the only work he's done in years."

But despite my flippancy it got to me. When I responded to what appeared to be my eighty-ninth uncalled-for forthwith, I had to retaliate. "Sarge, why don't you get off my back? What do you want from me? Twice you've done your damnedest to hurt me and got caught yourself; I'm not going to sit still while you try it again. If you're looking to set me up out in the field, I'll report into this office and just sit here from nine to five."

The answer to this set me back in time about fifteen years. I was assigned to guard a material witness who was being housed in a hotel right near the United Nations. Chaperone for the male detective who was actually the guard was really more like it.

Sonia Mendez and her two children Jaime, seven, and Carmen, five; Joe, the male detective; and I lived in the 3½-room suite. I always thought these details were a farce until one night, at about three in the morning, Sonia tiptoed out of her bedroom wearing a pair of see-through baby dolls and called me into the kitchenette.

"Maria, *parece cansado,* you look so tired. Why you no go lie in my room and sleep. You know there are two beds in there. Go, go sleep."

"Sonia, thanks, but I'm okay, really."

"Maria, listen, I love that Joe . . . he is beautiful, no? Maria, I have not had a man in two weeks. I have the hots for him. I hurt inside, it's been so long." She clutched her vaginal area. "You sleep, I'm going to make love to him, *es muy simpático.*"

"Sonia, Sonia. . . . Ha-ha, you're joking, right?" I was stalling for time and I moved back into the living room where Joe was watching TV. "Thanks anyway, Sonia, but I really don't feel like sleeping. Sonia said I could use the extra bed in her room, Joe, but I explained that I wasn't tired and besides, this is a good movie. Why don't you watch it, Sonia?" I got a string of Spanish curses as she flounced back into her room, slamming the door.

"What the hell's going on?"

"Lover boy, *tu eres muy simpático.* . . . I just saved your precious honor, that's what's going on." After I finished my little tale, I got a drawn-out "Jeeesus Chriiist."

"Whatever you do, don't leave me alone with her, she's desperate. You know yesterday she told the kids to call me Daddy, and when we went out to eat everybody was looking at me. Can you imagine if my wife ever hears about this?"

This was the baby-sitting I was reduced to, which was supposed to teach me not to open my big fat mouth. On the third week of it I was doing midnights. On school nights I'd go to classes and then go right in and give someone an early relief.

On Monday evening, November 20, I was fighting an unbearable pressure headache and trying to get to school. Every time I felt this way I used to swear that it was the sergeant sticking pins in an effigy he had hidden somewhere.

Going down on the Bronx River Parkway, I wondered if I'd had any homework. I was in the left lane so that I could get off and gas up at Motorcycle I, located on the parkway. There was a car in the center lane, less than a car length ahead of me, and traffic was rolling in an orderly fashion.

Until . . . the hood on the car in the middle lane suddenly flew up. He started braking and then, fearing a rear-end collision, decided instead to get the car off the parkway and onto the grass. He cut the car sharply into my lane, then became aware of the median barrier blocking him. Having no alternative, he just jammed on his brakes.

It takes longer to tell than to happen. Me, I saw a guy on my right whose hood flew up, then he cut in front of me and stopped dead. I climbed into his trunk.

When I recovered consciousness, the only thing I remembered was this man standing there wringing his hands helplessly saying, "I'm sorry, I didn't mean it. I couldn't help it . . . I couldn't see where I was going. What can I do?"

In the emergency room waiting, I remember thinking, "Thank God it's over. Everyone says things happen in threes. This is the third one. I'm still alive, knock on wood."

I'd never realized how ingrained some of the superstitious beliefs we inherit are. I'd often thought of my two freaky car accidents and said to myself, "That better be the end, kid, or the last one will be a beaut!"

Who says lightning doesn't strike in the same place twice? Baloney! To me it happened three times. Same injuries, same problems . . . only each time a little more serious.

When I got through with the hospital routine, I was back in the neck brace, taking traction, hydrocolator packs, Jacuzzi immersions, and loads and loads of medication.

Weeks later, I managed to get dragged in to visit the local police surgeon. Son of a gun, I was back on that crazy sick report cycle.

"Dejectedly I slumped into the unyielding couch in the police surgeon's waiting room, my neck encased in a three-inch brace as a result of an auto accident. *Some hotshot cop!*"

EPILOGUE

October 15, 1974. I'm still on sick leave from the Department, waiting for my case to come up before the Pension Board. All the medical reports will be reviewed as they try to determine whether I pick up the cudgel or stamp my file CASE CLOSED.